STEPHAN B. SHAFFER

FACTS, FICTIONS AND FANTASTICAL STORIES

—————— OF ——————

ANCIENT AMERICA

WRITTEN RECORDS, HIEROGLYPHS,
PICTOGRAPHS, ARTIFACTS AND
OTHER REMARKABLE DISCOVERIES

—————— OF ——————

NORTH, CENTRAL
AND SOUTH AMERICA

To those who wrote to preserve history
and to Bonnie, who has always stood beside me

Contents

PREFACE

MAN HAS ALWAYS BEEN A very inquisitive species. Just because some-one says something is so does not mean that man will simply accept it. Man has always tried to disprove or prove a theory. It's in his nature to be contrarian! Without contradiction he would simply stand still and do nothing but accept things as they are in the context of what he is told.

For many years we have been dominated by institutions like the Smithsonian, to name one of many. Although these institutions have served the people well in one sense, we are now learning that we have been duped and lied to by those in authority. The question is "WHY?" What purpose does that serve? Why lie to the people about their heritage or about fantastic inventions, ancient peoples and cultures, or even strange and unexplainable events? It serves no purpose at all except to hide the truth or advance another agenda.

The fact that this artifact or that writing, or a particular story has been proven to be true, shows us that those who write or teach otherwise are misinformed at best, or trying to re-write history at worst.

Main stream academia has so warped the minds of some people that they actually believe that no other answers exist other than what they've been told by the so-called scholars. Even after some academics have *seen the light* they continue to support their pet theories and ideologies out of habit or tradition.

Stories from the American Indians are said to be nothing more than legends, say the *experts* of American history! They scoff at the tales and stories handed down by the elders. Listening to the histories of the American Indian is needed and appreciated by those who thirst for knowledge. In *Documentos Mexicanos* by Francisco Lorenzanos we read:

It is now many days since our historians have informed us," said Montezuma, "that neither my ancestors, nor I, nor any of my people, who now inhabit this country, are natives of it. We are strangers and came hither from very distant parts. They also tell us that a Lord, to whom all were vassals, brought our race to this land, and returned to his native place. That, after a long time, he came here again and found that those he had left were married to the women of the country; had large families and built towns in which they dwelt. He wished to take them away, but they would not consent to accompany him, nor permit him to remain as their chief. Therefore, he went away. We have always been assured that his descendants would return to conquer our country, and reduce us again to obedience. You say you come from the part where the sun rises.

Modern day academia says that these legends are made up from tales and stories concocted to entertain the youth and tourists, but there is precious little proof of that theory. Similarly, mainstream scholars dismiss the history of the mound-builders and the Copper Cultures of the Midwest and Northeast of North America as found in the traditions and histories of the natives.

Obvious in the ancient record as testimony of advanced civilizations are myriad evidences of early cultures, whose monuments attest to their engineering prowess and skill—temples, stone pyramids, massive granite rings, blocks of hieroglyphics, circular walls of dwellings and ceremonial ruins.

At certain times of the day, for example, when the sun's rays make it possible to see arrows cut deeply into the face of the sheer rock walls along the canyon of the mighty Colorado River, such signs seem to indicate the remains of ancient cultures, some even suggesting Egyptian or Phoenician ruins at the head of the Gulf of California!

These artifacts and ruins represent—according to roamers who go hunting treasure westwards across the Gila Desert and the unpopulated, thirst-stricken and heat-crazed Arizona—extremely ancient races. In these arid and remote spaces are memorials of unknown peoples whose temples, lofty stone pyramids (seven of them within a mile square) and massive granite rings and dwellings, circular walls round venerable trees, and blocks of hieroglyphics.

It is the intent of the author to share some of the hidden truths, including evidences of ancient past cultures that inhabited North, Central and South America. The treasures are many, the knowledge is plentiful and the evidence is convincing—all we have to do is face it with an open mind, be willing to listen, and do the research.

—Stephan Shaffer

Foreword

IN CONTRAST TO TODAY'S WORLD of fast-developing stories, which change almost hourly, Stephan B. Shaffer provides simple, solid, honest and accurate information that challenges typical assumptions about our world, inviting the serious student of history to reassess conventional wisdom with some enticing and encouraging data based on careful but bold scholarship.

Beginning as a teen, Shaffer's interest and dedication to things ancient, mysterious and obscure has enabled him to create a remarkable archive of stories, histories, artifacts, photos and maps that provide background information for his lectures, writings and recordings. His latest book captures much of the intrigue related to ancient American cultures whose writings, engravings, burials and artifacts perhaps raise more questions than they answer, but the pursuit of those answers invites, entices and encourages further study, research and investigation.

This book includes a comprehensive index that references not only the names, places, dates and sources for items included in this volume, but also provides links to previous publications, lectures, recordings and histories cited in all his published works. This is an invaluable resource for the thoughtful researcher of ancient American history, including archaeology, epigraphy, Spanish symbology and glyphs research, including pictographs and petroglyphs.

In this volume you will learn of early explorers of this continent, their monuments, writings, and artifacts, including monumental earthworks, impressive burial mounds, and the testimonies of Native Americans, which all testify of the high degree of civilization attained by so-called "savages" based on a hunter-gatherer culture.

You will also be invited to review the centuries of Spanish atrocities committed in the name of religion and a "higher level of understanding."

And don't be surprised to read about the race of red-haired giants who populated this land and of their giant skeletons found from west to east across this continent and of the extensive conspiracy to keep such discoveries secret and evidences hidden.

If you are a student of the Book of Mormon, you will be pleased to learn of traditions, oral histories and even written records that recount stories very similar to those found in the LDS (Mormon) scriptures, including links to references of accounts passed down through generations of Native Americans.

Entire sections of the book are dedicated to describing the discovery, retrieval, examination and disposition of stone tablets and slabs with inscriptions both known and unknown, some of which armchair academics declare as frauds and forgeries, but whose provenance strongly suggests otherwise. Metal tablets and plates contain sometimes decipherable and at other times incomprehensible markings, with many of the glyphs being similar to those found on other continents, including Asia and Europe.

The author leads the reader gently to a greater grasp and understanding of the genius of previous civilizations from North, Central and South America and of the commonalities among and between the distinct cultures found therein and worldwide.

A unique aspect of this publication is the incorporation of a technology that enables readers to access additional information in the form of full color images, videos, lectures, source materials and other media. This revolutionary application is called *mbook* technology. In technical terms it is described as a "living, breathing part of the book," since it allows further exploration of topics much as someone would on the web, but within the confines of the printed book as outlined by the author. In essence, it transforms the printed book into a never-ending story—since updates, additions, corrections, resources, and even new discoveries can be appended continuously.

About the Author

A Utah native, Stephan B. Shaffer (born in Salt Lake City in 1947), developed an interest in things old and things ancient at a young age, finding the reading of histories—both mainstream and obscure—to hold a particular fascination for him.

As a teenager, he had the privilege of spending summers in the Uintah Basin with the Utes and Paiutes, befriending and becoming a blood brother to the Ute and Apache tribes. This friendship and trust has been instrumental in his pursuit of the true accounts of historical events that took place in the eastern part of the state.

Always on the lookout for the unusual—things out of place in time or geography—his natural curiosity has led to unique discoveries others have overlooked, including the finding of old maps used by the Spanish explorers and the interpretation of the symbols they used to document their discoveries.

His intellectual curiosity has led to extensive study of *lichenometry*, the study of dating based on the known growth rate of lichen on rock surfaces, to obtain an approximate date of the deposition of the surface, a technique especially useful in dating surfaces over the last 500 years—a period in which radiocarbon data is relatively inefficient.

In archaeology, paleontology, and geomorphology, lichenometry is a geomorphic method of geochronologic dating that uses lichen growth to determine the age of exposed rock, based on a presumed specific rate of increase in radial size over time.

He has traveled extensively throughout Utah and other western states learning everything he could about past outlaws, Spanish miners, hidden treasures and buried outlaw loot and more, keeping extensive journals of his expeditions and amassing a huge collection of photos of his adventures.

Shaffer worked with the Forest Service to document and preserve the Chalk Creek hieroglyphic panels on the site east of Fillmore, Utah, employing a microscope camera to record the markings and symbols before they are lost to vandalism or weather.

Shaffer is a contributing member of the Midwestern Epigraphic Society, an organization that researches the ancient migrations of mankind around the world through the study of inscriptions or epigraphs as writing. He has written scholarly papers on Spanish symbols documentation and ancient symbols identification.

The Midwestern Epigraphic Society researches the ancient migrations of mankind around the world—especially Pre-Columbian to the Americas and particularly to the Midwest US—as revealed by cultural similarities, archaic writing, ancient world history and evidence found by modern science. Epigraphy is the study of inscriptions on rocks, pillars, temple walls, copper plates and other writing material. Epigraphy is the science of identifying graphemes, clarifying their meanings, classifying their uses according to dates and cultural contexts, and drawing conclusions about the writing and the writers.

A wonderful companion and help meet has been his wife Bonnie Jane (Peay) Shaffer. She has been his staff, the *wind beneath his wings* and loyal supporter, constantly encouraging him to continue his work. He and Bonnie have been married thirty-one years and together have ten children and thirty grandchildren.

Shaffer has authored seven books and is continually working on others. He holds a Bachelor of Science degree in Archaeology and a Master of Arts degree in Education, as well as graduating from the North American School of Conservation. He is president and founder of the "We Nooch Society," based in Santaquin, Utah, a historical research and preservation organization. Since retirement he spends almost full-time in field research and writing. He lectures extensively and is engaged by many groups for his knowledge and experience in his field of expertise. He has appeared in several documentaries, including Tops of the Mountains, an Illustrated History of Utah; National Geographic Explorer; The Secret History of Gold; and others now pending release.

Among his many interests, he crafts reproductions of American Indian artifacts and weapons to sell or just as gifts for friends and family.

Shaffer is a combat veteran, serving our country in Vietnam with the 2nd Battalion, 16th Infantry Regiment Rangers during 1967-68.

Stephan B. Shaffer's book publications include:

Rumors, Facts and Fictions of Ancient America: Written Records, Hieroglyphs, Pictographs, Artifacts and Other Remarkable Discoveries of North, Central and South America, 2018

Utah's Hidden Treasure: Outlaw Loot in Every County, 2017

Treasures of the Ancients: Recent Discoveries of Ancient Writings in North America, 1996, 2013

Voices of the Ancients, 2012

Out of the Dust: Utah's Lost Mines and Treasures, 2006

Nachi: Man of Justice, Son of Warrior, 2001

Of Men and Gold: The History and Evidence of Spanish Gold Mines in the West, 1994

La Mina Del Yutas: The Lost Josephine Mine (out of print)

He has also produced a DVD series featuring lectures, photos, images, drawings and other artifacts from more than 50 years of research.

Editing this manuscript has been an education and a delight and we commend it highly for your enjoyment and enlightenment.

—David M. Tuttle, Publisher

SETTING THE STAGE

"As above, so below. That which hath been shall return again."
—Warning of an Ancient Mystery

MYSTERY SOLVING HAS BEEN PART of the human desire since time began. We all love a good mystery whether it is in the form of a good book or a legend handed down through generations. Many legends if not most, have a basic fundamental truth at their inception. That is to say, they are based on an actual fact or event. Then over time, many of those legends become embellished or they become diminished and sometimes forgotten. Stories handed down orally face the real possibility of embellishment or distortion but when they are written they stand a better chance of survival.

But even this assertion is open to debate, since many cultures insist that the verbatim learning of the story preserves the true intent. This is particularly true among various cultures that have been persecuted—the Languedoc, the Albigenses, the ancient Celts, and others—too numerous to name without lengthy exposition. These cultures argue that they are preserving their true history without distortion, but that their histories have been perverted and twisted by those who held power over them, particularly the powerful and dogmatic religions often enforced by the power of the state. These cultures made certain that the stories remained intact. Passing them down by oral tradition and by rote ensured that they remained so, and were made available only to the initiated.

It is an arrogant misconception among Western society that a non-literate culture is less developed than one which is literate. Few literate societies can match the memories of the sacred story bearers, be they Iroquois, Hopi, Lugbara, Mandinka—to name only a few societies around the world—all faithfully preserve their stories, and remarkably, they remain intact.

Many cultures have only oral transfer of stories and legends and they make certain the stories are told the same way each and every time. They recite the story then have the receiver of the story repeat it back. If there are discrepancies then the story is repeated until the receiver gets it right!

The Indians of North America have always relied on oral tradition to preserve stories and legends and at times used petroglyphic and pictographic signs to further illustrate the stories told verbally. Rock writing is sometimes baffling and mysterious, used as a widespread method of communication detailing the workings and daily life of those who chiseled, painted or carved these universal signs and symbols into rock faces, hides and sometimes even trees.

Many so-called professionals in rock art interpretation assert that rock art in a given area is meaningful only to those cultures that inhabited that particular area, and the meanings of the signs and symbols of significance only to the author and his tribe. Not so fast! The basic structure of Native symbolism—the basic signs and symbols—can be seen throughout much of the Americas. Nevertheless, many signs and symbols differ between tribes. Association of symbols can change the meanings as well.

Those stone panels inscribed in precise detail tell a compelling story that can alter the thinking of mainstream academics, provided they are open to further investigation. The old adage of signs and symbols being carved by lonely sheep-herders is a weak argument often used by those who are unwilling to acknowledge their inability to translate or transliterate certain signs and symbols.

The idea that Indian signs and symbols are unique and specialized is true only to a certain point. Additionally, we have discovered over time that many panels investigated show signs of foreign influences. Depending on where in North America you are situated determines in large measure what foreign culture may have influenced the art or writings of a particular tribe.

Hebrew, Chinese, Celt, Iberian, Norse and other diverse influences can be found on many panels throughout North America. The late Harvard Professor Berry Fell revealed that European and North African cultures were colonized in America's eastern seaboard. Also, Egyptian, Celtic, Ogham, Iberian-Punic script, Libyan, Nordic, and even Phoenician influences can be found throughout the continent. What does that say about the true historical events in North America?

The greatly misleading story of Christopher Columbus being the first European to grace the shores of the American continents has been so embedded into our collective cultural psyche that the very thought of other cultures coming to America long before Columbus is met with much skepticism if not outright repugnance! However, the voice of the open-minded researcher is making significant inroads on that long-held philosophy. How can mainstream academics turn a blind eye to the fact that hundreds if not thousands of sites, artifacts and rock writings have been discovered and proven to be from superior cultures that inhabited the land thousands of years before Columbus? We celebrate Columbus Day of course, but in our minds we should also celebrate the countless others that helped form the America we live in today.

Legends tell of encounters with people of enormous size, and there are documented accounts of skeletons unearthed that rival in size any found in modern times. Legends tell us of the hairy man-like creature we call Sasquatch or Big Foot that roams the mountains and remote, wooded areas. There are legends of dwarf-like creatures that inhabit areas of California, Utah and even South America! The Crow and Cheyenne of Montana also speak of these little men. Many stories have come forward of perpetual lights and tunnels that are illuminated by some strange force. There are stories of men that live deep underground in California, and of other peculiar and almost unbelievable creatures. True or not, every story warrants an investigation to either prove or disprove its authenticity. We cannot and should not dismiss a story or legend just because we think it too far out of our normal range of understanding or experience. We as a people thrive on mysteries, legends and stories; we have an innate desire to find truth no matter where it leads us. We therefore must follow those leads and try our utmost to find the truth. A bold or ignorant person who asserts that no such thing exists, blinded by personal narrow-mindedness, will never see past his own limits of observation or biases.

The dogmatic arrogance of many modern academics is due for a severe awakening; they are apt to forget what real scientists and inventors well know—that the bounds of knowledge are often advanced not by professionals or savants in learned societies and associations but by the less dogmatic and generally undistinguished amateur and layman and the modest or humble investigator.

ANCIENT AMERICA

Think about what we've been taught in school from a very young age. As mentioned, Columbus is credited with discovering America. Eighteen years before he set sail, Columbus had a map of the Americas, which he later acknowledged in his journal. Now, consider the explorer Magellan. Why is the strait named after Magellan, when all along the strait had been delineated on maps and charts before he set sail?

The Chinese are a culture to be recognized as having one of the greatest impacts on world cartography, inventions, navigation, astrology/astronomy and much more. Why is this not taught in our schools? We'll explore that further.

So, here we set the stage to explore the reasons why we have been misled regarding the world's history and to what purpose it may serve. What are the reasons to hide from the people the array of truths that could change the whole of historical events in America—and who may be the guiding hand behind all the subterfuge?

1

THE TESTIMONY OF
THE INDIANS

"Endeavor to live an upright life."
—Aztec Saying

IT SEEMS NOWHERE ELSE THAT a people's history and cultures have been so distorted that their history today is of little consequence. I speak of the American Indian! Long before the "Manifest Destiny" proclamation was issued, the Indian was portrayed as a slovenly and despicable race!

White man had been misled into believing the Indians were less than human because those in charge wanted no sympathy towards them in order to gain superiority over them and then take their lands, flocks, women and more! These unscrupulous men and women did everything possible to discourage pilgrims and pioneers from having contact with the native population and if they did, wanted them to shoot first and ask questions later. Horrible stories circulated amongst the white populations until the Indian seemed lost, with no hope, no dream and no sense of worth.

The Indians of the eastern part of the North American continent have a tradition that has not been accepted by mainstream academia until just recently. The tradition I speak of is *where* they came from. So bent on conquering and acquiring land and control, settlers had to maintain the fiction of the Indian as a *savage;* thus they did not listen to their traditions and had little interest in the truth. Insofar as they were concerned, the Indian's legends had no basis of truth in them. Oral traditions were considered as *"unverifiable hearsay evidence,"* and stories told around the Native campfire were simply to entertain those listening.

Many of the tribes claimed their ancestors came *from the East,* across the great waters. For years the only tribe that maintained that tradition was the Shawnee, but since that time many more tribes have joined that narrative.

Did the Indian believe in one God? Did he believe in chastity? Did he believe in cleanliness? The answer is yes to those questions. A savage? Not until he was made one! Did he believe in the return of the Great Spirit one day? Most certainly!

THE INDIAN MESSIAH

A true story of the Savior's visit with special witnesses of various Indian tribes has been logged in the annals of history by many different tribes. It has also been logged in a paper written by then U.S. Indian Agent Major James McLaughlin. McLaughlin penned testimonies from Chief Walkara (Walker), Ammon, Sitting Bull and Utahnahw. His testimony begins:

> *Chief Walker or Yah-Keera as most know him by, told me that there were 16 tribes represented at a great meeting held at Walker Lake, Nevada in 1855. This wasn't the first meeting nor will be the last according to Walker. Old Porcupine told us that there were several hundred Indians camped there and said they were Chiefs and Sub-Chiefs from tribes of the Cheyenne, Sioux, Arapahoe, Gros Ventres, Utes, Bannocks, Paiutes and some strange tribes that were white skinned from a far off land and had traveled a great distance. Walker said there they were shown somebody disguised as the Messiah and had spoken with him. Ammon, Walker's brother said 'I believe that there is more than one person impersonating this Messiah, as when the Sioux have spoken with him he replies in the Sioux language and so on with the talkers of each nation. This Messiah told us that when he comes to rein over us firearms will no longer be used, and that he will draw a line behind him which he will gather all Indians, and then he will roll the*

Figure 1 Chief Walkara

earth back upon the Whites. We were very excited. Chief Sitting Bull more than most!

The account continues with another chief:

Utahnahw of the White River Utah band and a Sub-Chief said the Messiah had come to save the White man, but they had persecuted him, and now he had come to deliver the tormented Indians. He was quoted as saying "All day the Messiah instructed us and gave us evidence of his powers. He showed us marks of spikes having been driven thru his hands; he offered to save the Whites and they refused to accept him, and now the day of the Indian who had been greatly wronged was about to come. He proposed to destroy the Whites and save the Indians who are to be restored to ownership of the land. He also taught us to be honest, peaceful, and cleanly and give up all bad habits."

McLaughlin then recounts the testimony of White Sitting Bull:

White Sitting Bull [or Short Bull] was quoted as stating that the New Messiah required them to simply work and behave themselves; not to quarrel, strike, and fight or shoot one another. The Whites and Indians to be all One People! .... The Christ talked to us all in our respective tongues. You can see him in your sleep any time you want to after you have met him and shaken hands with him. To dance only four days at the beginning of each New Moon was the Messiah's advice.

The story concludes with the following statement:

The day will come when the "Mighty Wise One" will come. He was crowned "Super Chief" and given the supreme authority over all Indian Chiefs, in that great Indian Meeting. I was told to show the Great Mormon where the Gold and Silver was hidden and when and where he was to take it and by who. There is more gold here in these mountains (Wasatch) than all of Nevada.

PORCUPINE'S ACCOUNT OF SEEING THE CHRIST

A righteous young Indian by the name of Porcupine from the Northern Cheyenne was inspired to make a pilgrimage to Walker Lake, Nevada, to see their Messiah. His story follows:

The fish eaters near Pyramid Lake told me Christ had appeared on the earth again; it appeared that Christ had sent for me to go there and that was why unconsciously I took my journey. I went to the [Indian] agency [office] at Walker Lake and they told us Christ would be there in two days. At the end of two days, on the third morning, hundreds of people gathered at this place. They cleared off a place near the agency in the form of a circus ring and we all gathered there.

The place was perfectly cleared of grass. We waited until late in the evening, anxious to see Christ. Just before sundown I saw a great many people, mostly Indians [some of the local whites including some "Mormons" joined in the Ghost Dance], coming dressed in white men's clothes. The Christ was with them. I looked around to find him, and finally saw him sitting at one side of the ring. They made a fire to throw light on him. I never looked around, but went forward, and when I saw him I bent my head. I had always thought the Great Father was a white man, but this man looked like an Indian. He sat there a long time and nobody went up to speak to him. He sat with his head bowed all the time. After a while he rose and said he was very glad to see his children. "I have sent for you and am glad to see you. I am going to talk to you after a while about your relatives who are dead and gone. I will teach you, too, how to dance a dance, and I want you to dance it." He was dressed in a white coat with stripes. The rest of his dress was a white man's except that he had on a pair of moccasins. Then he commenced our dance, everybody joining in, the Christ singing while we dance. The next morning when we went to eat

breakfast, the Christ was with us. He said, "I am the man who made everything you see around you. I am not lying to you, my children. I made this earth and everything on it. I have been to heaven and seen your dead friends and have seen my own father and mother." He told us also that all our dead were to be resurrected; that they were all to come back to earth. He spoke to us about fighting, and said that it was bad, and we must keep from it; that the earth was to be all good hereafter, and we must all be

Figure 2 Porcupine, Early Photo

friends with one another. He said that in the fall of the year the youth of all the good people would be renewed, so that nobody would be more than 40 years old. He said if we were all good he would send people among us who could heal all our wounds and sickness by mere touch, and that we would live forever. He told us not to quarrel, or fight, nor strike each other, nor shoot one another; that the Whites and Indians were to be all one people.

Even after the testimony of Major McLaughlin many people still believed the Indians were mere savages and had no God, no honor and were nothing short of barbarians. The very idea of having the Messiah visit a bunch of heathens was nothing short of blasphemous. Mainstream preachers tried in vain to subject the Indians to the waters of baptism to wash away their sins for trying to deceive others into believing they knew the Christ.

Those meetings referred to by McLaughlin and others of the many different tribes of Indians massing at Walker Lake, were in fact true. In actuality, those meetings have spanned many generations.

VARIOUS ACCOUNTS OF THE WALKER LAKE EXPERIENCE

So popular was the event in Nevada that the story was told and retold many times. The *Illustrated American* magazine contained a good deal of interesting information regarding the religious movement among the Indians, culled and condensed from a large number of sources.

The *Deseret Weekly* dated Saturday 27 December 1890, Volume XLII, gives us the following account regarding the Indian Messiah Movement:

[*The Illustrated American*] article is illustrated by a number of portraits of notable chiefs, the engravings being extra good. One of the likenesses

Figure 3 High Bear

is that of High Bear, one of the principal chiefs of the Oglalas, whose name has recently figured in the dispatches. He is large featured, the nose being especially ponderous, while the eyes are full and expressive. The mouth is the only feature which indicates a disagreeable trait, showing hauteur, and impatience with anything that would collide with his will.

One of the most striking portraits is that of Kicking Horse, the Indian who asserts that he was carried in the spirit to heaven. He also has a large, rather handsome face, with mild eyes, and especially pleasant appearance. [Photo appears later in chapter.]

Figure 4 Johnson Sides

Johnson Sides, the Indian who is credited with innocently being the cause of the present agitation is represented in his portrait as a man of gentle disposition, his face being devoid of the rugged aspect common to his race. He is known as the "Peacemaker."

The countenance of [White] Sitting Bull is a study. It is more like the face of a white man than of an Indian in its general contour, with the exception of the high cheek bones. Native intelligence and sagacity are expressed in every feature, as well as the deep lines of the face, impressed by habits of intense thoughtfulness. He would be regarded anywhere among observant people, judging from his portrait, as a most unusual man, with many superior points of character. Unprejudiced persons who are willing put themselves in his place, can come to no other conclusion, on the basis of his career and the traits exhibited by him in the event which terminated his life. This likeness in the *American* bears no resemblance to the miserable caricatures which are printed in the daily journals.

White Eagle, one of the leaders in the religious dances of the Indians, has a characterless countenance. The whole face, including the partly open mouth, disclosing the teeth, bespeaks the fanatic.

I here quote from the article in the *American*, which is titled The Red Christ:

Just when and where the present craze arose is uncertain. The evidence at present obtainable indicates that it has resulted more from a process of evolution than from the preaching of any one man. The first Indian who preached the coming of the Red Christ is a manner that attracted attention was Short Bull, or Sitting Bull, an Arapahoe who must not be confounded with Sitting Bull, the Sioux chief who took part in the Custer massacre, and who was also one of the most prominent leaders in the present agitation. This Sitting Bull, or Short Bull, arrived at the Shoshone Agency, at Fort Washakie, in Wyoming, about a year ago, and announced that he had seen Christ, the Messiah, he said, told of his previous life on the earth, nineteen hundred years ago, and of how the white people had refused to accept him, and showed the scars on his hands and feet where he had been nailed to the cross. He foretold the removal of the white men, and promised that the buffalo and other game should return in their former abundance. Then the Messiah gave the Indian buffalo meat to eat, and Sitting Bull fell asleep. When he awoke he found he had been transported a long distance in his sleep.

Indians do not communicate with one another by letters, but send their messages by runners. By word of mouth Sitting Bull's story was made known to many tribes, and a year ago a sort of council was held at a place supposed to be on the shore of Walker's Lake, in Western Nevada. At this council the Messiah showed himself. Representatives of sixteen tribes are said to have been present. Near the camp the sagebrush and rose bushes had been cut off close to the ground over a circle perhaps one hundred feet in diameter. Here is one account of the appearance of the Christ:

> The next day, as the sun was getting low, the people all assembled about this circle, and presently a man was seen walking into it. The people stood about until he had reached the middle of the circle, and then they went in to meet him. He stood in the midst and talked to them, appearing to be able to talk all the languages and to make himself understood by all the tribes present. He told the people that things were going to be changed; that the game and the buffalo would be brought back; that they

should again have their own country, and that the world should be turned upside down and all the whites spilled out.

He closed his speech by saying that in the night he should go up to heaven to see God. Next morning about nine or ten o'clock the people again gathered about the circle, and presently the Messiah walked in among them. He told them that he had just returned from heaven, where he had seen God.

Among the Indians present at this council was Porcupine, a Northern Cheyenne, who has since been one of the foremost prophets of this new Messiah. His story is as follows:

What I am going to say is the truth. The two men sitting near me were with me, and will bear witness that I speak the truth. I and my people have been living in ignorance until I went and found out the truth. All the whites and Indians are brothers, I was told there. I never knew this before. The fish-eaters near Pyramid Lake told me that Christ had appeared on earth again. They said Christ knew he was coming; that eleven of his children were also coming from a far-land. It appeared that Christ had sent for me to go there, and that was why, unconsciously, I took my journey. It had been foreordained. They told me when I got there that my Great Father was there also, but I did not know who he was. The people assembled, called a council, and the chiefs' sons went to see the Great Father, who sent word to us to remain fourteen days in that camp, and that then he would come and see us. At the end of two days on the third morning, hundreds of people gathered at this place. They cleared a place near the agency in the form of a circus-ring, and we all went there. Just before sundown I saw a great many people (mostly Indians) coming dressed in white men's clothes. The Christ was with them. They all formed in this ring and around it; they put up sheets all around the circle, as they had no tents. Just after dark some of the Indians told me that Christ (Father) was arrived. I looked around to find him, and finally saw him sitting on one side of the ring. He was dressed in a white coat. The next morning he told us he was going away that day, but would be back the next morning to talk to us. I heard that Christ had been crucified and I looked to see, and I saw a scar on his wrist and one on his face, and he seemed to be the man; I could not see his feet. He would talk to us all day. That evening we all assembled again to see him depart.

The following morning the Christ was back with us and wanted to talk with us. He said: "I am the man who made everything you see around you. I am not lying to you, my children. I made this earth and everything on it. I have been to heaven and seen your dead friends, and have seen my own father and mother." He spoke to us about fighting, and said that it was bad and that we must keep from it; the earth was to be all good hereafter, that we must be friends with one another. He said if any man disobeyed what he ordered his tribe would be wiped from the face of the earth. Ever since the Christ I speak of talked to me I have thought what he said was good. I have seen nothing bad in it. When I got back I knew my people were bad and heard nothing of all this, so I got them together and told them of it, and warned them to listen to it for their own good. I told them just what I have told you here today.

Porcupine's tale met with belief wherever he told it, and other missionaries labored incessantly with equal success. It will be observed that Porcupine's account of the Red Christ's message makes it one of peace. The Sioux changed its tenor to hostility towards the whites. They were much taken with the idea of the Messiah, but they thought they ought to do something to help remove the whites. The *American* article continues this amazing saga:

The next development of the belief was furnished by Kicking Horse, whose visit to heaven has been compared with that of Tecumseh's brother,

the Prophet. Kicking Horse is a Sioux. To him are accredited the features of the craze involved in the belief of the resurrection of all dead Indians, and of the overwhelming of the whites. His story is that he was taken to heaven through a hole in the clouds, and talked with the Great Spirit, who told him that his children, the Indians, had suffered long enough, and the time had come when they should occupy the earth again. They must not kill or molest the whites, the Great Spirit said, for he himself would wipe them off the face of the earth by sending a wave of mud, twenty

Figure 5 Kicking Horse

feet or more in depth, over the country. All dead Indians would be restored to life and there would be buffaloes and horses in the plenty. Kicking Horse further declared that while he was talking with the Great Spirit, the devil appeared, in the shape very tall with immense knee-joints, a monstrous mouth, and long teeth.

Following is the account given in the *American* of the experience White Sitting Bull, or Short Bull, claims to have passed through:

While hunting alone near the Shoshone Mountains he became lost, and for a long time wandered about aimlessly. Finally a strange feeling came over him, and he involuntarily began to follow a certain star, which moved before him and led him many miles out into the mountains. Just at daybreak the star became stationary over a beautiful mountain valley, and he sank to rest on a couch of moss. While he rested, a strange vision appeared before him. He saw a Great Spirit dance, and the participants were dead Arapahoe warriors, led by the dead chiefs of the past. Suddenly he was awakened by a voice, and saw before him a strange being, dressed in a blanket of pure white. The strange being said that he was the same Christ who was upon the earth nineteen hundred years ago to save the white men, and that he would soon return to save the red men. The whites, who had so long persecuted and robbed the Indians, would be driven out of the land across the sea, never to return again. All day the Messiah conversed with [White] Sitting Bull, revealing to him many things, also showing him the scars of nails in his hands and feet and the wound in his side. When night came on the Messiah disappeared.

The Federal Government was so concerned that the Indian Nation would once again rise up against them that they kept a close eye on everything they did. They sent spies acting as news reporters or aspiring authors to cover all the proceedings of the different tribes. Chief Porcupine was most interesting to the Government, for he seemed to carry a lot of weight with many tribes.

A REPORTER'S STORY

It was during the time of much turmoil in the LDS Church and the Messiah craze was in full swing that F.K. Upham, a reporter for the *Boston Journal*, arrived at Fort Custer, Montana 1 July of 1890. He intended on gaining more information on the Indian Christ. His report was later printed in the *Latter-Day Saint's Millennial Star* Volume 52, p. 532-5, August 25, 1890, under the title The Indian's Christ:

> *The reading room of the officers' club at Fort Custer on Saturday night was a scene of unusual interest. Hither had come the general who commands the post and his adjutant, these occupying a prominent position near to the entrance of the long room in question. Seated by the walls, along the sides and ends, were the officers of the garrison, with their wives and members of their families; added to all of these was a sprinkling of civilians, somewhat noticeable owing to the absence of the blue and gilt of the customary uniforms at a military post. Perhaps forty persons had so assembled.*

> *The occasion of this was the appearance of the disciple (Apostle) Porcupine, a Cheyenne Indian, recently returned from a pilgrimage to visit the new Christ of the Indians at some remote and mysterious point toward the setting sun. For months past the various Indian tribes of the Northwest have been greatly exercised over the coming of this Messiah, so great has been this interest, that from way down in the Indian Territory and Texas have some messages of inquiry from the Southern Indians asking information from their Northern brethren, saying that they, too, had received the*

Figure 6 Chief Porcupine, Disciple

> *"glad tidings of great joy," and were prepared to come and sit as the feet of this great stranger. The wild Western air has been filled with strange rumors of super-naturalism, and a feeling of intense anxiety has found its way among all the Indian tribes.*

> *Sometime last winter this Cheyenne Indian, Porcupine by name, without the permission of his agent, started on his pilgrimage to find the "Great One" of whom the Indians heard. He had neither money nor a supply of food, and was*

accompanied by his faithful squaw and two other Indians from the reservation of the Northern Cheyenne, on Tongue River, Montana, 60 or 70 miles from here. They traveled far to the westward, and saw much they had never seen before, after reaching the railroad, going much of the way by rail—on which they were permitted to ride without charge—at other times on foot; though always without money, both Indians and white men giving them food as they journeyed. But like certain wise men that once before made a pilgrimage, they found their reward and were content.

The recent return of Porcupine to the reservation made the Cheyennes, more than usually restless and excited. Early in May the Indian agent had called for military protection, and Major Carroll, with three troops of the first cavalry, was sent to his agency by General Brisbin from this post, where they have since remained. Cattle belonging to the settlers had been killed. A man by the name of Ferguson suddenly coming on a party of Cheyennes at a remote place in the hills in the act of cutting up one of his steers which they had just shot, was himself killed that he might not be a witness against them. The Indians were duly arrested and turned over to the civil authorities, and they now await their trial in the jail at Miles City. A general feeling of alarm existed among the scattered settlers in the surrounding country, many of them moving their families to Miles City for safety. The settlers armed themselves for the protection of their isolated ranches, and the races watched each other anxiously for a time. It is believed, however, that the presence of the troops will prevent further trouble, and matters can be adjusted by the authorities at Washington, which, it is claimed, can best be accomplished by the removal of the Cheyennes.

The reappearance of Porcupine among such conditions added to the complications with which the Indian agent had to contend, and he requested by telegraph of the Interior Department at Washington that Porcupine might be arrested by the troops, which request was at once responded to by the War Department, and the arrest promptly ordered. Porcupine immediately expressed his willingness, and in fact a wish, to go without delay to Fort Custer and explain his position, and what he knew of the Savior who has come to his people. The agent withdrawing his request for the arrest, Porcupine came to Fort Custer. To hear his story was the occasion of the assembly on Saturday night, already referred to. This somewhat lengthy explanation seems necessary to a full understanding of the matter.

He was an erect, handsome, and perfectly developed young Indian, standing fully six feet in height, with a pleasant, sprightly face, the mobility of his features indicating anything but the traditional Indian. Clad in a garment of striped wool, red and white, the stripes several inches broad, evidently made from blankets, belted at the waist and extending to the knee, with a tuft of eagle feathers knotted in his scalp-lock, certainly he was not lacking in the picturesque. Squatting, after the fashion of his race, near the centre of the room, just in rear of him his squaw and the two companions of his pilgrimage, through an interpreter he told what he had seen of the Christ who had now come.

His story was prefaced—as all Indian "talks" are—by the information that what he was now about to say was "the truth," and pointing to his mouth, he indicated that his words would go straight to the front, "neither to the right nor the left;" he had "no forked tongue." Then rising to his full height, he assumed the exact attitude which we have been taught to believe that Jesus took when blessing the disciples, the upper portion of the body slightly inclined forward, the arms extended to full length, with the hands dropping downward, the eyes closed. Then he trembled violently from head to foot, alternately changing the position of his hands to across his breast, then to the waist with the left hand, the right dropping by the side. In this position he remained fully five minutes, during which the heads of his Indian companions were dropped in silence, and the room was so still that the fall of a pin might have been heard. Having completed this, seemingly a silent prayer, he resumed his former place on the floor and began.

On the wall hung a large military map of the United States, indicating the various army posts of the West, and so nearly as the mysterious location could be established where the Christ had been found, it was possibly in the vicinity of Walker's or Pyramid Lake in Nevada. It was in the mountains. Porcupine found himself with many strange Indians, whose language he could not speak, and who, like himself, had come from far off, but all had come to see the Christ. At sundown the Indians collected in large numbers, and after it became dark He appeared to them, a large fire being built to throw the light on him. He was not as dark as an Indian, nor as light as a white man, and his dress was partly like each. He sat for a long time in perfect silence, with his head bowed, during which time the Indians neither moved nor spoke. They were told that if they even whispered the Christ would know it and be displeased. After a time he raised his head, and then Porcupine saw that he was fair to look upon, that his face had no beard, and was youthful, and that his bright hair extended to the waist. Porcupine had heard that the Christ of the white man had been nailed to a cross, and, looking, he was able to see the scars of the nails in the hands of the Indian's Christ when he raised them. In his feet he could not see the marks of the nails by reason of the moccasins, but he was told they were there, and that in his side were spear marks which were concealed by the shirt he wore. Porcupine was told that his own coming had, with eleven others, been foretold by the Christ, who had sent for him, and that was why he had involuntarily taken the long journey; that all the heathen tribes there represented had been influenced in the same manner, though all had not been individually called, as he had.

The Christ spoke to them and took Porcupine by the hand, and told them that they were all his children. He talked to them until it was day, telling them that he had made them, and all the things around them; that in the beginning God had made the earth, and after a time had sent him on the earth to teach the people what was right, but the people were afraid of him, and "this is what they did to me," showing his scars. He said when he found the children were bad he went back above, and promised to return after many hundred years. Now the time was up, and God had told him the earth was old and worn out, and had sent him again to renew it, and make things better. He said that all the dead were to be resurrected and brought back to life on this earth, which was now too small to hold them all, but he would do away with heaven and make the earth large enough to hold them all. He spoke about fighting, that it was bad, and that Indians must not do it anymore; that the earth here-after was to be all good and everybody must love one another. He said he would send those among them who could heal wounds and cure the sick by a laying on of the hands, and that the good would live here forever and the buffalo would come back. He said it was wrong to kill men of any kind, that here-after the whites and the Indians would become one people; that if any man disobeyed these teachings he would be banished from the face of the earth; that the Indians must believe all that he now told them, and not say that he lied, for he would know their thoughts, no matter in what part of the world they were, and they could not expect to deceive him. Among those whom Porcupine saw were some who seemed like white men, but they all seemed Christ said to them.

During Porcupine's stay of many days the Christ several times repeated these talks, and told the Indians that when they returned to their people they must tell them all these things. But he was not at all times visible, and could disappear at will. "He is here among us tonight, and knows all that we are talking about," said Porcupine.

Porcupine continued: "When I heard all these things I came back to my people, and they listened to me. Ever since I heard these things from the Christ I have thought they were good. I can see nothing bad in them. I knew my people were bad, and I got them together and told them. I warned them to listen, for it was for their own good. I talked to them four nights and five days, and said just what I said here tonight. I told them these were the words of the Almighty God, who was looking down on them and knew what was in their hearts. I wish some who are here had heard my words to the Cheyennes. They have been bad and fools, and the sin of the killing of Ferguson will be visited on the whole tribe. I am sorry to say that there are one or two Cheyennes who do not believe what I have said. I wish these, and some of you, would go back with me and see that I have spoken the truth. When you have seen the Christ once you can see him in your sleep, that is, if you have shaken his hand; and through him you can go to heaven and see your friends who are dead. I see him often in my sleep and he told me there was trouble for the Cheyennes. The next night he came to me and told me that all would be well in the end."

Of Porcupine's sincerity there can be no doubt. As he says himself, he is "no medicine man," and seems to have no wish to become one. That he has seen the person whom he describes as "The Christ" there seems to be no question. [F. K. Upham, in the Boston Journal]

It may be of interest to members of The Church of Jesus Christ of Latter-day Saints to note a prophecy by President Joseph Smith Jr. who made this statement at a conference held at Ramus, Illinois, on April 2, 1843. Sometime prior to Feb. 14, 1835, he had asked the Lord when the second coming was to take place.

I earnestly desired to know concerning the coming of the Son of Man & prayed, when a voice said to me, 'Joseph, my son, if thou livest until thou are 85 years old thou shalt see the face of the Son of Man. Therefore let this suffice & trouble me no more on this matter.

I was left to draw my own conclusion concerning this & I took the liberty to conclude that if I did live till that time He would make his appearance. But I do not say whether He will make His appearance or I shall go where he is. I prophecy in the name of the Lord God, & let it be written, that the Son of Man will not come in the heavens till I am 85 years old 48 years hence or about 1890." (Also see Doctrine and Covenants 130: 14-16.)

THE GREAT WHITE CHIEF

[Note to reader: Much of the information included here is excerpted from the unpublished manuscripts, journals and papers of Zula Marian Clegg Brinkerhoff (a sister to Vernon Henry Clegg), including her book *God's Chosen People of America*, published in 1971.]

On May 15, 1959 a spokesman for the Cherokee Nation paid a visit to his friend Vernon Henry Clegg of Salt Lake City, Utah, to give him information pertaining to "The Coming of the Great White Chief" that had been handed down for generations.

The spokesman told him that Natoni Nez-Bab, PhD, a graduate of Carlyle and Haskell Universities, was a full blooded Navajo and a fully authorized member of his tribe's High Council of Sixteen, holding the position of Tribal Historian. Mr. Nez-Bab had majored in archaeology and conducted scientific research and had since served on many archaeological expeditions throughout North, South and Central America with the Smithsonian and Carnegie Institutions. He was also a linguist of considerable ability, speaking some three or four modern languages and twenty-seven Indian dialects.

During an archaeological expedition to Monte Alban, near Oaxaca in Southern Mexico in 1935, Dr. Nez-Bab first heard and came into contact with the "Great White Chief" and his legendary "White Indians" who had since come into exceptional news prominence to Latter-day Saint people. Subsequently, Nez-Bab was commissioned as Tribal Delegate to represent the Navajo people at the great Indian conventions which had been held in Mechoagan [Michoacan], Mexico, and the United States of America, and which had resulted in the complete amalgamation of all Indian tribes and nations on the Western Hemisphere as a united people under the Great White Chief.

So impressive was this Great White Chief that he had been elected as Chief of all Chiefs! He was called *Eachata Eacha-Na,* to be interpreted Mighty and Wise One. He was the law giver and teacher. Under him the Indian nations determined to be and remain a united people by casting aside all enmity, hatred, malice, and bickering, recognizing the blood brotherhood of their people under one God and one leadership.

Nez-Bab had several extended visits with the Great White Chief and his people, and had found unusual favor with him in that the Mighty and Wise One adopted Natoni Nez-Bab as his own son in a sacred Indian ritual. Therefore, Natoni Nez-Bab spoke with authority in telling the history of the Indian movement to all those that would hear. Following is the personal account of his visit to the White Indians of Mexico:

> *Chigaragu Indians are a nation of white or very light-skinned Indians living in the Southern part of Mexico. Their walled city lies in an almost inaccessible section of the high mountainous region near the border of Guatemala. To reach this Shangri-La of the New World where White man's civilization has not totally penetrated due to his complete exclusion, one much go first to the capital city of Oaxaca, State of Oaxaca, then to the ancient ruined city of Mitla to where dirt roads and trails lead to this fantastic city.*
>
> *After five days of almost continuous climbing, one comes upon some high table land that opens up into a magnificent valley of transcending beauty. It lies at an elevation of about 12,800 feet. Within this valley is secluded the beautiful walled city of the White Chigaragu Indians where it has remained untouched and unspoiled by the evils of civilization since it was built long before the times of Christ.*
>
> *Their habitations cover an area of about 9.5 miles long by 11 miles wide, or about 100 square miles. At the northern end of the valley steep rock cliffs some two or three hundred feet high complete their protective encirclement with guarded gates being the only entrance and exit.*
>
> *The law of Chigaragu has been that only those who speak the Indian languages and in whose veins flows Indian blood shall enter into their domain, and the White Man has been thus far effectively barred as well as war-like tribes of Indians.*

All the buildings, homes, and temples are very light or white in color on the inside as on the outside and present a very attractive appearance, forming a city which approaches perfection in its layout and architectural designs.

The people are tall and stately in stature, being from five foot eight to six feet one in height. Their skins are very light, their hair brown to very black. Their eyes vary from hazel to deep blue and black. Their clothes are all woven by hand and differ considerably from all other Indian tribes. Instead of wearing the customary shirts and trousers, they wear long white robes that reach almost to the ground and which they fasten down the front with three sets of strings. A girdle is wrapped about the waist and long sleeves are sometimes tied at the elbows with a draw string. Certain symbolic marks are placed upon the robe, over the breast, naval and knee and on the head over the forehead. A cowl-like hood is worn over the head, and white, tanned moccasins cover the feet. These people regard these symbols as very sacred.

Men and women, for instance, put everything they raise into the great storehouse. The wool weaver, pottery maker, leather workers do likewise with their products, and then all is made available for the common use of all the people as needed. They have no money and need none for them-selves. All commerce with other Indian tribes is carried on by the barter or exchange system. Among themselves there are no rich or poor, and every-one shares the abundance they have. Once when I was presented with a beautiful pair of moccasins I offered a handful of pesos in return for them, only to be rebuked by the Great White Chief with the soft spoken words, "My son, our hills are full of that metal, and we find it useful only for tools and ornaments."

They are a very clean people, having no vices or bad habits, such as the use of tobacco or liquor. They live principally upon a vegetarian diet and fruits and melons and raw vegetables. And all are very healthy and beautiful in their appearance, walking erect with excellent posture that gives the impression of almost effortless motion or a gliding movement.

They are very devout and pray several times during the day and night, each prayer being very sincere, they follow the belief that 'I am my broth-er's keeper.' Should any sickness or injury or sorrow fall upon one of them, everyone else is ready to do all possible for the unfortunate one, as each person feels he or she should be responsible for each other's feelings. No ill feelings or misunderstandings exist among them. All are very happy and they know not of greed, or hatred, or malice, or corn. Theirs is the perfect life.

THE LEGEND

This mode of living has been with them many generations just as the firm traditions and beliefs have been handed down from generation to generation that they should live this way, Nez-Bab continued:

Many years ago, according to their belief, as there are stars in the sky, a great event happened to their ancestors living in this valley. The legend reveals that there was a great storm with fearful earthquakes and thick darkness for several days. Then after the darkness was lifted a Great White God de[s]cended to them from heaven. He was draped in a beautiful robe made of the feathers of the quetzal bird. The Great Being stayed with the people for a short time, and taught them how they should live and put away their evil ways by living the law which he taught them. Then before he departed, he promised that if they would live faithfully by these laws and abide by His teachings, some day He would return and live among them again.

During rain storms or heavy wind and hail storms that are attended by darkness which might remind them of the legendary times when their Great White God came to them, the Chigaragu people prostrate themselves in prayer upon the earth, for they firmly believe in the return among them. To keep their faith alive they have proclaimed the quetzal bird as a sacred symbol of Him for they believe that the robe was made of feathers from the bird. Consequently, severe punishment and torture [is] meted out to anyone harming the quetzal bird.

They have a set of records written in books made of buckskin which have been handed down from generation to generation. The records are regarded by them as highly sacred, for they contain the history of their people for many generations prior to the coming of the Great White God. They are the only Indian tribe, as far as I know, who possess a set of records originating in B.C. times. They are written in a language no longer spoken by them except by the Mighty and Wise One who learned it from his father as a responsibility handed down from the beginning by their family.

They also followed an unusual custom which has become a fixed law with them for generations, and which has resulted in their population remaining limited to the present size of about 8,000. This custom or law requires that a woman may bear a child only once every seven years. Hence, the birth and death rate has remained about an even balance so they have not spread from the lights of their walled city and their own culture and custom.

EACHATA EACHA-NA (THE MIGHTY AND WISE ONE)

The Chicaragu Indians are presided over by a Great White Chief called Eachata Eacha-Na meaning The Mighty and Wise One. This title has been held by this Chieftain's fathers before him for many generations. The Great White Chief is old but looks like a middle aged man and is stout. He walks very erect, and with such ease that he seems to float rather than plod as men of age do. He has a very commanding figure, and one immediately senses in him deep spiritual qualities that make him a man of majesty amidst thousands.

Yes, millions of his worshipful followers look to him for guidance and leadership when he speaks, and it is what the Great Spirit whispers into his mind; one instinctively desires to obey his words.

THE GREAT AMALGAMATION OF INDIANS

In May of 1938, Eachata Eacha-Na, Chief of the Chicaragu Indians, called his runners to the great Council House and told them to deliver a special message to the Indian tribes nearby, and to have them in turn deliver it and relay it as far as a bird flies to the North and to the South, until all Indian tribes receive it. His runners took his message to the Chiefs of the nearby tribes and told them that at the beginning of 1939, the Chiefs were to send representatives to the Great Indian Conference to be held at Lake Patzcuaro in Michoacan. Each Chief in turn was to send runners to the tribes beyond them until the message had reached all tribes throughout the Hemisphere.

The response to his message was tremendous; when the conference was held in April of 1939, government officials of Old Mexico estimated that more than 130,000 Indians, representing every tribe on the continent had gathered at Lake Patzcuaro in the state of Michoacan in order to attend this mighty conference at the request of the Great White Chief.

After meeting together for one week, during which time good will was firmly established among them, The Great White Chief invited them to return again in 1940, during the same season. Accordingly in 1940, a similar large number of Indian delegated from all tribes of all the continent responded, and this time by unanimous vote, they determined to merge one great nation with Eachata Eacha-Na as Chief of all Chiefs, and Great Chief of all Indian Nations. This was done with the result that now every Indian everywhere holds Eachata Eacha-Na, the Mighty and Wise One, in great esteem, and all of them look to him for guidance and leadership.

One year since then as the Mighty and Wise One called them to his great annual conference where he had presided over them, and has taught all of his ways and his laws for more righteous living. The Indian delegates take this teaching back to their tribes where they endeavor to live up to them and teach them to their brothers.

A GREAT WELFARE PROGRAM

During these times a great welfare plan has been put into effect involving the storing of food, grain, vegetables, fish, meat, etc. There has been great activity among all tribes in the land with dehydration of food supplies and storing them away in concealed places until now. They have sufficient durable food supplies to last them five to seven years. Tribes with surplus of any commodity have exchanged or shared with other tribes who have shortages or a surplus, until all their supplies have become well balanced and well distributed among them. This has been done under well-organized leadership, which has involved delegated authority to predominate tribes in large geographical centers. Leadership in South America, for instance, has been given to Quio and Quinche tribes under Chief Etaha Donab, while all of Central America goes to the responsibility of the Quenches under Chief Chiche Suma who, incidentally is second in power to Eacha-Na himself. Mexico is presided over by the White Chief and all United States Indians are under the Navajos with Chief Lone Tree at their head, while all Canadian and North Western Indians come under the leadership of the Sioux, with Chief Black Pony at the head.

A MAGNIFICENT TEMPLE

During the great conference of 1940 at Lake Patzcuaro, the Mighty and Wise One advised all Indian delegates that the time had come, according to the voice of the Great Spirit, for them to build a magnificent temple to His name in fulfillment of the promise and tradition that had been handed down by them, that the Indians should do this thing. He showed them the plans for this great and beautiful structure, which, when completed would cover as much ground as [a] Salt Lake City, [Utah] block.

Five great quarries were selected in Mexico, Central America, and the northern part of South America, and some 20,000 Indians went to work cutting and polishing beautiful stone for this purpose. One quarry is in the Northern part of Columbia near Soldada. Another is Estaciono Mario in Honduras, another in Chiantla, Guatemala, a fourth at Autian, Hidalgo, Mexico, and the fifth at Labiaco, Jalapa, Mexico. All stone is of white marble, but each quarry cuts a separate and distinct size to the finest specifications. Special key stones are also cut and shaped somewhat like a dumbbell, which interlocks each stone above and below and to the side with its neighbor stones like a chain, so that even a strong earthquake would not dislodge them.

At several places in Old Mexico at the present time, Indian people of various nations are hand polishing woodwork for the interior trim of this great temple, while in other places in Mexico and Central America other Indians are polishing precious stones such as Jasper, Moleschito Turquoise, and forming these with beautiful inlaid work of exquisite and intricate design to be used for the interior adornment of the temple. All preliminary work that can be done is rapidly nearing completion, and the finished materials are sent to the seashore for shipment by water to the temple site.

THE GREAT MIGRATION

Plans for the great migration are now being revealed that will involve the movement of tens of thousands of Indians from Mexico, Central and South America to their promised temple site.

To take care of this migration, great preparations have been made which involves the careful selection of special camp sites where great stores of food have been secreted. Indian tribes along the route have made exten-

sive preparations to assist their brethren in this great migration, and are ready to offer them whatever aid they may need. Then the first group will journey many, many days toward the rising sun, until they come to the mighty river that flows from North to South. They are to go up this river until they come to the special stone which will indicate to them where they are to build the temple, and there they will stop and commence the shipping of their supplies and materials to this location.

The second group is to journey to the west not many days until they find a range of mountains where only the morning sun shall strike. They shall follow these mountains to the North many, many days until they meet with another white people who do not speak their language, but whom they will recognize by certain marks, signs, and symbols, the two shall amalgamate together and become one certain people under one leadership. After this, they shall travel together many, many days toward the rising sun where they will find their brethren and they shall assist them in building the great temple, and the beautiful city within a wall.

Later, as time goes on, other bodies of Indians will arrive at this spot and addition after addition will be erected in the city. The entire city, homes and public buildings will be built of stone from native surroundings, but the stones for the temple with the polished wood and furnishings, will be transported by barges and ships from the quarries heretofore mentioned.

At the last Indian Conference at Lake Patzcuraro, the Great White Chief repeated his strong prediction again. "What the water has taken from the land, and the land has taken from the water, what man has taken from man, each by the command of the spirit, shall come back to its own." By this he meant that all things shall revert and be restored to its original state as God first designed, in a great restitution of all things. He repeated this statement on several occasions, and at the last conference he spoke of the years that go by so fast by saying, "another milestone has passed and there is so much to do with but little time to accomplish it."

A SIGNIFICANT LETTER

On August 8, 1945, in the magazine section of the *Salt Lake Tribune*, a letter from "The Mighty and Wise One" to the President of The

Church of Jesus Christ of Latter-day Saints was published. The text of that letter follows:

To my Brother, The Great White Leader, salutation: When He, the Mighty and Wise One comes among you, He shall speak and all shall listen unto Him only. All things shall be given unto Him such as properties and possessions, etc. He shall have everything at His disposal to do with as the Great Spirit directs.

All things which the Indian people have shall be placed at the top, and those who are at the top shall be placed at the bottom for you have rejected and left behind the things which the Great Spirit has given you in times past. He and the Mighty and Wise One will select the men who are best fitted for each office and position.

All wealth and possessions will be used by both sides under His directions. All wealth of the Indian people will be combined with your wealth; all food supplies shall be used by both sides as needed. Neither sides shall hoard or keep anything hidden from the other side, but all shall have a share equally of the total.

Great farms will be worked by both white and Indian people. Flocks and herds will be raised by them both. Great large buildings shall be built by both sides, together, and all will worship the same God together at the Great Place or site where the mighty temple shall be built. White people and Indian people shall work together and build the beautiful city also. Many shall remain here and many shall go from here. Several years more will be required to complete all things on the temple. Many will refuse but many will accept. And those who I shall take will be as a handful of sand on the seashore. Some will deny or refuse me. Many will not understand; many will not care. Nevertheless, all things shall be done, and all laws of the Great Spirit shall be obeyed in good faith.

The righteous shall do great things, and the wicked among you shall be destroyed. All things shall be done in a quiet way. We shall come peacefully as we are accepted peacefully, but if we are not accepted peacefully, we will come to destroy, for those who hold these things in scorn and derision shall be destroyed. It is the Voice that speaks even the Voice of the Great Spirit has spoken to him. He asks that He be reconciled with His people in this great amalgamation, for you and they shall be one.

He has spoken. It is finished.

(Signed) Eachata Eacha-Na, The Mighty and Wise One.[1]

The question here is why haven't the masses been told of this great event that shall come to pass? Why would an obscure letter in a newspaper magazine not be on the front page if it was so important to those it was intended? I would surmise it was treated as a lame threat from a semi-reclusive group of people and that mainstream religious fellows gave it little thought and they certainly gave the message of the letter faint recognition because it didn't, and still doesn't, fit into their political or religious agenda.

It seems that most all Indian prophecies, visions, legends etc., are looked upon as nothing more than tribal fantasies to enthrall their little ones or to keep the masses in check with stories of evil deities, strange gods, and boogie men. Nothing is further from the truth. It takes some research and closeness with the various tribes to learn to appreciate their truths and religious beliefs.

WHITE INDIANS AND OTHER INDIAN RACES

To further the idea of a white Indian race we have a most interesting letter concerning the late Milton R. Hunter, a general authority of the LDS Church. Hunter was given a letter the First Presidency had received from an Indian Chief of the Pottawatomie Nation. The First Presidency wished to have Hunter research this letter and to go visit the chief at his home. The letter the First Presidency received reads thusly, addressed to the Church on League of Nations Pan-American Indians letterhead:

Most Honored Brothers:

In that you are brothers of we, the Indian race of the Americas, that you believe the books in the Book of Mormon to be the revealed history of my fathers, and in that you of all the followers of Jesus Christ our Lord do have the true faith, and have built his temple on earth, and that I, Chief Shup-She as defender of my father's faith, and a student of our records, do tell men you are truly builders of the Temple of the Lord.

And word reaches my ear of the good that you do for my blood brothers of the Ute, Shoshone and Navajo Nations makes my heart glad as their councils are also with our League. And because of this good service we of the League shall give service to your church and Chiefs, and ask that your Church be the State Church of our Nations and we ask that you give answer to our League, by me, that I may in like manner answer to our Church. And I must tell you in the wealth of this earth we are poor and our League made up of poor men is poor. We use the monies we collect from our members to fight for our people's rights. If we were to win 1/10 of what the U. S. Government owed us, we would be rich. And in turn your Church also. And I ask one more service of you in this first letter, would you give me the name of one of your people who is versed in the laws of the U. S. Government who has been admitted to the federal bar, we could trust him and he would receive 1/10 of all he won us, plus fees for individual tribes that he worked for on local cases from such tribes.

I have asked much, but we will give our records and histories to you and do service into your Church in like turn.

In peace I close.

(Signed) S.H. L. LaHurreau,

Chief Shup-She, Pottawattomie Nation

On June 15, 1951, Milton R. Hunter, President Carl C. Burton, president of the Great Lakes Mission, and Elder Evan Hale, mission secretary, visited with Howard L. LaHurreau, Chief of the Pottawatomie Tribe at his home at Fort Wayne, Indiana. Hunter's comprehensive report follows:

Visit[ed] with Howard L. LaHurreau, Chief of the Pottawatomi Indians and treasurer of the Inter-National and National Chiefs Grand Council of League of Nations Pan-American Indians June 15 1951. On the evening of June 15, 1951, Pres. Carl C. Burton President of the Great Lakes Mission, Elder Evan Hale, mission secretary, and I spent three and one half hours in the home of Howard L. LaHurreau visiting with him and his wife. It was a very interesting experience and I hope it results in much good for the Church in helping to further missionary work with the Lamanites. LaHurreau is the Chief of the Pottawatomi Indians. His Indian Chief name is Chief Shup-She. He appears to be a man in his thirties. His ancestors are Pottawatomi Indians with cross of French. He is as white as the average white man.

LaHurreau's wife is a beautiful full blood Cherokee Indian. She is also white and her mother, who was at the home visiting, is as white as any of the white people. Chief and Mrs. LaHurreau have four children, two boys and two girls, ranging from eight to four years of age. One of the boys has blue eyes and the other three dark brown eyes, and they are also all as white as the average white children. The four year old boy has curly hair and is really a handsome little chap. Throughout the entire evening the children stayed in the room with us and were unusually well behaved. Mr. LaHurreau made the remark that he and his wife wanted their children to stay out of bed "to be present and hear good men talk."

The Indians of Canada, United States, Mexico and South America have organized into what they term the League of Nations Pan-American Indians. The purpose of this organization seems to be furthering the cause of the Lamanites and to work for their spiritual, economic, social and political advancement.

Figure 7 Howard L. LaHurreau, Chief Shup-She, Pottawatomi Nation

The Indians have an International and Nations Chief Grand Council which is composed of Tribal Chieftains from each of the Americas. Chief Howard L. LaHurreau is the treasurer of the United States Central Committee of the Chiefs' Grand Council. He is in a position of authority of sufficient importance to do the Church much good in furthering our program of carrying the Gospel of Jesus Christ to the Indians. Before the evening's conference was concluded, LaHurreau informed us of the fact that the League of Nations Pan-American Indians were going to hold an International Council of the Chiefs at Independence, Missouri, during the last week of August of this year. He extended to me an invitation for the Indians Relations Committee of The Church of Jesus Christ to attend that council of the Chiefs and informed me that the Chiefs would grant us equal voting powers and the rights of speech which are enjoyed by all of the chiefs who will be delegates at that Grand Council. He claims that that is the highest honor the Indians are capable of bestowing on us. He said that he would send us a written invitation when definite arrangements have been made. I advised him to send the invitation to the chairmen of the Indians Relation Committee, and he agreed to do so.

I am waiting with great anticipation to see what happens at that Grand Council for the Indian Chiefs and the five new members of their council—the Indian Relation Committee members of The Church of Jesus Christ of Latter-day Saints. It may be that the time has come for the Lord to open the way whereby we can really take the gospel message to the Lamanites and have them as a nation give a receptive ear to the same. We shall hope and pray that that is the case.

A REMARKABLE OUTCOME

One of the most interesting things that Chief LaHurreau told us during the course of the evening's conference was that at last council meeting of the League of Nations Pan American Indians that many reports were made by the Navajos relative to the kindness of The Church of Jesus Christ of Latter-day Saints in sending that people many articles they badly needed to relieve them from their distress. On the other hand, no other churches paid any attention to the terrible distress. He said that the decision was made at that convention or council meeting to "adopt The Church of Jesus Christ of Latter-day Saints" to be the State Church of all Indian Nations. He, LaHurreau, had been appointed by the Indian delegates at the council of the Chiefs to make the foregoing offer to the Church. Another very interesting thing that Chief Howard. LuHarreau told us was that there was a city of "White Indians" located in Guatemala. He showed us the exact location on the map. The city is called the "Star God City" in commemoration of the visit of the White-bearded God who had visited the ancestors of the White Indians in that city, when the White God appeared to the ancient Americans of Guatemala, on the shores of a lake. At the present time it has a population of approximately 200 white Indians. The city has a wall around it made of limestone. It has four gates in the wall, one in each of the four walls. There are four temples in the city. The language of the people in this city is that of the Mayan people, or, LaHurreau thinks, the original tongue of the Lamanites and Nephites. He advised that if one went to the city he would need to have two interpreters, one versed in Spanish and one in Mayan. According to the report of LaHurreau, the people of the Star God City are anxiously looking for the second coming of the "Star God" or Jesus Christ and the building of a holy city in which the Star God will dwell. He says their belief is similar to ours regarding the New Jerusalem. They think that this holy city or the New Jerusalem will be built somewhere in North America, but they do not know the exact spot. We informed him that the spot had been dedicated by the Prophet Joseph Smith at Independence, Jackson County Missouri, and he replied that that spot would be in harmony with the beliefs of his people and very favorable to them. Furthermore, LaHurreau claims that the White Indians are busy at the present time collecting and cutting stones of various kinds to be used in the construction of the temple in the New Jerusalem. Chief LaHurreau claims that these things he has told us are all facts and not hearsay. He knows through actual experience and testified that he was not lying. He was selected as one of the chiefs of one of the North American Indian tribes to go to that city and receive education in the traditions of the Indian people. Indians from various parts of the country are sent there to be trained before they take over in their home tribes as chiefs. LaHurreau spent eighteen months in the Star God City as part of his training to become a Chief of the Pottawatomie Indians.

IS NATONI NEZ-BAB ACTUALLY TONI NESPAH?

Being aware of the claim made by Toni Nespah, I asked him questions regarding Toni. He claims that Toni Nespah was also trained in the Star God City representing the Navajo Indians. When the young Indian Chiefs who are trained in that city leave the holy city to return to their various tribes they take a vow never to lead white men to that city. LaHurreau claims that Toni Nespah of the Navajo Indians broke his vows by speaking to the Mormon people and also to the Reorganized Church members at Independence, Missouri, about the sacred city and especially by offering to take any of them to the city of the Star God. He also made the remark that

Nespah was not a good man in many other respects; therefore, the Indians had rejected him as had the members of The Church of Jesus Christ of Latter-day Saints. LaHurreau claims that the Shite Indians in the Star God City have always had the priesthood [and] that it came down through their people from the ancient Americans. He claims that it is the Aaronic Priesthood that these people had. Of course, we took advantage of the opportunity to explain to him regarding the apostasy in ancient America and the loss of the priesthood and the restoration of the priesthood to the Prophet Joseph Smith. I believe that we convinced him, but he remarked that our job would be to convince the other chiefs of the various other Indian tribes. There is one more important idea that I forgot to mention in regard to the building of the temple in the New Jerusalem. The white Indians have the tradition that they are merely to assist in the erection of the temple. They have been told that another people will arise in the United States and work with them on that temple. LaHurreau also told us that the white Indians in the Star God City have been visited from time to time by three men with long white beards dressed in white robes and that their priests had received direction from these three men as occasion would require. He also claims that these three men have visited Indian tribes in almost every part of North America on various occasions and through their council have saved the Indians many times from calamites. Chief LaHurreau also claims that the white Indians in the Star God City who live there have been protected by the Star God. The Spaniards have not been able to capture that city or to destroy the culture of the people. He believes that someday members of the true Church of Jesus Christ who hold the (Higher) Priesthood will be permitted to visit that ancient holy city, but that will not happen until the Lord wants them to. Naturally we took full advantage of the opportunity to again assert we belonged to the true Church of Jesus Christ and were holders of the Holy Melchizedek Priesthood.

NO PRIESTHOOD AUTHORITY?

Clarence L. Wheaton, A Delaware Indian, and one of the twelve apostles in the Hedrikite Church, or the Church of Christ at Independence, Missouri, and his wife made an attempt this year [1951?] to visit the Star God City. Mr. Wheaton received letters to the Mexican Government officials from LaHurreau and also from Dr. Danial Reuben Barbeolis of the Instituto Nacional de Antropologia. LeHurreau claims that Dr. Borbella was the most important man in Mexico to assist the Church of Jesus Christ if we desire to work with the Indians in Mexico or visit the Star God City. Mr. Wheaton left in January for Guatemala in his endeavor of visiting the Star God City and he very recently arrived back at Independence. He never reached the city of White Indians but arrived near the city. On account of illness he was forced to return to the U. S. He and his wife are both ill and are in the hospital at Independence at the present time. A son of one of the Mayan Chiefs dreamed three nights straight that Mr. Wheaton was coming and in response to that dream he walked forty miles from his home in Yucatan to the airport and was there to meet Mr. Wheaton when the plane arrived. He was able to recognize him from his dreams. We ask[ed] Chief LaHurreau why he thought that Mr. Wheaton had not reached the city of White Indians. He replied that probably Mr. Wheaton did not hold the High Priesthood and probably God did not want him to reach the city. We assured him that we were certain that Mr. Wheaton did not hold the Priesthood and we would agree with him that probably God did not want him to reach the city.

RECORDS ON METAL PLATES

Mr. LaHurreau stated that not only did the Indians in Guatemala keep records on metal plates, but most of the tribes in North America did the same thing. For example, the Chippewa's or Ojibwa tribe of Indians in Wisconsin have a depository of records. This depository is located near Shawano, Wisconsin, near the city limits. These records are composed of copper and the writing is engraved on forty eight plates, engraving being on both sides of the plate. The writing is a pictorial writing but there are men in the tribe who know how to read it. The record begins with the arrival in America of the ancestors of these Indians and comes on down to the present time. These Indians have the practice of writing the main events of their history while they live in one place on one plate. Every time they move on another section of the country, they write on another plate. LaHurreau claimed that the Indians in the northeastern part of the U. S. wrote on lead plates. He claims to have seen some of the Indian records. He thinks that through proper contact that we might induce the Indians to let us see their records, I mean, some of the Indian records. We asked Mr. LaHurreau many questions regarding the traditions and beliefs of the Indians. He said that probably their most universal belief was the tradition of the visit to Ancient America of the "White Bearded God" and of his promise to return. The Indian tribes from Peru to Canada are looking forward to the return of the Savior. We mentioned as a proof to this tradition that the ancients had built a statue of the crucified Lord at Mileta, Mexico, which showed Christ's wounds. We asked if the Indians believed in the bestowal of the Holy Ghost. The answer was yes, but he was under oath not to repeat their ceremony of baptizing the [receiving of the] Holy Ghost. He said that these ordinances are secret ordinances such as our temple ordinances.

Chief LaHurreau also claimed that the foregoing ordinances and many others were at one time performed by their priests in their temples in ancient times when they had temples. The sweat house substituted for the temples.

MIGRATIONS FROM THE EAST

We were very interested in Mr. LaHurreau's explanation of the migration of people to ancient America. He said that the Indians had traditions of their ancestors living in America continuously from Adam's time, and that the population on this land had been augmented from time to time by four or five migrations. These migrations all came to America from the East. It is evident that the Indian's tradition agrees with the Book of Mormon in several important respects. The people who came here were led by the Lord, according to LaHurreau and also according to the Nephite record; he said that one group of colonists came to America about 4,000 years ago in boats, like tortoise shells. This migration would compare favorably with the Jaredites. Chief LaHurreau explained that their traditions also told of groups of colonists who compared favorably with the Nephites and Mulekites. He also told of the coming of the yellow race and that they brought to America the bad practices of scalping, real human sacrifices and much sex immorality. Part of these people married and merged with the Indians and became the Aztec Indians of Mexico and others moved eastward across the U.S. and became the Algonquin.

The most wicked portion of the eastern Orientals that came to America however, were driven northward by the Indians and became the Eskimos of today. He claimed that because of their gross wickedness of such practice of trading wives, drinking blood, eating raw flesh, and many other similar wicked practices, the Eskimos were hated by the North American Indians. Indians will not associate with nor will they think of marrying them.

Chief LaHurreau reported to us that there are 40 families of Pottawatomi Indians living at or near Athens, Michigan, and about 8,000 other Indians living in other parts of Michigan. To get in touch with Indians at Athens, we should contact Elbert Hackety. He also said that there were 300 families of Indians at Mimi, some at Ft. Wayne and others living at other places in Indiana. Their headquarters are at Peru, Indiana. To get in contact with these Indians we should do so through Chief Isa S. Godfrey, R.F.D. No 1, Peru, Indiana. At the end of our evening's visit we asked Chief LaHurreau if he desired us to pray with the family. He and his wife seemed highly pleased. They asked me to be mouth in offering the prayer. Pres. Burton, Elder Hale and I joined with the family in a circle. We kneeled and I offered the prayer as requested.

I was greatly impressed with this Indian family. Chief LaHurreau seemed to be telling the truth. Pres. Burton, Elder Hale and I all felt a very good spirit in their home. In fact we returned to the mission home with the feeling in our hearts that we had had a wonderful, and we hope had a profitable evening. It is out hope that great good will come from this conference in visiting or opening the way to spread the gospel of Jesus Christ among the Lamanites.

Milton R. Hunter filed a complete report with the President of the Quorum of the Twelve Apostles, Joseph Fielding Smith. It is unclear how this report was received, but little has ever been said about it. A post script gives us insight about how Hunter felt regarding the meeting with LaHurreau.

P.S. June 21, 1951. This evening we held a conference at Ft. Wayne, Indiana. Chief LaHurreau and his wife were in attendance at the meeting. They were highly impressed. Following the meeting we had another interesting conversation with these good people. Chief LaHurreau told me that he would do anything in the world that I should ask him to do except guide me to the Star God City. He was under oath not to do that. He mentioned that if I wanted any letters of recommendation to any chiefs in Yucatan, to any of them who possessed records, or to the officials of Mexico, if I should be assigned or decide to visit the Star God City, he would be pleased to write such letters of recommendation. He also mentioned the fact that if there were any other services he could render, he would feel it an honor to do so. He was highly impressed with the conference session and believed the doctrine taught by the speakers. He again reminded me that the Indians Relations Committee of the Church was invited to attend the Internation[al] and National Chiefs Grand Council in August at Independence, Missouri, and that occasion would furnish the Church a wonderful opportunity to teach the Indian Chiefs the story of the Book of Mormon and the fact that the gospel had been restored. He mentioned the fact that if he could convert the chiefs to the Church, the people would come in too.

It seems obvious that the Indian people for the most part had always wanted peace with others and were willing to do anything to promote it. By European standards their life was simple and quite backwards, but this is far from true! The Indian was far more sophisticated than he appeared. He had religion, he had God, he loved his family, he loved nature, he never took more than he used, and he always gave to the poor of his tribe. True, they did war one with another over issues that are no different by today's standards. But all in all they were quite a peaceful people.

ORIGINS OF DIFFERENT AMERICAN INDIAN TRIBES

Milton R. Hunter, a general authority of The Church of Jesus Christ of Latter-day Saints, gave the following report to the Indian Relations Committee and to the President of the Quorum of the Twelve Apostles on June 15, 1951: [2]

.....this comment has another part as told by the Iroquois of New York. The historical Indians we call *Delaware* which anciently were known as the Lenni Lenapees, did indeed come from the west in great numbers. That in times past they desired to return to their original homeland in the east along the Atlantic seaboard. These "Delaware" Indians had many, many years ago lived in the eastern portion of present day United States but had at one time, picked up and moved far to the western regions of this land. It is here, in this western land area that the influx and mixing with the yellow race occurred according to their own history as recorded [through oral tradition] "mouth to ear;" they decided to return to the land of their forefathers to the east. It is only common sense that any investigator who researches into the lives, history and origin of the American Indian is to listen to their own oral histories and written word! Why should an investigator solely rely on previously written works or ideas of origin according to mainstream academia? We should always do our own research and come to our own conclusions by interacting with the principles we are researching. This is not saying that all research done is bogus but we need to authenticate it first if at all possible.

There are many histories from American Indians across America that hardly anyone hears or reads about. There are authors that have written about these histories and they have made an impact with many others who thirst for such knowledge. However, our schools—from elementary through college—refuse to acknowledge the works of these great researchers, authors and historians.

In order to rectify this situation insofar as possible, I submit a few articles from different tribes as to their origin and histories.

ORIGINS OF THE SIOUX ACCORDING TO THEIR HISTORY

From an interview by the late Fred Rydholm, author of *Michigan's Copper: The Untold Story,* he learned from a Sioux Chief named Herbert Welsh (grandson of Sitting Bull), his wife Mrs. Welsh and Tom Wastaken, that Indians did not migrate over the Bering Strait land bridge as so many scholars claim. Chief Welsh remarked:

> *Do you see my eyes? Can you see this epicanthic fold so characteristic among oriental people? I (my ancestors) came from that direction (west). My wife does not have this eye characteristic because her people (Algonquians) came from the other direction (east). Your archaeologists have concluded that all Indian Nations came from the west, but had they asked us, we would have told them both directions are correct. Both Mrs. Welsh and Mr. Wastaken, both Ojibwas, confirmed that this was true. Wastaken then added that he was always told that his ancestors long ago came from the "land of the rising sun." The scientists can believe what they want but all the tribes have many differences of customs, traditions, and language.*

Wastaken said he could always tell Indians apart tribe by tribe. He knew immediately when he entered Cree country as they all look just like white people except their hair and eyes are always dark.

MENOMINEE TRIBAL BELIEFS

Dr. James P. Scherz, PhD, interviewed a member of the Menominee tribe concerning his beliefs, asking specific questions:

Did you get the little horses from the Vikings?" "No," was the Indian's reply, "from the Chinese." Becoming more excited, he said, "Look, we knew about people across both the western and eastern seas. We were not isolated savages as they teach in the schools. We were part of a world community and knew it. We knew about other peoples of the world. People from across the seas came to visit and we went there to visit. And we knew about the man you call Jesus long before the coming of the Black Robes (Jesuits). We called him East Star Man. In the old language he was referred to as Wa Pahn, and there are many place names honoring Him. His religion was called Wa Pah Nu. The white authors say there is a Wa Pah Nu tribe. It was not a real tribe but just a religious group of many different tribes. We knew all about your Jesus and how he had been fastened to a tree with nails though his wrists. And we know all about his teachings. But we did not have the white man's sacred book, the Bible. We knew such things verbally. We kept such things in our hearts.

In an interview with Fred Kennedy, a Seneca Elder of New York, Dr Scherz asked about race and the tradition of Jesus. Kennedy had this to say:

That long ago in New York State there was a major confrontation between his people and another people of lighter skin. They fought over who would control God! These other people lost. We won the fight.

Dr. Scherz then asked him "Why was this fight so important?" Fred said it involved the Wau-Pa-Nu.

The Wau-Pa-Nu is our priesthood. These men could go among all the tribes to act as arbitrators, messengers and spiritual leaders among our many people. The Wau-Pa-Nu had their beginning when East Star Man appeared. He set up new laws, healed the sick and ended blood sacrifice. Now we use tobacco in place of blood to offer sacrifice.

Fred Kennedy then stated that the word Oneida (which is a tribe of the Iroquois nation) means "keepers of the stone" or "keepers of the hill." The hill he refers to is Oneidah Hill.

EAST STAR MAN ON THE SHORES OF MISHEE-GAHME

Dark Thunder, Chief of the Ojibwa, spoke of this divine visitor, or the Prophet, as he called him:

Very well, let us speak of the Prophet. He was bearded, and pale of feature, without doubt a White Man. His eyes were as grey-green as the still green water, and just as changeable in their color. He came to us one day at dawning and the light touched His hair with the sheen of red-gold until it shone like newly mined-copper. Yet He was not as the men of your people. This one was a god, with high soul-stature. If He touched a man who was wounded, that one became healed.

His robe was long and white down to the hemline which almost hid His golden sandals. Everyone wished to make him white robes, for then He would leave behind the old ones, and all that He touched was enchanted with His god-like power of healing. He came alone. He organized churches, changed the temples, taught the priesthood. Some say He taught them a secret language with certain signs of greetings. He came to us when we had cities more than a thousand winters before the days of the Black Robes (Jesuits) and the Long Knives (English and French). The city we call sacred is not far from here. Its history is longer than that of England's London. Once we had books and priests to read them. Books are of stuff which can be swept to oblivion. Since then we have places our stories in the chants of our people, but now even these are being forgotten." (See He Walked the Americas for additional details.)

SUMMARY STATEMENT

The evidence is mounting that the Indian people were much more than what is being taught in our public schools. As a society we would do well to lend an ear to the written and oral histories of the Indian people, including those of ancient origin. We need to learn and grow in the knowledge that they, for the most part, were God-fearing religious people with ideals, morals, and family ties that surpass those of many so-called civilized people of today. They cared more about their religious beliefs, family, honor, life, flora and fauna than most people do today. It would take volumes to give a complete history of each tribe that has lived upon "this land" and to provide a narrative of their mortal existence. They are of the Tribe of Israel as are many others living upon this land that God has seen fit to give to His chosen people, the Children of Israel!

2

THE SPANISH LEGACY

"For ye know that ye were not redeemed with corruptible things as silver and gold."
1 Peter 1:18

MUCH HAS BEEN WRITTEN ABOUT the Spanish invasion of the New World. Scores of books, papers and movies have plagued us since we were young and learned about them in school. However, how much of what we learned is really true?

History tells us a little bit of the major Spanish explorations and expeditions into the land of milk and honey of the west. Of course we know the tale of Christopher Columbus and his adventures in the Gulf of Mexico and the Caribbean Ocean. After he made his mark upon the land then came a host of others. Listed below are names of explorers and when and where they explored:[3]

Explorer	Area/Lands/Impact
Juan de Grijalva	Coast of Mexico
Hernando Cortez	Conquest of Mexico
Panfilo de Narvaez	Coast of Florida
Cabeza de Vaca	Florida, Arizona, Mexico
Juan de Asuncion/Fray Nadal	Arizona and Cibola
Melchior Diaz	Gila River, Arizona
Hernando DeSoto	Gulf Coast, Mississippi Valley
Hernando Coronado	North to Cibola, Quivira
Hernando de Alarcon	Colorado River and Arizona
Pedro de Tovar	To Tusayan, Colorado River

Garica Lopez Espejo	Grand Canyon, Southern Utah
Francisco de Ibarra	The Land of the Yutas
Antonio de Espejo	New Mexico and Colorado
Gaspar de Sosa	Mines of New Mexico
Fray Augustin Rodriguez	Mission, New Mexico
Gaspar de Sosa	Slave Trader
Luis de Carabajal	Illegal mining in the north
Juan Humana	Explores Wyoming
Juan de Onate	Mining in New Mexico
Marcos Farfan	Mining the San Juan River, Utah
Juan de Onate	Sierra Azul, Teguayo
Fray Estevan Perea	North into Ute Country
Vincent Saldivar	Mapped Teguayo
Fray Geronimo Salmeron	Utah Valley, Wasatch Range
Fray Bartolomé Romero	Builds Mission, San Juan River
Fray Alonso Benavidas	Locates mines at Teguayo
	Dates inscribed at Glen Canyon
Fray Alonzo Posada	Describes Utah Valley
Diego de Peñalosa	Explores North Platt River
Juan de Archuleta	Slaving in Wyoming
Alvarez de Leon	Mining in Uinta Mountains
Antonio de Oterman	Makes Treaty with the Utes
Don Juanillo	Escapes from Utes, Utah Valley
Pedro de Abalos	Mines in New Mexico
Fray Alonzo de Posada	Second trip to Utah Lake
Diego de Varga	Re-conquest of Ute Country
Rogue de Madrid	Slaving in Colorado
Juan de Uribarri	Slaving in Northern Utah
Juan de Uribarri	Mining in Northern Utah
Juan de Uribarri	Discovers ancient mines, Utah
Don Diego Garcia	Uinta Mountains, Utah

Pedro de Villasur	Utah and Wyoming Missions
Don Pedro	Mining gold in Utah
Fray Carlos Jose Delgado	Maps Northern Utah
	Ute-Spanish Treaty Utah-Colorado
Padre La Rue	Mining San Andreas Mountains
Juan Maria de Rivera	Central Utah, Sevier Lake
Juan Maria de Rivera	Northern Utah, Idaho
Marquis de Rubi	Inspects Northern Missions
Antonio y Ramariz	Maps Teguayo, Utah Lake
Teodoro de Croix	Inspects Northern Mines
Gregorio Sandoval, Munez	Uinta Basin, Utah Mines
Dominquez-Escalante	Great Basin Expedition
Juan Bautista de Anza, Governor	Slaving in Colorado
Juan Bautista de Anza, Governor	Arrests Illegal Miners Utah Area
Juan Bautista de Anza, Governor	Illegal Mining Parties Utah-Colorado
Juan Bautista de Anza, Governor	Ute-Spanish Treaty
Fray Augustin de Morfi	Northern Missions
Manuel Maestes	Trading, Utah Lake, Utah
Captain Joaquin Garcia	Hoyt Peak Gold Mines
Jose Rafael Sarracino	Seeks Lost Mission, Utah
Mauricio Arze, Lagas Garcia	Slaving Utah Lake area.
Ute Rebellion	Utah Forts, Mines, Missions burned and concealed

Of course there was the great Pueblo Revolt that took place in 1680. Historians, inaccurate in their presentation of this revolt, have stated that New Mexico's seventeenth-century experience displayed the actions and motivations of its most numerous and yet historically almost silent participants of the revolt, the Pueblo Indians; attest to their facts that the Indians of that time were non-literate in pre-modern times. Historians claim that the people of the five major language groups—Piro, Hopi, Zuñi, Tano (including its three subgroups Tiwa, Tewa, and Towa), and Keresan, known collectively as the Pueblo Indians of northern New Mexico—have " . . . left little tangible record of their early past."

THE PUEBLO REVOLT OF 1680

The Pueblo people, Native Americans living in what is now New Mexico, rose up against Spanish conquistadores in the wake of religious persecution, violence, and drought. The uprising aimed to reclaim Pueblo religious practices, culture, and land, which had been obliterated by Spanish conquistadores.

Although the Pueblo uprising ultimately failed to take back Santa Fe from Spanish colonizers, the Pueblo people made a lasting impact on the dominant culture of the Southwest.

Having found wealth in Mexico, the Spanish looked north to expand their empire into the land of the Pueblo people. The Spanish expected present-day New Mexico to yield gold and silver, but they were mistaken. Instead, they established a political base in Santa Fe in 1610, naming it the capital of the Kingdom of New Mexico. It became an outpost of the larger Spanish Viceroyalty of New Spain, headquartered in Mexico City.

As they had in other Spanish colonies, missionaries built churches and forced the Pueblos to convert to Catholicism, requiring native people to discard their own religious practices entirely. They focused their conversion projects on young Pueblos, drawing them away from their parents and traditions.

The Spanish demanded corn and labor from the Pueblos, but a long period of drought impeded production, escalating tension in Santa Fe. The Pueblo also suffered increased attacks on their villages by rival native groups, which they attributed to the Spanish presence.

Popé, a Pueblo leader and medicine man led a response to the persecution and violence—a return to native customs. He popularized the idea that "when Jesus came, the Corn Mothers went away." This was a succinct way of describing the displacement of native traditions by the culture and religion of the Spanish.

Taos Pueblo served as a base for Popé during the uprising.

A member of the Six Nations Reserve recounts an intriguing alternative story from a ceramist:

I recall a Pueblo artist who crafted a series of pots in the ancient style, but the story as told within his pueblo was that Popé was a cacique, a priest or holy man, who was whipped by the Franciscan priests trying to enforce Catholicism. Incensed by the disrespect and humiliation against one who should have been honored as a wise elder, to say nothing of the total invalidation of sacred beliefs, Popé plotted his revenge—the total overthrow of the Spanish overlords. History records that the timing was a series of knotted cords—much like the Inca, but the story given to the ceramic artist, as told within his pueblo, differs significantly. Rather than knotted cords, it was beans, a humble staple, not likely to attract attention regarding the time of the attack. I tend to be biased in favor of the storyteller, rather than the writer of history, as history's tale lies within the realm of the victor.

The plan was ingenious—Popé gathered a number of leather bags, into which he counted the exact same number of beans. He then sent runners who would travel to a pueblo carrying a bag of beans, removing one bean for each day they traveled. The bags were then given to the leader with specific instructions. At each respective pueblo, they were to remove one bean each day. When the bag of beans was empty, then they would revolt. The plan was largely successful—the hated Spanish were kept out of the Pueblos for years—and the level of persecution and control was never the same. One might reasonably state that the short-term victory of the 1680 Revolt passed on down through the years—time was forever changed in this aspect.

That's the best of my account—just wish I had my sources, but it was in some art history/human nature/natural history venue. I remember seeing the art pieces commemorating the revolt as told from the artist's prospective—more than thirty years ago (compliments of Gordon Soaring Hawk of the Six Nations).

So, on that fateful day in 1680, the Pueblo launched a coordinated attack on the Spanish. Pueblos, Navajos, and Apaches from the region congregated and planned to strike Santa Fe when the Spaniards were low on supplies. They laid siege to the city for nine days and cut off the

Spanish water supply. The uprising, also known as Popé's Rebellion, killed over 400 Spaniards and drove the remaining 2,000 Spanish settlers south toward Mexico. Participants in the rebellion also destroyed many mission churches in an effort to diminish Catholic physical presence on Pueblo land. Pueblo historian Joe S. Sando calls the movement "the first American revolution."

The Pueblo reestablished their religious institutions and a government of their own for the next 12 years of independence. However, as droughts and attacks by rival tribes continued, the Spanish sensed an opportunity to regain their foothold. In 1692, the Spanish military returned and reasserted their control of the area. (See Khan Academy Spanish Colonization 1491-1607 for more details: https://www.khanacademy.org/humanities/us-history/precontact-and-early-colonial-era/spanish-colonization/a/pueblo-uprising-of-1680.)

EXPLOITATION

The Spanish deemed anyone who was not of pure Spanish bloodlines as infidels to be wiped out, after they were baptized of course! The Indians of the land were not illiterate as I have demonstrated in the previous chapter. Cortez knew this as well. He had to save face in front of his men by playing the Master over all! Gold! Gold! Gold! was on the minds of the Spanish!

At Mexico City, Cortez found hoards of treasure which had been hidden by its citizens, and also recovered part of Montezuma's ransom, which had been thrown into the lake when his soldiers were forced from the city. Only a small part of the treasure was recovered, but still it was a fabulous fortune. Recovered were "150,000 castellanos of gold, 88,000 pesos in gold bars, thousands of gold plates and a mass of jewels." From the sealed treasure room found by his soldiers, Cortez took *"gold worth more than 600,000 ducats, which we melted into bars three fingers wide."* During the next two years Cortez sent ten tons of gold to Spain as the King's Quinto, his one-fifth share, which was more than all of the nations of Europe then possessed, except Spain!

It mattered little to Cortez or his men how many natives they killed in the process of getting gain! Did they *really* want to save the Indians from themselves? Did they *really* want to save them from a certain hell? Or did they only want the spoils of a defeated nation?

In a letter written by Cortez to the King of Spain he described some of the Royal Fifth. "*Of all the gold smelted, one-fifth was put aside for the Royal Treasury, as well as jewels, 33,000 ounces of gold in ingots and 60,000 ounces of gold castellanos. I also sent a field piece made entirely of silver, which cost me in metal working alone some 35,000 ounces of gold; this I sent as well as certain gold and silver ornaments, jewels and gems.*" Of the richness of the land, Viceroy Marques de Montesclaras later wrote, "Truly the land is overflowing with wealth, so that it is deemed easier and cheaper to arm men and to shoe horses with silver than it is with iron!"

The earliest explorers, even before the 16th century arrival of the Spanish, quickly learned that the new world was a virtual treasure house of precious metals and gem stones. Thus, they just as quickly became adept at exploiting this new treasure trove.

The Spanish were fairly restricted from working mines of wealth because of their lack of numbers. Not more than 150 men usually came with each galleon, and their numbers were decimated by disease and warfare with the Indians who greatly outnumbered them. In one case involving 1,300 Spanish soldiers sent to the new world, the Indians killed 862 of them and many of these were the victims of cannibals along the Mexican coast.

Balboa had described the state of affairs to the king, "*Two days journey from here there is very beautiful country, inhabited by a very evil race, who eat as many of our men as they can get. They have no chief and are the lords of the mines, which are the richest in the world. These Indians have deserved death a thousand times over, for they are a very evil race who has killed many of our Christians. I would not make slaves of so bad a people, but would order them to be destroyed, both old and young, so that no memory of them might remain!*"

ENCOMIENDA

About 1495, the problem of having little or no labor to work the mines was solved when a system known as "Encomienda" was implemented. This law, for the most part, was in force within the Indies for more than 300 years. The Spanish overlords used this system to enslave the local Indians and made them provide labor and tribute to the King's agent in order to receive Christian instruction—but it was just another name for "slavery."

Columbus himself imposed a tribute on the Indians. He taxed each "a hawksbill of gold of an arroba (25 lbs) of cotton every three months." The King of Spain authorized the branding of slaves, but stipulated that they should not be branded on the face! It was the Encomienda system that gave legal justification for the slavery imposed, thus making it possible for the legal looting of the wealth of the Americas. Consequently, the Indians were soon being forced to work in mines or on Rancherias under the most horrid conditions! This slavery of Indians continued up until the Great Revolt of 1680.

While this was going on in the western part of the country, significant events were occurring in the eastern part of the country. In 1585-86 the great, well-known artist John White spent fifteen months in what is now North Carolina, painting more than seventy watercolors of people, plants and animals. His work was later distributed in a series of romanticized engravings. His illustrations of the Native peoples were always portrayed in superb health and in excellent physical condition—nothing like his European counterparts that were contemporaneous. These Indians were impressive to the Europeans with their well-organized villages and huge gardens of corn, squash, potatoes, and beans.

Why these great organizations were not brutalized like their western brothers is because of their heritage and beliefs. They also relied on various tribal confederacies and allies to help in case of crisis. However, they were at the mercy of the European onslaught that was upon them.

It had been noted in many journals concerning the stature and height of some of these eastern seaboard Indians and their complexions as well. The Natives had a strict duty to cleanliness and bathed sometimes twice a day. They were disgusted by the stench of the Europeans and how they let themselves go dirty for so long. The Europeans were equally disgusted by the way the Indians presented themselves—using multicolored textiles, skins and hair hanging from their bodies, bear fat or eagle fat smeared on their skin and hair to ward of harmful sun rays, wind, and insects. The robes of the chiefs were adorned with animal heads, snake skins belts, and bird wing or tail feather headdresses. Tattooing was used on their faces, arms and legs with many elaborate geometric designs. They assumed the Pilgrims of the time were less intelligent than they and were quick to announce it.

What a contrast between the Indians from one side of the country to the other. Yet, they all had a common desire—simply to be left alone!

The Spanish and other Europeans had other ideas, and in not too many generations the Native Indian's way of life would be greatly and forever altered.

LOST CITIES AND GOLD

That the Spanish came to the southwest to harvest gold and silver is an understatement! They wanted total control of the populace and all that the land had to offer. Legends flowed out of the mouths of friendly Indians about lost gold mines from ancient times and the fabled *Lost City of Cibola*. This only managed to further drive the Spaniards' greed to an all-time high!

During the second half of the seventeenth century, the slave trade was flourishing as never before! In 1661 Governor Diego de Peñalosa asked the King's permission to lead an expedition to locate a quicksilver mine told to him by Natives in the Teguayo, not far from Sierra Azul, in the Blue Mountains of Silver. Many thought the Governor was a liar, that he really did not do much with the permission granted him by the King.

It wasn't until 1856 that a document was discovered in the Spanish archives at Seville revealed the truth. The document was recorded by Franciscan Father Nicholas de Freytas in 1663 describing the discoveries made by the Governor. More importantly, the document spoke of the mines located in the northern mountains which he learned of but was not allowed to investigate.

In 1662, Peñalosa led a force of eighty Spaniards with Captain Michael de Noriega, and of course a friar whose name was Father Freytas. Besides the above mentioned soldiers, they took some 1,000 plus Indian slaves and burden carriers with two dozen two-wheeled carts to carry their supplies. Instructed to investigate a report of the French encroachment upon Spanish territory, Peñalosa turned northeast. Eventually they arrived at the Missouri River then turned up towards the Platte River. Along their route they encountered strange Indians that gave him accounts of the country further ahead that excited him. The reports gleaned from those Indians told of great mines near the great land they called Aca-nada or Canada, *"where the abundance of silver and gold is such that all vessels are made of silver, and in some cases of gold."* During the visit of these Indians, he also learned of a great lake called "Copalla" where the richest mines in the region were located. The Indians showed him gold nuggets that came from those mines which the Governor purchased from the Indians. Longing to reach this great region he found himself separated by a serious obstacle: "*...we stand separated by a very lofty sierra, which the inhabitants of these regions do not know the termination of.*"

Peñalosa decided to try another route to the land of "Copalla," but upon his return to Santa Fe, he was taken prisoner by the interrogators of the Inquisition and charged with blasphemy. He was imprisoned two and one-half years, and upon his release, all accounts of the lands he discovered were gone and he was banished to Spain—never to return again.

However, records indicate that his dream of finding the lake called Copalla was still in the minds of others that followed after him. Spaniards went north to find the riches of the land. Many slaves were captured and used in the mines, smelters, and arrastras (ore crushing machines). To prevent escape, some unfortunate Indians lost their toes on one foot so that running was not an option. Women were used and abused and then discarded. However, as long as they were baptized before killing them, it was right with the Church.

These practices caused a Catholic padre who sympathized with the Indians to write "there we saw many Indians laboring in the mines. The soldiers are sometimes harsh in their treatment of the Indians, neither is it strange then for the Indians to flee from the Spaniards to escape laboring in the mines. Liberty means much to these primitive people, who have always known liberty."

Many who managed to escape took Spanish horses and arms with them. Old records in the archives tell of parties being sent into the far reaches of the Ute Indian country to capture runaway slaves.

In 1664, the Governor sent Juan de Archuleta with troops of soldiers to pursue these runaway slaves. They pursued them into Colorado and into Wyoming and were able to capture many of them. He was surprised to find out while in this pursuit that certain mines the Indians knew about were not *Indian* mines, but very ancient mines, which he was told dated back some 5000 to 6000 years. Ancient timbers from wood not found on the mountains at that time were used as mine supports. Strange mining techniques perplexed the Spaniards.

It is obvious they had little or no knowledge of the superior mining techniques and ways of smelting and purifying metals possessed by the ancient inhabitants, something that was not really studied until the late 19th century.

As the Spanish acquired more information concerning lost mines and treasures they began hearing about an ancient race that had great wealth and that it was hidden in caverns and caves throughout the land. Using their *normal*, meaning torture tactics of gleaning needed information from the Indians, they moved forces into lands where these ancient inhabitants flourished. They heard rumors of red-haired giants that had inhabited the land, as well as other beings of huge stature. They heard of their riches, and this naturally made the Spaniards anxious to obtain this great wealth for themselves.

SANPETE VALLEY

One such site is situated in Central Utah and known as Sanpete Valley. It is here that The Church of Jesus Christ of Latter-day Saints built a Temple, the area having been settled in modern times under the direction of then President Brigham Young. It is not a surprise that this valley was chosen, for it is said to be a sacred place that had once been the home of Nephites and Jaredites of Book of Mormon fame. Many strange archaeological discoveries have been made here.

In 1850 the Spanish came to Sanpete looking for a site they were told about. This information was said to have been gleaned by the death of an Indian Chief's son as he was being torn asunder by two horses pulling him apart! Nevertheless, the information was now theirs. The search for these chambers of wealth was ongoing from the time the Spanish entered into the depth of the continent until they were finally expelled.

The story tells of a Spanish train coming out of Utah's high Uinta country with a store of gold on its way to Santa Fe. In addition to the gold, the Spanish brought information about a cave situated in the mountains, at the edge of Sanpete Valley. With Ute Indians as guides, they pushed ahead into the valley only to turn and go up a side canyon choked with brush, rock and steep cliffs. The difficulty of traversing the canyon was treacherous and foreboding.

They finally reached the top of the mountain where they were told of the site on a nearby hill not too far from their present position. Gathering a few men, the Spaniards took six Indians and went to the site of the cave. The rest of the Spaniards stood guard over the train and its cache of gold.

The Spaniard in charge was Antonio de Reinaldo. He had spent a great deal of time in Utah's Uinta Mountains mining gold and silver; however, the thought of getting it already mined was a bonus for him. And this time through the valley he had an eye witness.

Unbeknownst to Reinaldo, the Ute Indians had other ideas about him taking the treasures of the Ancients from its sacred place. Under the direction of Ute Chief Walker, a force of Indians sneaked up what is now Chicken Creek in the Sanpitch Mountains, surrounding the pack train and their guards.

Meanwhile, Reinaldo and his men got into the cave and began carrying out everything they could. They then killed the Indian guides and stashed their bodies in the cave with the remains of several giant mummies—with red hair! As they came off the mountain to join their companions, the band of Utes attacked, brutally killing all of the Spaniards and their animals. To ensure the spirits of the animals could not return to this place, they cut the hooves off the horses, mules, donkeys and cows. The mutilated bodies of the Spaniards, along with the treasures they stole, including two sets of Spanish armor, were then placed in the cave of the dead and sealed up. In an act of stewardship in deference to the ancients, they then took the gold from the packs and hauled it to its rightful place in the Uinta Mountains.

When word got to Brigham Young that there had been a massacre at Chicken Creek, he sent a number of troops to the site to investigate. The leader of that group was Thomas Rhoades. He and the others "buried the Mexicans and heaped up their animals." A few of the items the Spanish had with them survived the massacre, including two or three maps by Reinaldo showing the rich mines and treasure sites in the Uinta Mountains of Utah.

There were other such places the Spanish attempted to pilfer but each time they were met with disaster! Many Indians kept those places sacred and would give up their lives to protect them. They were keenly aware of those ancient people and they knew their history. They also knew that they themselves had lost much of their ancient knowledge because of wickedness and warring one with another for no other reason than to possess something not belonging to them.

SPANISH MISSION SITES

To save the Indian for himself, the King of Spain caused hundreds of mission sites to be constructed in various parts of New Spain. By Royal Decree the purpose of the missions was to convert, to civilize and to exploit. In 1574, Lopez de Velasco, the Geographer of New Spain, reported there were estimated to be several thousand Indian towns with as many as five million inhabitants, all subject to conversion and paying tithing or tribute.

Research conducted by Dr. Donald Moorman of Weber State University at Ogden, Utah, uncovered new information on Spanish Mission sites constructed as far north as Wyoming territory. His research revealed that some 13,000 Indians had been baptized in some of those northern missions as early as 1615. By 1626 some 34,000 Indians had been baptized. To ensure that the missions had sufficient clergy, King Philip III instructed the Archbishop of Mexico, Don Juan de la Serna, to establish Jesuit colleges to train missionaries. Schools to train the "lost" Indians in the rites of Catholicism were established at many of the northern mission sites.

A man by the name of La Perouse described conditions at certain missions he visited. He wrote that the Indian's day was divided between manual labor and prayer. If any Indian wavered from that scheduled task he was severely punished! La Perouse wrote "... I saw many Indians who had been cruelly beaten; some with their noses or hands cut off, some were in chains, and I witnessed whippings!" He also wrote that the padres told him that punishment was a suitable penance for the salvation of their souls. Indians were forced to do all of the manual labor in return for some ration of "bread and broth." If one attempted to escape and was caught he was whipped.

Slavery of the American Indian became rampant, and miners and priests captured Indians that were not "branded" to work in their own mines. All Indians were required to carry the King's brand on them and if a mine owner or priest was caught with unbranded slaves he was required to pay tax on them and then see that they were properly branded. If a slave committed murder of a Spaniard or priest he was hanged.

George A. Thompson, author of *Lost Treasures on the Old Spanish Trail* [1985], recounts another revolt that was only partially successful, as perceived through the eyes of the victors:

When the Indians witnessed the Spaniard's greed for gold, and saw that if necessary every Indian who was captured would be forced to work in the mines until they died, they not only hid their own gold and silver objects and denied any knowledge of such metals, they even went to great effort to conceal their own mines and hide all evidence of veins of ore from the Spaniards. At each mine and mission the Indians soon learned that to refuse the orders of the mine owner or padre quickly resulted in severe punishment or death. Medicine men that had great influence over their tribesmen skillfully planned revolts to overthrow their oppressors. Usually any attempt by the Indians to overcome their Spanish masters failed, but in 1616 the first organized revolt took the Spaniards by surprise.

With great intrigues and enchantments this old hechicero warped the minds and souls of the Indians, and with his chiefs he plotted a simultaneous uprising throughout the sierras, attacking at once the reals of mines and churches in each place and driving away the miners, padres and their Christian Indians. The attack was planned for the time of the Festival of the Virgin. A beautiful statue of the Virgin had been sent from Mexico City, and the Indians believed that all of the Spaniards would be away from their mines to attend the festival, and would not be carrying arms during the celebration. The precise date for the attack was fixed for the 21st of November. By Friday, more than 500 Indians had gathered to join the attackers. They set fire to the entire settlement and made a fierce assault. The house of the padres they set on fire with burning arrows. When everything was going up in flames, an Indian named Michael, who the Spaniards trusted, shouted to the besieged that those wishing to escape could surrender with assurance their lives would be spared. There being no other recourse, they laid down their arms, and with their families gathered at a place near the church. The mission Padre carried in his arms the reliquary of the church while another carried an image of the Saintly Mother.

They began speaking kindly to the savages, when suddenly a voice rose from the multitude, shouting that God of the Christians was not their God. The Indians were put in a frenzy and began attacking the helpless prisoners. The images of our Holy Mother and of our Saviour were trampled into the earth, and all of the Spaniards were murdered except for three who escaped. Their fury was then turned upon the Padre, who was seized while the savages in derision recited words from the Holy Scriptures which they had learned from him. Thus he was held exposed until an arrow pierced his body. Finally he was killed with a blow from an ax, but as he died he cried to his tormentors, "Do as you will, I am in the hands of God!"

On the day following, the savages attacked at the houses where some Spaniards had taken refuge. They soon opened some holes in the roof and walls and through these openings fired burning arrows. The defenders climbed to the roof, but finally they were compelled to surrender. No mercy was given; even worse, the savages exercised the most extreme cruelty on men, women and children while murdering them. Of 300 persons, only two escaped. Here also died some 600 faithful Christian Indians. But once the Spaniards gained control the Indians were once again put into bondage.

Sixty Indians were identified as being among those participating in the revolt and were hanged from trees. Except for a few stubborn ones, those who had taken part in the terrible rebellion were once more cultivating fields, working in the mines or rebuilding churches. The cost to the Royal Coffers of Spain was 800,000 pesos of eight Reales each, without taking into account the lives lost, the mines and churches destroyed and the many souls lost to heaven.

Although killing off the Indians was not on the minds of the Spaniards because of the manual labor they would provide, many thousands died inadvertently through the ravages of plague, smallpox, syphilis, and other epidemics; lethal cruelty, and egregious racism pale in comparison to the damage caused by the great waves of disease, the kinds of diseases that cause a vibrant, industrious people to become nothing more than skin on flesh.

The Spaniards spoke of the atrocities and horrid practices the Indians afflicted on their own kind as well as captives. The same was spoken of by the Europeans that came to America's east coast as well with such statements as "dirty devils, the heathen, barbarians," etc. But really, who were the devils, the heathens and barbarians?

EYE WITNESS ACCOUNTS

I will here refer to an account discovered in the writings of historian Bartolomé de las Casas, titled *A Brief Account of the Destruction of the In-*

dies, which explains the massacres, butcheries and all manner of horrid cruelties committed by the Popish Spanish Party on the Indians from the isles of the West Indies to the shores of Florida. This narrative was first written in Spanish by Bartolomé de las Casas, a Bishop and eye-witness of these barbarous cruelties. It is rather lengthy but worthy of the read. Please see Appendix A for this account, which is presented there as originally written, without corrected spelling or grammar.

In summary, de las Casas attempted to curtail the cruelties of the Spanish taskmasters but without immediate success. From Wikipedia we learn that:

Arriving as one of the first European settlers in the Americas, he initially participated in, but eventually felt compelled to oppose the atrocities committed against the Native Americans by the Spanish colonists. In 1515, he reformed his views, gave up his Indian slaves and encomienda, and advocated, before King Charles V, Holy Roman Emperor, on behalf of rights for the natives. In his early writings, he advocated the use of African slaves instead of Natives in the West-Indian colonies; consequently, criticisms have been leveled at him as being partly responsible for the beginning of the Transatlantic slave trade. Later in life, he retracted those early views as he came to see all forms of slavery as equally wrong. In 1522, he attempted to launch a new kind of peaceful colonialism on the coast of Venezuela, but this venture failed, causing Las Casas to enter the Dominican Order and become a friar, leaving the public scene for a decade. He then traveled to Central America undertaking peaceful evangelization among the Maya of Guatemala and participated in debates among the Mexican churchmen about how best to bring the natives to the Christian faith.

Traveling back to Spain to recruit more missionaries, he continued lobbying for the abolition of the encomienda, gaining an important victory by the passing of the New Laws in 1542. He was appointed Bishop of Chiapas, but served only for a short time before he was forced to return to Spain because of resistance to the New Laws by the encomenderos, and conflicts with Spanish settlers because of his pro-Indian policies and activist religious stances. The remainder of his life was spent at the Spanish court where he held great influence over Indies-related issues. In 1550, he participated in the Valladolid debate in which Juan Ginés de Sepúlveda argued that the Indians were less than human and required Spanish masters in order to become civilized. Las Casas maintained that they were fully human and that forcefully subjugating them was unjustifiable.

3

GIANTS IN THE LAND

"And the giants of the land, also, stood afar off: and there went forth a curse upon all the people that fought against God."
—Book of Moses

THE HISTORY OF GIANTS BEGINS with Genesis chapter six in the Bible. Giants have been the subject of tales, stories and folklore since that time. One of the greatest historians of all times, Josephus, noted in his *Antiquities of the Jews*, that fallen angels and women produced children with superhuman strength. He linked these creatures to Greek mythology (Josephus, Antiquities, 5.2.3).

CENTRAL AND SOUTH AMERICAN GIANTS

Giants were also seen in many parts of the world including the Americas. Not only did Amerigo Vespucci and Magellan speak about their encounters with giants but so did Sir Francis Drake, Coronado, Narvaez, De Soto and many others. Tales of giant men and women encountered on their journeys and eyewitness accounts have been documented throughout the world. However, as noted by some writers, mainstream academics seem to do their best to hide the truth from the public. Dr. Glen Kimball in his book *Giants in America,* noted that.....*"Pedro de Casteñada who accompanied Coronado, wrote of the Cocopa Indian tribe that there were giants who could carry logs that six of the Spaniards couldn't budge."* Of other accounts we read where two huge mummies lay in glass coffins at the Gold Museum in Lima, Peru. Their golden robes that were found with them are on permanent and prominent display. Amazingly, the artifacts include crowns so large that a slight man could step into with both feet, and golden gloves with fingers ten inches long! Their mummies have measured nine and one-half feet tall.

3

As the reader can see by the photograph below, the head of the mummy is huge in comparison to modern men. Notice the arrows pointing to the shadowy figure to the right. He is a normal sized man. Even as the Spanish entered into the realm of the Aztecs he was confronted with giants in the land. One of the most feared men of the Aztec Nation was Txilacatzin, who was very tall, above average height by some several feet! Spanish chroniclers noted:

> ...the whole army marched into the very heart of Tenochititlan. Wherever they went, they found the streets empty, with no Indians anywhere in sight. Then the great captain, Tzilacatzin, arrived, bringing with him three large stones of the kind used for building walls. He carried one of them in his hand; the other two hung from his shield. When he hurled these stones at the Spaniards, they turned and fled the city.

Tzilacatzin took the actions of the Spanish as cowardice, so he saw an opportunity to drive the Spanish from the land. The following was taken from an Aztec/Nahuatl manuscript known as the Florentine Codex, as preserved by Fray Bernardino De Sahagun:

> Tzilacatzin's military rank was that of Otomi (captain), and he clipped his hair in the style of the Otomies, a people who inhabited the Valley of Mexico since ancient times, long before the Aztecs. Sometimes he wore only his cotton armor, with a thin kerchief wrapped around his head. At other times, he wore a plumed headdress with the eagle symbol on its crest, and gleaming gold bracelets on both arms, and circular bands of gleaming gold on both ankles. At still other times, he wore his lip-plug, his gold earring and all the rest of his full regalia, but left his head uncovered to show that he was an Otomi.

As noted, Tzilacatzin was not Aztec but was from a presumably vanished race of people. He wore a beard and had "*tremendous stature*" and carried an unusually large arsenal of weaponry.

Other claims of encounters with giants come from various sources such as published books by Don Cieza de Leon who visited South America in 1553 and 1555. They told of an ancient giant race that came to South America on raft like boats, and were so tall that from the knee down they were as big as a normal man. Their eyes were huge, like unto a plate. Their mode of dress was near naked or fully naked. They had no women with them. Remnants of these giants were still living when Cortez invaded Mexico.

In the summer of 1931 Monsignor F. Lunadi organized an expedition into the jungles of San Agustin in Colombia. He found traces of a very ancient South American empire known to the old British buccaneers of the seventeenth century. These men were giants who had knowledge of electricity which they used in various forms. This race of ancient giant white men was called the Viracochas. It was said they came long before the Incas began to reign. The natives called these white men "Titicaca," the name of one of South America's largest lakes and the world's highest navigable body of water, located in the mountains between Bolivia and Peru at an elevation of 12,507 feet. There are huge statues of these giants near the city of Tiahuanacu [alternate spelling Tiwanaku] and most notably is that they are depicted with six fingers and toes. They were also noted for having huge hands with very long fingers.

NORTH AMERICAN GIANTS

The North American Indians early on believed that the first race of humans were giants. They claimed that these giants were three times larger than a normal man and were able to run down a buffalo and carry it with one hand. Of course we, being more educated and unlikely to believe such nonsense, cast that notion aside as being nothing more than children's stories. However, keep in mind that proof has surfaced to support the claims of huge men in North America. Could it have been that a man of this stature could have thrown or captured a buffalo single handedly?

Let's take a look at many claims of the existence of giants besides those mentioned already. In a chronicle by Antonio Francesco Pigafetta, who was with Magellan on his expeditions, we read:

We had been two whole months in this harbor without sighting anyone when one day (quite without warning) we saw on the shore a huge giant, who was naked, and who danced, leaped and sang, all the while throwing sand and dust on his head. Our Captain ordered one of the crew to walk towards him, telling this man also to dance, leap and sing as a sign of friendship. This he did, and led the giant to a place by the shore where the Captain was waiting. And when the giant saw us, he marveled and was afraid, and pointing to the sky, believing we came from heaven. He was so tall that even the largest of us came only to midway between his waist and his shoulder; yet with all he was well proportioned. He had a large face, painted round with red; his eyes were ringed with yellow and in the middle of his cheeks were painted two hearts. He had hardly any hair on his head, what little he had being painted white . . .

Another quote was from author Rupert Gould who quoted Magellan in his book, *Enigmas,* that *"...this man was so tall that our heads scarcely came up to his waist, and his voice was like that of a bull."*

P. Joseph Tarrubia wrote in his work *Gianthologia,* published in Spain in 1761, that some utensils found in South America were of such enormous size that they could only have been used by a race of giants. He also noted that many Spaniards told of huge men ranging from nine to ten feet in height and perhaps taller.

Quoting from *Gianthologia* we learn that:

...South Americans had a body of soldiers, consisting of about four hundred men, the shortest of whom was not shorter than nine feet and the tallest about eleven feet. Years before came Amerigo Vespucci and with fellow sailors sighted many giants off the coast of Venezuela. Vespucci wrote:

Thus sailing along, we came upon an island which was situated fifteen leagues from the mainland. At our arrival, since we saw no people and the island looked favorable to us, we decided to explore it, and eleven of us landed. We discovered a trail and set ourselves to walk on it two leagues and a half inland; we met with a village of twelve houses in which we did not find anyone except seven women. They were of such great stature that there was not one of them who was not taller than every one of us. The chief one of them, who was certainly a discreet woman, by signs hauled us up to a house and made them give us refreshments. When we saw such noble women, we determined to carry off two of them, who were young women fifteen years of age, and make a present of them to the king. They were creatures whose stature was certainly about that of average men. While we were thus plotting, thirty-six men arrived, who entered the house where we were drinking, and they were of such lofty stature that each of them was taller when upon his knees than I was when standing erect. They were of the stature of giants in their great size and in the proportion of their bodies, which corresponded with their height.

When the men entered, some of our fellows were so frightened that at the moment they thought they were done for. The warriors had bows and arrows and tremendous oar blades, finished off like swords. When they saw our small stature, they began to converse with us to learn who we were and whence we came. We gave them soft words for the sake of amity and replied to them in sign language that we were men of peace and that we were out to see the world. In fact, we judged it wise to part from them without controversy, and so we went by the same trail by which we had come. They stuck with us all the way to the sea and until we embarked.

OHIO RIVER VALLEY

In North America evidence of giants is primarily through the study of skeletal remains excavated from mounds and other sites. In Ohio the first recorded evidence of a giant race can be traced back to 1829 when material to be used in the construction of a hotel in Centerville, came from one of the many mounds extant within that region of the country.

While digging in a particular mound, workers dug up a large human skeleton. It was recorded that a local physician examining the remains said that the skull could have easily fit over a normal man's head with little difficulty. Another peculiarity of the skeleton was the additional teeth it had compared to modern man.

In the Ohio River Valley at a mound site called Bates Mound, three skeletons were unearthed and all measured from eight feet to ten feet in height, but most amazingly they all had double rows of teeth! In a hometown newspaper called *The Ironton Register* [from a small Ohio town] dated May 5, 1892, it was stated that: "Where Proctorville now stands was one day part of a well paved city, but I think the greatest part of it is now the Ohio River. Only a few mounds, there; one of which was near the C. Wilgus mansion and contained a skeleton of a very large person, all double teeth, and sound, in a jaw bone that would go over the jaw with the flesh on, of a large man. The common burying ground was well filled with skeletons at a depth of about 6 feet. Part of the pavement was of boulder stone and part of well-preserved brick."

Scientific American, the oldest continuously published magazine in the United States, published the following in 1883:

Two miles from Mandan, on the bluffs near the junction of the Hart and Missouri Rivers, says the local newspaper the Pioneer, is an old Cemetery of fully 100 acres in extent filled with bones of a giant race. This vast city of the dead lies just east of the Fort Lincoln Road. The ground has the appearance of having been filled with trenches piled full of dead bodies, both man and beast, and covered with several feet of earth. In many places mounds from 8 to 10 feet high, and some of them 100 feet or more in length, have been thrown up and are filled with bones, broken pottery vases of various bright colored flint, and agates . . . showing the work of a people skilled in the arts and possessed of a high state of civilization. This has evidently been a grand battlefield where thousands of men have fallen . . . Five miles above Mandan, on the opposite side of the Missouri, is another vast cemetery, as yet unexplored. We asked an aged Indian what his people knew of these ancient grave yards. He answered: "Me know nothing about them. They were here before the red man."

In the *History of Marion County, Ohio*, numerous accounts were published of giant skeletons and legends from local Indians attesting to the fact that giants once indeed roamed their lands. In one article published in 1883 the editor reported of three skeletons found at the mouth of Paw Paw Creek. A man named Jim Dean, accompanied by some other laborers, were digging for a bridge foundation and found bones at the lower end of what was called Buffalo Wallow. The remains were exposed to the weather for just a short period of time when they began to turn black and soon turned to dust. However, before this happened, the skeletons were measured and found to be eight feet long.

Other accounts tell of a Cherokee by the name of James Wafford, who was born in Georgia around 1806. He told a reporter that his grandmother, who was born in middle of the 18th century, told him that she had heard tell from the old people that long ago, before her time, a group of giants had once come to visit the Cherokee. They were huge! Almost twice as tall as a Cherokee man and had strange eyes that set slanting in their heads, so the Cherokee called them "TsunilA' kaluA' *the slant-eyed people*" because they looked like the giant hunter by the same name. The giants said they came from the west where the sun goes down. They stayed with the Cherokees some time before leaving to return to their home in the west.

Most researchers of giants know the story of Sarah Winnemucca, the Northern Paiute, who wrote the book *Life Among the Paiutes*. She wrote the following:

Among the traditions of our people is one of a small tribe of barbarians who used to live along the Humboldt River. It was many hundreds of years ago. They used to way-lay my people and kill and eat them. They would dig large holes in our trails at night, and if any of our people traveled at night, which they did, for they were afraid of these barbarous people, they would other times fall into these holes. That tribe would even eat their own dead—yes, they would even come and dig up our dead after they were buried, and would carry them off and eat them. Now and then they would come and make war on my people. They would fight, and as fast as they killed one another on either side, the women would carry off those who were killed. My people say they were very brave. When they were fighting they would jump up in the air after the arrows that went over their heads, and shoot the same arrows back again. My people took some of them into their families, but they could not make them like themselves. So at last they make war on them. This war lasted a long time. Their number was about 2600. The war lasted some three years. My people killed them in great numbers, and what few were left went into the thick bush, and my people set the bush on fire, right above Humbolt Lake. They could not live there very long without fire. They were nearly starving. My people were watching for them all around the lake, and would chase them as fast as they could on land. At last one night they landed on the east side of the lake and went into a cave near the mountains. It was a most horrible place, for my people watched at the mouth of the cave, and would watch them as they came out to get water. My people would ask them if they would be like us, and not like coyotes or beasts. They talked the same language, but would not give up. At last my people were tired, and they went to work and gathered wood, and began to fill up the mouth of the cave. At last my people set it on fire; at the same time they called out to them, "Will you give up and eat like man, and not eat people like beasts? Say quick, and we will put out the fire." But no answer came and in ten days some went back to see the fire had gone out. They came back to my third or fifth great grandfather and told him they must all be dead, there was such a horrible smell. My people say the tribe had reddish hair.

Sarah went on to say that she still had some of their red hair that had been handed down from father to son. She told of a dress that had been in their family for many years trimmed in the reddish hair of the giants.

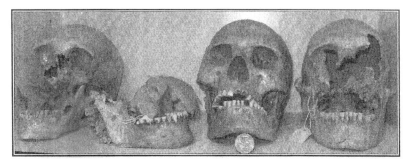

Fig. 8 Some of the large skulls from the Lovelock, NV cave of giants.

The over-whelming evidences of giants can fill volumes. Yet, it seems that modern-day academics have literally sealed the doors to that real history so effectively that only a select few are given access to secreted vaults full of the proof of these long lost civilizations. It seems that such history should be opened to all for the purpose of research and education and not concealed because of some political or personal purpose. And why turn oral history of the American Indian into "folklore," knowing full well it is more than that? It makes little sense.

CURIOSITIES OF SANPETE VALLEY

In Utah's Sanpete Valley, some 120 miles southeast of Salt Lake City, lies an area full of mystery. This little valley has more hidden history within its region than one might think.

When the Mormons first arrived in the valley they found it was inhabited by Ute Indians led by the Great War Chief Walkara, commonly called Walker. Then-governor Brigham Young and leader of The Church of Jesus Christ of Latter-day Saints, commissioned several families to leave Salt Lake City to settle Sanpete Valley at the request of Chief Walker. The head of this group of spirited souls was Isaac Morley, a deeply religious man admired by Brigham Young, confident that he, if anyone, would keep peace with Walker's band.

Two months after Walker's request to have Sanpete Valley settled by the Saints, Brigham Young sent Parley P. Pratt to explore Sanpete Valley. One objective was to select a site where Morley's company could develop a productive settlement. The report received back to Young was very positive so no time was wasted in getting Morley's company on the road.

It was in November of 1849 when Morley's company topped the hill west of Sanpete. It was early winter, and the valley they viewed before them appeared to be a winter scene none of them wanted to see. However, they made their way down into the valley where they would stay and live and endure hardship after hardship for the sake of their religious beliefs.

Little did they know that they had taken up residency in a valley once inhabited by cultures long extinct! Giants once roamed the land and others who came after built temples and mounds throughout the valley. Strange writings left in stone, records of lost cultures lay hidden in dusty tombs of the dead, and strange rock edifices and monuments dotted the landscape. However, the pioneers had little time to explore ancient sites and if they did see them, they never mentioned it in their journals.

To the east of this valley, rising from the valley floor is the Wasatch Plateau with its mountain peaks towering over 10,000 feet. Over a dozen streams enter the valley from the east and the north giving plenty of water for irrigation, animals and human consumption. To the west are the San Pitch Mountains named after Chief Walker's brother. A few dry washes enter the valley from this range and only during the spring runoff do any of them have water in them. At the south end of the valley the San Pitch River enters a narrow canyon and then eventually ties into the Sevier River. All along these rivers Indians hunted, fished and lived for many generations as did those who came before them. It was in these mountains that many of the secrets of the ancients lay hidden from view.

As men began herding their cattle and sheep into the mountains and cutting wood for more homes, corrals and fences, they began to take notice of their surroundings. During church meetings and gatherings the men talked of their discoveries, including large stone patios, steps carved from solid rock and strange inscriptions on stones high in the mountains above the valley. Soon reports came that strange rock walls were discovered in the sage covered flats along the western edge of the valley. During a lumber operation in what is now called Manti Canyon, a stone sarcopha-

Fig. 9. Manti Canyon Sarcophagus

gus was discovered and brought out of the canyon. There was no lid on the sarcophagus and no bones, but it was indeed made for a burial. And, it was over seven feet long!

Mounds were noticed by some that had similarities to mounds in Ohio and Illinois. One mound near present day Ephraim, Utah, was partially excavated and during that little excavation a few Ute Indians stopped by to speak with the pick wielding excavators. They told them of a race of giants that once roamed the land and had been killed off by their ancestors and buried in the mountains on both sides of the valley and their houses were covered up with dirt with all their children and women inside. Although the men didn't believe the Indians, nevertheless they kept on digging. On the northwest side of the knoll at a depth of six feet they discovered the remains of a human skeleton, stone knives, smoking pipe, clay jars and couple of gorgets (an article that covered the throat). Deeming the work was too hard for what they got, they soon abandoned the idea of doing any more excavation and returned to their lives as farmers. The items they recovered floated around the valley for many years until all that was left was one knife that was owned by the late R.G. Huntington.

TEMPLE HILL

South of Ephraim is the town of Manti, named after the ancient City of Manti found in the Book of Mormon. It is uncertain why Isaac Morley chose to erect the first dugouts on the south side of what would be known in history as "Temple Mount," but it is assumed he had spiritual guidance in that choice. It was later revealed that Chief Walkara told Morley about an ancient rock altar that sat on the hill above the dugouts and that it was erected by an ancient race of people. It was further noted that he also talked of tunnels and secret places beneath the hill. The Utes of the valley deemed the hill sacred.

Brigham Young directed the building of a Temple on the hill because as he stated it was the site that the Book of Mormon Prophet Moroni had dedicated the land for a temple site. In his writings Morley stated that " . . . *the very hill where the Nephites had sacrificed Nehor on the sacrificial altar for the sake of the preservation of the ancient church. Here once an ancient temple stood, and here one day again would stand another in these last days . . . This was, even as Chief Joseph Walker (Chief Walkara) said, a sacred hill, and so I called the place Manti, even as it was called in days gone by."*

When the Mormons began construction on the Temple they began a rock quarry behind the Temple Mount where they discovered strange inscriptions on rock faces. Some thinking the characters were of Nephite origin knew in their hearts that this site was indeed a sacred place. However, even though the site is a sacred place, the inscriptions are not Nephite in origin but from a period before them. And to the north from the quarry is a site that is thought to be the remains of an ancient building with huge stones as the foundation. Was this a temple used by Nephites or Jaredites?

Following is a lengthy excerpt from The Life and Contributions of Isaac Morley, a Master's thesis submitted by Richard Henrie Morley to The College of Religious Instruction, Brigham Young University, July 1965. From chapter eight of the thesis, entitled "Colonizing Among the Lamanites," we read.

> Father Isaac Morley was chosen to lead the first group of colonizers to settle among the Indians in Sanpete County, Utah. On June 14th 1849, Chief Walker, of the Utah Nation, requested the Mormon pioneers settle Sanpete Valley. According to Brigham Young, "When Walker had filled his pipe, he offered the Lord the first smoke, pointing the pipe and stepping toward the sun." Walker, after recognizing his sun god, passed the peace pipe around the ring, first to the elders present and ending with the Indians. This ceremony signified peace between the Mormons and Walker's tribe, and from that time plans were laid for a group of Saints to move into Sanpete Valley.
>
> About two months after the Walker interview, Brigham Young sent a party, led by Parley P. Pratt, to explore Sanpete Valley. One objective was to select a site where Brother Morley's company could develop a productive settlement. Sanpete, according to Elder Pratt's report, had potential for becoming an asset in the Great Basin empire.[3]
>
> There were three Mormon colonies in Utah which preceded the one in central Utah. These were: Salt Lake City, Ogden, thirty-eight miles north of the Mormon mecca, and Provo, forty-four miles south of church headquarters. The latter two colonies preceded the one in Sanpete Valley by only a few months.
>
> In order to gain a better understanding of the Indian people, one should examine a few incidents in the life of Chief Walker and the mountain tribes. Walker was born in or about the year 1808, on the banks of the Spanish Fork River in a location known by the natives as PEQUI-

NARY-QUINT, which signifies "Stinking Creek." The odor which the name suggests is created from warm sulphur springs which flow into the river from one of the canyons through which it passes. Walker, was one of seven sons who, with the exception of one who was physically maimed, were all exceptionally good athletes. His brothers, each of whom displayed other qualities of leadership in the tribe, were Arapeen, Groceepeen, Sanpitch, Ammon, Tibbinaw, and Yankawalkits.

The name "Lamanite" is given to some of the western American Indians. The Book of Mormon identifies some of these Indians with descendants of Lehi's family who left Jerusalem in 600 B.C. and sailed to America. [See II Nephi 5:20-25 for details.]

Other Indians may have worshiped the sun. When the first Mormon settlers reached the Provo River in March, 1849, a band of Timpanogos Indians met them. Dimick B. Huntington was required to raise his right hand and swear by the sun that his people would not drive the Indians from their land or deprive them of their rights. Roberts, *CHC*, III, pp. 460-461.

Walker was so adamant that settlement not only be in Sanpete where Manti now stands but be established in proximity to the Temple Hill, that he actually alienated a number of the others, who preferred more convenient places to settle. But Father Isaac Morley would have none of it and told the people that this particular hill was "our God-appointed abiding place...."

Why was this hill so important to Morley and Walker? Walker informed them that this hill was where the *"Old Ones" had once erected an altar, and so this hill was considered sacred to the Ute people. It is believed that Morley heard from Walker in a private conversation that the hill had tunnels and caverns underneath it and more in the surrounding area. It is said that both men knew that there would be a temple built on the hill and that it would be the "Second Temple" that once stood on or near the hill.* It is said by some that Morley secretly discovered an entrance to an underground vault or cavern which he sealed up after he explored it. Prior to his death in 1865, Morley gave specific instructions to his son, Isaac Morley Jr., that his remains be brought back to Manti and interred at the foot of Temple Hill, for according to him it was a sacred place, *"in proximity to the secret of the Lord."*

The Google image does not allow the reader to actually see at this elevation the details that make this a very probable site for an ancient

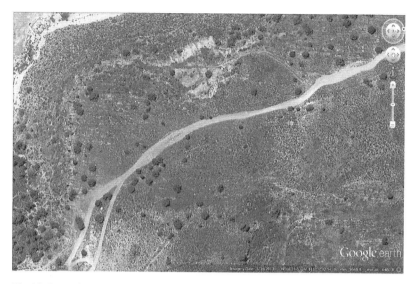

Fig 10 Site of Ancient Structure?

building. There are numerous rectangle slabs of stone laid side by side and end to end measuring as long as 16' x 4' wide. There are rocks that have been removed in some areas and there is an impression within the foundation that could have been the remains of a baptismal font. There are cuts in the surfaces of the slabs that are either round or square. South of this site are two hieroglyphic panels that were discovered at the time of the construction of the temple in 1880.

Figure 10 shows the location or probable footprint of ancient building or temple site as noted by Chief Walker and Morley. This area site is north and east of the present LDS Temple Hill at Manti.

Fig. 11 Panel of Inscriptions

This panel of inscriptions is found in a narrow passage that leads to the quarry used for the construction of the Manti LDS Temple and shows evidence of ancient usage as well.

Fig. 12 Panel of Damaged Hieroglyphs

Across the quarry to the south is another panel of hieroglyphs, now almost completely destroyed due to human hands, rubbings and abuse.

Will we really ever know whether or not these hieroglyphic panels were carved by giants or by others that inhabited the land? Mainstream academia. however, typically dismisses these artifacts as frauds and fantastical and amateurish hoaxes.

BREWER'S CAVE

Skipping ahead to the 1950s we find a young man by the name of John Brewer hunting arrowheads along the foothills of Sanpete Valley when by chance he over turned a rock to find it engraved with strange symbols and characters on it. Soon he discovered more—for a total of four large stones—all with strange symbols and characters on them.

By using these stones as a map or key, he discovered a series of caves, tunnels and tombs. One cave held the remains of two large entombed mummies, one man and one woman. According to Brewer, the pair measured up to seven feet tall, the man had red hair while the woman had blond hair; both mummies sported fabulously beautiful head-dresses. The man had a sword with him that was almost five feet in length from the hilt!

The cave was full of stone boxes filled with lead, copper and gold tablets with strange script on them. These two mummies looked as if they might be of Mongolian descent. Although no photos have ever been seen of the two mummies, Brewer's son drew pictures of them, indicating that every time he attempted to photograph them, something would go wrong with the camera. Be that as it may, the artifacts are real and one has to assume the mummies are as well. Some think these mummies could be Jaredites as written about in the Book of Mormon. We'll explore this story more in depth further on in this book.

WEST COAST GIANTS

California is not exempt from the giant craze. In fact, it has its fair share of tales surrounding lost cities, mummies, giants and more. We turn to an account told about two geologists, Ken Moore and Steve Korolyi from Coos Bay, Oregon. Moore and Korolyi traveled to the hot dry deserts of southern California in search of a lost River of Gold beneath the rugged Kokoweef Peak and Dorr Peak just southwest of Ivanpah Mountain.

The pair had heard the story of Earl P. Dorr who had discovered a subterranean canyon deep beneath Kokoweef Peak that had gold bearing black sands that he panned and removed from the underground river in 1927. The gold bearing black sand was valued at $2,145.47 per cubic yard at that time. According to Dorr in a signed affidavit, a hand drawn map was included that indicated a crystal cave entrance that led to an amazing tunnel system leading 2,000 feet down to an underground canyon. His altimeter indicated this was another 3,000 feet deep and the "river of gold" was flowing at the bottom.

It was during this time that Dorr claims he met and conversed with a huge red-headed giant who lived in the canyon with other giants. The voice of the giant sounded ...."*as hollow as a man ascending a cave.*" He was taken down stream where he saw two giants sitting at a table tallying gold ingots. They hardly paid any attention to him. The men were dressed in red robes and the women in white. All were exceptionally tall.

He was told he could get the gold he needed then leave and never come back. Dorr had no intention of returning, but he didn't want others to find what he had, so after he left the underground caverns he dynamited the passageway shut. He figured he could easily find another way down, but try as he might he never did.

Korolyi and Moore were very intrigued with the story Dorr told, so they organized an expedition to Kokoweef Peak. Apparently these two experienced geologists found another entrance into the bowels of Kokoweef. They had a third partner by the name of Roger Villaneuve who paid them to stake a gold claim on their discovery.

The two men purchased a great quantity of equipment for spelunk-ing and underwater dredging from a prospecting store in Las Vegas. They hinted that they had found the mother lode of mother lodes and they were rich beyond anyone's wildest dreams! That was the last time anyone ever saw the two men.

Villaneuve told police he had been waiting to meet with the men in Tonopah, Nevada, but they never showed up. Villaneuve was the owner of the mining and forestry company called Oregon Villaneuve & Associates. He hoped the two men were still alive or just stranded some-where because their find was estimated to yield hundreds of millions of dollars in gold revenue.

Did Karolyi and Moore run into the giants of the *River of Gold*? Perhaps they were taken captive by them or were killed. Earl Dorr swore up and down that what he saw in the bottom of Kokoweef Peak was true. He never changed his story. Stories of giants come from all across the country and some are worth the time to investigate and to read about. Here are some of those stories. [See http://mojaveproject.org/dispatches-item/kokoweef-still-searching-for-the-lost-river-of-gold/ for an update on this project.]

GIANTS OF CRYSTAL LAKE MICHIGAN

From the *Bruce Herald*, March 19, 1899, we read of a prehistoric man eleven feet tall. This is a description of the contents of mounds opened in Montcalm County in Michigan.

The mounds on the south side of Crystal Lake in Montcalm County, Michigan, have been opened, and a prehistoric race un-earthed. One contained five skeletons and the other three. In the first mound was an earthen tablet, five inches long, four wide, and half an inch thick. It was divided into four quarters. On one of them were inscribed queer characters. The skeletons were arranged in the same relative positions, so far as the mound is concerned. In the other mound there was a casket of earthenware, 10 1/2 inches long and 3 1/2 inches wide. The cover bore various inscriptions. The characters found upon the tablet were also prominent upon the casket. Upon opening the casket a copper coin was revealed, together with other types, which the inscription or marks upon the tablet and the casket had evidently been made. There were also two pipes, one of stone and the other of pottery, and apparently of the same material as the casket. Other pieces of pottery were found, but so badly broken as to furnish no clue as to what they might have been used for. Some of the bones of the skeletons were well preserved, showing that the dead men must have been persons of huge proportions. The lower jaw is immense. As ordinary jaw bone fits inside with ease. By measurement the distance from the top of the skull to the upper end of the thigh bone of the largest skeleton was five feet five inches. A doctor who was present stated that the man must have been at least eleven feet high. One of these mounds was partially covered by a pine stump, three feet six inches in diameter, and the ground showed no signs of ever having been disturbed. The digging had to be done among the roots, which had a large spread.

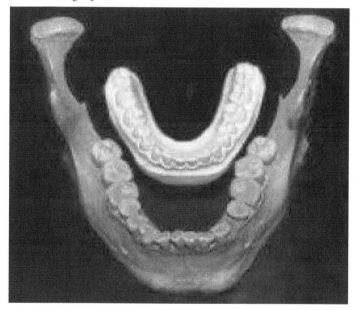

Fig. 13. Skeletons of extraordinary height have been recorded.

We have seen where countless eye witnesses have borne testimony of giants throughout the Americas. Many newspaper articles have been written such as the one above to describe to their readers what these ancient inhabitants might have looked like. Unfortunately, dozens of the remains taken to museums and in private holdings, have long since been lost or forgotten.

Some professionals try to explain away the reasons why these ancient skeletal remains are so out of the norm. They tell us the bones are those of a distorted few or an enigma that really has no bearing on history. These academics summarily dismiss the oral histories of the Native Indians and those who actually saw living giants as folklore or speaking from the bottle. Why is that so? What is wrong with being wrong? It is amazing that so much of our history is hidden from us. Giants in our land? Of course! Why not?

NIAGARA'S ANCIENT CEMETERY OF GIANTS

From the *Daily Telegraph* of Toronto, Ontario, Canada, with the date of 23 August 1871, comes an astounding headline:

A REMARKABLE SIGHT. Two hundred skeletons of ANAKIN in Cayuga Township; a singular discovery by Torontonian and others. A vast Golgotha opened to view some remains of the Giants that were in those days. From our own correspondents:

Cayuga, August 21. On Wednesday last, Rev. Nathaniel Wardell, Messers, Orin Wardell (of Toronto), and Daniel Fredinburg, were digging on the farm of the latter gentleman, which is on the banks of the Grand River, in the township of Cayuga. When they got to five or six feet below the surface, a strange sight met them. Piled in layers, one upon top of the other, some two hundred skeletons of human beings nearly perfect, around the neck of each one being a string of beads. There were also deposited in this pit a number of axes and skimmers made of stone. In the jaws of several of the skeletons were large

Ceremonial stones, scratched with the sign of the cross, show Spanish influence. Skull is of a giant Indian who was seven feet tall

Fig 14 Giant Skull and Stones

stone pipes; one of which Mr. O. Wardell took with him to Toronto a day or two after this Golgotha was unearthed.

These skeletons are those of men of gigantic stature, some of them measuring nine feet, very few of them being less than seven feet. Some of the thigh bones were found to be at least a foot longer than those at present known, and one of the skulls being examined completely covered the head of an ordinary person. These skeletons are supposed to belong to those of a race of people anterior to the Indians.

Some three years ago, the bones of a mastodon were found embedded in the earth about six miles from this spot. The pit and its ghastly occupants are now open to the view of any who may wish to make a visit there.

Another account of this discovery on the Fredinburg farm dated August 22, was chronicled in *Ancient American Magazine* Issue No. 41.

There is not the slightest doubt that the remains of a lost city are on this farm. At various times within the past years, the remains of mud houses with their chimneys had been found; and there are dozens of pits of similar kind to that just unearthed, though much smaller, in the place which has been discovered before, though the fact has not been made public hitherto. The remains of a blacksmith's shop, containing two tons of charcoal and various implements, were turned up a few months ago.

The farm which consists of 150 acres, has been cultivated for nearly a century, and was covered with a thick growth of pine, so that it must have been ages ago since the remains were deposited there. The skulls of the skeletons are of an enormous size and all manner of shapes, about half as large again as are now to be seen. The teeth in most of them are still in almost perfect state of preservation, though they soon fall out when exposed to the air.

It is supposed that there is gold or silver in large quantities to be found in the premises, as mineral rods have invariably, when tested, pointed to a certain spot and a few yards from where the last batch of skeletons was found directly under the apple tree. Some large shells, supposed to have been used for holding water, which were also found in the pit, were almost petrified. There are no doubts that were a scheme of exploration carried on thoroughly the result would be highly interesting. A good deal of excitement exists in the neighborhood, and many visitors call at the farm daily.

ANCIENT AMERICA

The skulls and bones of the giants are fast disappearing, being taken away by curiosity hunters. It is the intention of Mr. Fredinburg to cover the pit up very soon. The pit is ghastly in the extreme. The farm is skirted on the north by the Grand River. The pit is close to the banks, but marks are there to show where the gold or silver treasure is supposed to be under. From the appearance of the skulls, it would seem that their possessors died a violent death, as many of them were broken and dented.

The axes are shaped like tomahawks, small, but keen, instruments. The beads are all of stone and of all sizes and shapes. The pipes are not unlike in shape the cutty pipe, and several of them are engraved with dog's heads. They have not lost their virtue for smoking. Some people profess to believe that the locality of Fredinburg farm was formally an Indian burial place, but the enormous stature of the skeletons and the fact that pine trees of centuries [of] growth covered the spot goes far to disprove this idea.

NEWSPAPER ACCOUNTS OF GIANTS IN THE LAND

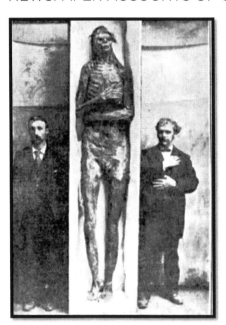

Fig. 15 Large Corpse from San Diego

Appearing in an article dated 7 October 1895 and printed in *The World*, we read the following headline: *Nine Feet High and Probably a California Indian. Measurement Well Authenticated. Other Big Men and Women of Fact and Fable Who are Famous Types of Giantism.*

The article then continues, describing the find, the scientific investigation and the results, although the claims seem somewhat exaggerated:

The corpse of the biggest man that ever lived has been dug up near San Diego California. At all events there is no satisfactory read in ancient or modern history of any human being nearly so tall. The mummy-for in such a condition the remains were found-is that of a person would have been about nine feet high in life. This makes allowances for the shrinkage, which may be pretty closely calculated.

As to the accuracy in the estimate there can no question, as the cadaver has been carefully inspected and measured by Prof. Thomas Wilson, Curator of the Department of Prehistoric Anthropology in the Smithsonian Institution, and by other scientists. The tapeline even now registers the length from heel to top of the head at eight feet four inches.

The mummy is that of an Indian and is almost certainly prehistoric, though its age cannot be determined with any sort of accuracy. Historical records of the part of California where it was found go back for at least 250 years, and they make no mention of any man of gigantic stature. How much older the body may be must be left open to conjecture. Its preservation, is not matter of surprise, in that arid region the atmospheric conditions are such that a corpse buried in the dry season might very well become perfectly desiccated before the arrival of the rains, and thus be rendered permanently proof against decay.

The body was found in a cave by a party of prospectors. Over the head are the remnants of a leather hood. The man was well advanced in years.

It has been stated that the man must have surpassed in height any giant of whom there is an historical record. This is unquestionably true so far as the last two centuries are concerned, and accounts of older dates are not well authenticated. Indeed they grow more and more apocryphal as distant in time increases.

Here is another newspaper account from the *New York Times* with publication date of 20 December1897.

WISCONSIN MOUND OPENED.

Skeleton Found of a Man Over Nine Feet High with an Enormous Skull.

MAPLE CREEK, Wis., Dec. 19.—One of the three recently discovered mounds in this town has been opened. In it was found the skeleton of a man of gigantic size. The bones measured from head to foot over nine feet and were in a fair state of preservation. The skull was as large as a half bushel measure. Some finely tempered rods of copper and other relics were lying near the bones.

The mound from which these relics were taken is ten feet high and thirty feet long, and varies from six to eight feet in width.

The two mounds of lesser size will be excavated soon.

The New York Times
Published: December 20, 1897
Copyright © The New York Times

Fig. 16 Large Skeleton Found in Wisconsin Mound

Another more recent account from the same newspaper gives the date of July 14, 1916, concerning the discovery of giant size remains in a mound excavated in Pennsylvania.

Finally, yet another account describes the discovery of a metal helmet, nine foot sword and skeletal remains indicating the man "must have stood eighteen foot in his stockings."

Arthur Schopenhauer penned a universal truth when he said, "All truth passes through three stages. First it is ridiculed. Second it is violently opposed. Third, it is accepted as being self-evident."

GIANTS' BONES IN MOUND.

Scientists Unearth Relics of Indians Who Lived 700 Years Ago.

Special to The New York Times.

BINGHAMTON, July 13.—Professor A. B. Skinner of the American Indian Museum, Professor W. K. Morehead of Phillips Andover Academy, and Dr. George Donohue, Pennsylvania State Historian, who have been conducting researches along the valley of the Susquehanna, have uncovered an Indian mound at Tioga Point, on the upper portion of Queen Esther's Flats, on what is known as the Murray farm, a short distance from Sayre, Penn., which promises rich additions to Indian lore.

In the mound uncovered were found the bones of sixty-eight men which are believed to have been buried 700 years ago. The average height of these men was seven feet, while many were much taller. Further evidence of their gigantic size was found in large celts or axes hewed from stone and buried in the grave. On some of the skulls, two inches above the perfectly formed forehead, were protuberances of bone. Members of the expedition say that it is the first discovery of its kind on record and a valuable contribution to the history of the early races.

The skull and a few bones found in one grave were sent to the American Indian Museum.

The New York Times
Published: July 14, 1916

Fig. 17 Newspaper Article on Discovery of 68 Men

ALLEGED DISCOVERY OF THE SKELETON OF A GIANT

The Oil City (Penn) "Simet" is responsible for the following : — While William Thompson, assisted by Robert R. Smith, was engaged in making an excavation near the house of the former' about half a mile north of West Hickory, preparatory to erecting a derrick, they exhumed an enormous helmet of iron which was corroded with rust. Further digging brought to light a sword which measured nine feet in length. Curiosity incited them to enlarge the hole, and after a little time they discovered the bones of two enormous feet Following up the "lead" they had so unexpectedly struck, in a few hours time they had unearthed a well-preserved skeleton of an enormous giant, belonging to a species of the human family which probably inhabited this and other parts of the world at the time of which the Bible speaks, when it says "and there were giants in those days.' The helmet is said to be in the ruins of those found among the ruins of Nineveh. The bones of the skeleton are remarkably white. The teeth are all in their places, and all of them are double and of extraordinary size. These relics have been taken to Tionesta, where they are visited by large numbers of people daily. When his giantship was in the flesh, he must have stood eighteen feet in his stockings. These remarkable relics will be forwarded to New York early next week. The joints of the skeleton are now being glued together. These remains were found about twelve feet below the surface of a mound which had been thrown up probably centuries ago and which was not more than three feet above the level of the ground around it. Here is another nut for antiquarians to crack.

Fig. 18 Newspaper Article of Eighteen Foot Giant

4

THE PEOPLING OF AMERICA

"Stranger tales than these are told,
But none so tempting, true, or bold!"
—Anonymous

IN SCHOOL WE WERE TAUGHT that Christopher Columbus discovered America, Fathers Dominguez and Escalante were the first Spaniards to the shores of Utah Lake, the pilgrims were the first to have a party with the Native Indians and that they ate turkey, mashed potatoes, yams, corn, etc. We were taught that the native inhabitants were wild, scary, and vicious, spoke gibberish and used sign language; we were taught that the indigenous peoples did not know God or know how to write. The list goes on. How thankful they must have been when the Europeans taught them how to be civilized! How wrong our teachers were. How wrong indeed!

I echo the words the author of *America BC*, the late Berry Fell: ". . . except that the two dates every American remembers are 1492 and 1776. Hence there can be no American history prior to 1492, *quod erat demonstrandum*."

QED (AS WILL BE SHOWN)

I could never understand why my questions as a youth went unanswered when I questioned my teachers as to "why" and "when." They were the teachers yet they had no answers for my questions. It was this lack of academic knowledge of true historical events that led me to thirst after knowledge and the truth surrounding the beginnings of our nation. Since that time I have learned a great deal more than I had ever expected to learn. Thanks to the tireless research of true historians, we now have so much more information at our finger tips. One can now literally punch a computer key and all sorts of information come to light. However, one must be careful as to what is true and what is not; so, the research continues but with much greater ease.

There are many books, papers, essays and articles written about America's history. Many reports are factually true while others are more or less opinions based on the author's political or religious ambitions. The latter seems to be the norm. Even some modern historians say that histories written by early historians have become antiquated and nothing more than folklore.

Josiah Priest, author of several publications and looked upon by some scholars as the master historian has exhibited bias based on his religious preferences. Henry Schoolcraft had inside help when he penned his *Aboriginal Knowledge* because he was married to the granddaughter of an Ojibwa Chief. However, his observations were limited to what the Ojibwa and Chippewa knew as "historical." His writings show that he thought all nations were much alike throughout the Americas. The idea that the American Indian believed in God or the Great Spirit wasn't seen as that but of some god other than the one most of us acknowledge as such. Even more was the repugnant idea of a trilogy of gods. Some thought this was absolutely ridiculous!

Fig. 19. An engraving by Theodore De Bry from a John White drawing

For instance, his bias and narrow view of history is showing in this quote:

There is a strong resemblance between the northern and independent Tartar, and the tribes of the North American Indian but not of the South American. Besides this reason, there are others for believing our aborigines of North America were descended from the ancient Scythians, and came to this country from the eastern part of Asia.

Explorers and clergy in the early history of America had a predisposed notion of how things were and how they would stay. They believed that since the Scythians customs of scalping their prisoners, and torturing them to death, their construction of canoes, implements of war, and of the chase, with the well-known habit of marching in "Indian file" and their treatment of the aged—the American Indian had to be akin to that culture.

During the adventures of Capt. John Smith in 1608 he describes his encounter with members of the Algonquian tribes in the vicinity of the falls of the Rappahannock River where they were attacked by Indians. This group of Indians were known as the Manahoac; a branch of the Algonquian. During the battle one of the Indians was found severely wounded and was taken to their boat, where he could be interviewed. However, this interview almost never happened because Mosco, a lusty Savage of Wighcocomoco tried to outright kill their captive. Mosco was an old friend of the English who was destined to serve them as guide and interpreter. Being unsuccessful in his quest, the English preserved the wounded warrior's life. Capt. John Smith and others soon began their interview with the Manahoac once his condition was stable:

. . . he looked somewhat chearefully, and did eate and speake . . . Then we desired Mosco to know what he was, and what countries were beyond the mountaines; the poore Salvage mildly answered, he and all with him were of Hassininga, where there are three Kings more, like unto them, namely the King of Stegora, the King of Tauxuntania, and the King of Shakahonea, that were come to Mohaskahod, which is onely a hunting Towne, and the bounds betwixt the Kingdome of the Mannahocks and the Nandtaughtacunds, but hard by where we were.

We demanded why they came in that manner to betray us, that came to them in peace, and to seeke their loves; he answered, they heard we were a people come from under the world, to take their world from them.

We asked him how many worlds he did know, he replyed, he knew no more but that which was under the skie that covered him, which were the Powhatans, with the Monacans, and the Massawomeks that were higher up in the mountaines. Then we asked him what was beyond the mountaines, he answered the Sunne; but of anything else he knew nothing; because the woods were not burnt.

These and many more such questions wee demanded, concerning the Massawomeks, the Monacans, their owne Country, and where were the Kings of Stegora, Tauxsintania, and the rest. The Monacans he sayd where their neighbours and friends, and did dwell as they in the hilly Countries by small rivers, living upon roots and fruits, but chiefly by hunting. The Massawomeks did dwell upon the great water, and had many boats, and so many men that they made warre with all the world. For their Kings, they were gone everyone a several way with their men on hunting. But those with him came thither a fishing till they saw us, notwithstanding they would be all together at night at Mahaskahod.

For his relation we gave him many toyes, with perswasions to goe with us; and he as earnestly desired us to stay the comming of those Kings that for his good usage should be friends with us, for he was brother to Hassininga. But Mosco advised us presently to be gone, for they were all naught; yet we told him we would not till it was night. All things we made ready to entertain what came, and Mosco was as diligent in trimming his arrows.

The night being come we all imbarked; for the river was so narrow, had it beene light the land on the one side was so high, they might have done us exceeding much mischiefe. All this while the King of Hassininga was seeking the rest, and had consultation a good time what to doe. But by their espies seeing we were gone, it was not long before we heard their arrowes dropping on every side of the boat; we caused our Savages to call unto them, but such a yelling and hallowing they made that they heard nothing, but now and then we shot off a peece, ayming so neare as we could where we heard the most voyces. More than 12 myles they followed us in this manner; then the day appearing, we found ourselves in a broad Bay, out of danger of their shot, where wee came to an anchor, and fell to breakfast. Not so much as speaking to them till the sunne was risen.

Being well refreshed, we untyed our Targets that covered us as a Deck, and all shewed our selves with those shields on our armes, and swords in our hands, and also our prisoner Amoroleck. A long discourse there was betwixt his Countrimen and him, how good wee were, how well wee used him, how wee had a Patowomek with us, who loved us as his life, that would have slaine him had wee not preserved him, and that he should have his libertie would they be but friends; and to doe us any hurt was impossible.

Upon this they all hung their Bows and Quivers upon the trees, and one came swiming aboord us with a Bow tyed on his head, and another with a Quiver of Arrowes, which they delivered our Captaine as a present: The Captaine having used them so kindly as he could, told them the other three Kings should doe the like, and then the great King of our world should be their friend; whose men we were. It was no sooner demanded but performed, so upon a low Moorish poynt of land we went to the shore, where those foure Kings came and received Amoroleck: nothing they had but Bowes, Arrowes, Tobacco-bags, and Pipes: what we desired, none refused to give us, wondering at everything we had, and heard we did content them with other Commodities. And so we left foure or find hundred of our merry Mannahocks, singing, dauncing, and making merry, and set sayle for Moraughtacund.

INITIAL ENCOUNTERS

Thus ended the first encounter between the English and Chiefs of several Manahoac tribes. Other colonists may have entered the country above the falls of Rappahannock, but not until after the native villages had been abandoned and the Indians had left the valleys. Explorers and settlers traversed the ancient territory of the Manahoac and left records of their journeys into the wilderness, now known as Virginia.

Smith wrote of other tribes he visited or knew about near the falls of the Rappahannock and when he navigated the river called Toppahanock some 130 miles. His interpreter, Mosco the Algonquian, went with him. When referring to the several tribes Smith wrote:

Upon the head of the river of Toppahanock is a people called Mannahoacks. To these are contributers the Tauxsnitanias, the Shackaconias, the Outponcas, the Tegoneaes, the Whonkentyaes, the Stegarakes, the Hassinnungas, and the diverse others; all confederats with the Monacans, though many different in language, and be very barbarous, living for most part of wild beasts and fruits.

Nowhere did Smith or his subordinates speak or write about "*Mounds*" being discovered and if they did see them they must have felt they were a natural occurrence. Practically nothing was known of the sparse evidences of pre-historic occupancy of the western extension of Virginia, where a few mounds and other major remains are known to exist. Smith had no idea of the ancient historical evidence that lay at his feet—that the American Continent was peopled by a superior race long before modern Indians came on scene. Some opened-minded modern scholars have reported oral histories by descendants of different Indian tribes that inhabited the eastern mountains and forests of America.

The late Dr. Paul R. Cheesman, a professor of ancient scripture in the Department of Religious Instruction at Brigham Young University, spoke of an old Indian chief—who kept the temple—told him that his race came from the south and west indicating Mexico and the southern region, and that they were driven into this land, and at that time *white* people filled the entire land with cities and villages.

Fig. 20   Capt. John Smith takes the King of Pamavukee Prisoner.

ANNIHILATION OF TRIBES

The Ojibwa have a legend of a people they called the Mun-dua. William Warren, an Ojibwa man who wrote a history of his people in 1858, penned the following:

One tradition, however, is deemed full worth of notice, and while offering it as an historical fact, it will at the same time answer as a specimen of the mythological character of their tales. During their residence in the East, the Ojibwa have a distinct tradition of having annihilated a tribe whom they denominate Mun-Dua. Their old men, whom I have questioned on this subject, do not all agree in the location or details. Their disagreements, however, are not very material, and I will proceed to give, verbatim, the version of Kah-non-dum-a-win-so, and the old chief of Sandy Lake.

There was at one time living on the shores of a great lake, a numerous and powerful tribe of people; they lived congregated in one single town, which was so large that a person standing on a hill which stood in its centre, could not see the limits of it. This tribe, whose name was Mun-dua, were fierce and warlike; their hand was against every other tribe, and the captives whom they took in war were burned with fire as offerings to their spirits.

All the surrounding tribes lived in great fear of them, till their Ojibwa brothers called them to council, and sent the wampum and war club, to collect the warriors of all the tribes with whom they were related. A war party was thus raised, who's line of warriors reached, as they marched in single file, as far as the eye could see. They proceeded against the great town of their common enemy, to put out their fire forever. They surrounded and attacked them from all quarters where their town was not bounded by the lake shore, and though overwhelming in their numbers, yet the Mun-dua had such confidence in their own force and prowess, that on the first day, they sent only their boys to repel the attack. The boys being defeated and driven back, on the second day the young men turned out to beat back their assailants. Still the Ojibwa and their allies stood their ground and gradually drove them in, till on the eve of the second day, they found themselves in possession of half the great town. The Mun-duas now became awake to their danger, and on the third day, beginning to consider it a serious business, their old and tired warriors, mighty men of valor, sang their war songs, and putting on their paints and ornaments of battle, they turned out to repel their invaders.

The fight this day was hand to hand. There is nothing in their traditional accounts to equal the fierceness of the struggle described in this battle. The bravest men, probably, in America, had met one party fighting for vengeance, glory, and renown; and the other for everything dear to man, home, family, for very existence itself!

The Mun-dua were obliged at least to give way, and hotly pressed by their foes, women and children threw themselves into, and perished in the lake. At this juncture their aged chief, who had witnessed the unavailing defense of his people, and who saw the ground covered with the bodies of his greatest warriors, called with a loud voice on the Great Spirit for help. Besides being chief of the Mun-duas, he was also a great medicine man.

Being a wicked people, the Great Spirit did not listen to the prayer of their chief for deliverance. Immediately a dark and heavy fog arose from the bosom of the lake, and covered in folds of darkness the site of the vanquished town, and the scene of the bloody battle. The old chieftain, by his voice gathered together the remnants of his slaughtered tribe. The whole day and ensuing night they traveled to escape from their enemies, until a gale of wind, which the medicine men of the Ojibwa had asked the Great Spirit to raise, drove away the fog; the surprise of the fleeing Mun-duas was extreme when they found themselves standing on a hill back of their deserted town, and in plain view of their enemies.

It is the will of the Great Spirit that we should perish," exclaimed their old chief; but once more they dragged their wearied limbs in hopeless flight. They ran into an adjacent forest where they buried the women and children in the ground, leaving but a small aperture to enable them to breathe. The men then turned back, and once more they met their pursuing foes in a last mortal combat. They fought stoutly for a while, when again overpowered by numbers, they turned and fled, but in a different direction from the spot where they had secreted their families; but a few men escaped, who afterward returned, and disinterred the women and children. This small remnant of once a powerful tribe were the next year attacked by an Ojibwa war-party, taken captive, and incorporated in this tribe. Individuals are pointed out to this day who are of Mun-dua descent, and two are members of the respected family whose totem is the Marten.

In this story we can understand how vast the town was and how many people there were. It was a major event in ancient history. Accordingly, this event took place in the Great Lakes region and parallels an account in the Book of Mormon. (Book of Mormon: Mormon; chapters 1-6)

ORAL TRADITIONS AND PARALLELS

Who were these ancient warriors? Some accounts say they were a race of *white* men. An old Indian Chief named Cornstalk gave the following account, from the book *The Prehistoric Men of Kentucky*, by Colonel Bennett H. Young, published in 1910:

> . . . *that long ago in Ohio, Kentucky, and Tennessee that the country had been inhabited by a white people who were familiar with arts of which the Indian knew nothing, that these whites, after a series of bloody contests with the Indians, had been exterminated. He also stated the burial graves were of an unknown people; that the old forts had not been built by the Indians, but had come down from a very long ago people, who were of a white complexion, and skilled in the arts.*

Obviously, the white man did not migrate from Mexico as some suggest but rather came from across the Atlantic long before the arrival of the Jaredites found in Mormon literature. This parallels the Book of Mormon with testimonies of some Indians attesting to the fact that their histories have much in common. Father James Savage, a Bishop in the Roman Catholic Church made this claim:

There was a tradition among the Attiwanderons, that their fathers utterly exterminated a great white people, taking their cattle and their lands. These same Attiwanderons were themselves exterminated by the Iroquois about 1650. A similar tradition obtained among the Chippewa Indians. Chief Shop-na-gun, an aged Indian residing at Grayling, Michigan, tells with apparent pride how his fathers killed off white men, way back, taking much cattle and land.

Mr. Soper showed him a ceremonial artifact taken from a mound below Grayling, and asked, "Indian made that?" He answered indignantly, "NOT! Indian no make; white man make long ago, way back." He asked, "Where you get?" We told him we dug it up. He looked at me indignantly, and coming forward, his hand extended and index finger pointing, called my attention to a large Bible on his desk, saying, "See book, book say no dig'em up; let them rest!"

In *American Antiquities, Discoveries in the West,* by Josiah Priest (1884), Priest writes concerning one "Mr. Sargon" who had been enlisted by the London Society to give an account of the people who reside in Bombay, Cinnamore, and their vicinity *"who are evidently the descendants of the Jews. Calling themselves Beni Israel, and bearing almost uniformly Jewish names, but with Persian terminations. This gentleman, feeling very desirous of obtaining all possible knowledge of their condition, undertook a mission for this purpose to Cinnamore; and the result of his inquiries was, a conviction that they were not Jews of the one tribe and a half, being of a different race to the white and black Jews at Cochin, and consequently, that they were a remnant of the long lost Ten Tribes."*

Continuing the account, Priest provides some very intriguing information:

> This gentleman also concluded, from the information he obtained respecting the Beni Israel, or sons of Israel, that they existed in great numbers in the countries between Cochin and Bombay, the north of Persia, among the hordes of Tartary, and in Cashmere; the very countries in which, according to the paragraph in the German paper, they exist in such numbers. So far, then, these accounts confirm each other, and there is every probability that the Beni Israel, resident on the West of the Indian peninsula, had originally proceeded from Bucharia. It will, therefore, be interesting to know something of their moral and religious character.

The following particulars are collected from Mr. Sargon's accounts, according to Priest:

- In dress and manners they resemble the natives so as not to be distinguished from them, except by attentive observation and inquiry.
- They have Hebrew names of the same kind, and with the same local termination as the Sepoys in the ninth regiment Bombay native infantry.
- Some of them read Hebrew, and they have a faint tradition of the cause of their original exodus from Egypt.
- Their common language is the Hindoo.
- They keep idols and worship them, and use idolatrous ceremonies intermixed with Hebrew.
- They circumcise their children.

- They observe the Kippur, or great expiation day of the Hebrews, but not the Sabbath, or any of the feast or fast days.
- They call themselves Gorah Jehudi, or white Jews; and they term the black Jews Colla Jehudi.
- They speak of the Arabian Jews as their brethren, but do not acknowledge the European Jews as such. They use, on all occasions, and under the most trivial circumstances, the usual Jewish prayer "Hear O Israel, the Lord our God is one Lord."
- They have no Cohen, (priest) Levite, or kais, among them under those terms; but they have a kais, (reader) who performs prayers, and conducts their religious ceremonies; and they appear to have elders and a chief in each community, who determine in their religious concerns.
- They expect the Messiah, and that they will one day return to Jerusalem. They think that the time of his appearance will soon arrive, at which they much rejoice, believing that at Jerusalem they will see their God, worship him only, and be despised no more.

These particulars, we should presume, can scarcely fail to prove interesting, both in a moral and religious, as well as in a geographical point of view. The number of the scattered members of the tribes of Judah, and the half tribe of Benjamin, rather exceed than fall short of five millions. Now, if this number be added to the many other millions to be found in the different countries of the east, what an immense power would be brought into action, were the spirit of nationality once roused, or any extraordinary event to occur, which should induce them to unite in claiming possession of that land which was given to them "for an heritage forever," and to which, in every other clime of the earth, their fondest hopes and their dearest aspirations never cease to turn.

ALTERNATIVE VIEWS OF TEN TRIBES

But although the opinion that the American Indians are the descendants of the lost Ten Tribes is now a popular one, and generally believed, yet there are some who totally discard this opinion. And among such, as chief, is Professor Samuel Rafinesque, [a self-taught polyglot, researcher, botanist and published author] whose opinions on the subject of the flood of Noah not being universal, and of the ark, we have introduced on the first pages of this work.

This gentleman is decidedly, and we may say severely, opposed to this doctrine, and alleges that the Ten Tribes were never lost, but are still in the countries of the east about the region of ancient Syria, in Asia. He ridicules all those authors who have attempted to find in the customs of the Indians, traits of the Jews, and stamps them with being egregiously ignorant of the origin of things pertaining to this subject. This is taking a high stand, indeed, and if he can maintain it, he has a right to the honor thereof. Upon this notion, he says, a new sect of religion has arisen, namely, the Mormonites, who pretend to have discovered a book with golden leaves, in which is the history of the American Jews, and their leader, Mormon, who came hither more than 2,000 years ago. This work is ridiculous enough, it is true; as the whole book of Mormon bears the stamp of folly, and is a poor attempt at an imitation of the Old Testament Scriptures, and is without connection, object, or aim; shewing everywhere language and phrases of too late a construction to accord with the Asiatic manner of composition, which highly characterizes the style of the Bible, and how can it be otherwise as it was written in Ontario county, New York.

Professor Rafinesque continued his opinion on why the American Indian was anything but from the tribes of Israel. It is obvious that he was unaware of the great cities, commerce, trading, governments, and religious beliefs of the ancients on the Americas. He places them in a box whence they can see no light, no honor and no deliverance. Priest continues:

As reasons, this philosopher advances as follows, against the American nations being descended from the Ten Tribes of ancient Israel.

1. These Ten Tribes are not lost, as long supposed; their descendants, more or less mixed with the natives, are yet found in Media, Iran, Taurin, Cabulistan, Hindostan and China, where late travellers have traced them calling themselves by various names.

2. The American nations knew not the Sabbath, nor yet the Sabbattical weeks and years of the Jews. This knowledge could never have been lost by the Hebrews. The only weeks known in America, were of three days, five days, and half lunations, (or half a moon) as among the primitive nations,

before the week of seven days was used in Asia, which was based upon the seven planets, long before the laws of Moses.

Here is another manifest attempt of this philosopher to invalidate the Scriptures, in attempting to fix the origin of the ancient Jewish and present Christian Sabbath, on the observances of the ancient nations, respecting the motions of the seven primary planets of the heavens; when it is emphatically said, in the Hebrew Scriptures, that the week of seven days was based on the seven days' work of the Creator, in the creation of the world. And as the Creation is older than the astronomical observations of the most ancient nations of the earth, it is evident that the Scriptures account of the origin of the seven day week ought to have the precedence over all other opinions since sprung up.

3. He says, the Indians hardly knew the use of iron, although common among the Hebrews, and likely never to be lost; nor did they, the Indians of America, know the use of the plough.

4. The same applies to the use of writing; such an art is never lost when once known.

5. Circumcision was unknown, and even abhorred by the Americans, except two nations, who used it . . . the Mayans of Yucatan, in Central America, who worshipped a hundred idols, and the Calchaquis, of Chaco, [Argentina] of the same country, who worshipped the sun and stars, believing that departed souls became stars. These beliefs are quite different from Judaism; and besides this, the rite of circumcision was common to Egypt, Ethiopia, Edom, and Chalchis.

But to this we reply, supposing circumcision was practiced by all those nations, and even more, this does not disprove the rite to be of pure Hebrew or Jewish origin, as we have an account of it in the Scriptures written by Moses, as being in use quite two thousand years before Christ; long enough before Abraham or his posterity knew anything of the Egyptians; it was therefore, most undoubtedly introduced among the Egyptians by the Jews themselves, or their ancestors, and from them the custom has gone out into many nations of the earth.

Again, Mr. Rafinesque says, one tribe there was, namely, the Calchaquis, who worshipped the sun and the stars, supposing them to be the souls of the departed. This notion is not very far removed from or at least may have had its origin with the Jews; for Daniel, one of their prophets, who lived about 500 years before Christ, expressly says, respecting the souls of the departed righteous: "They that be wise shall shine as the BRIGHTNESS of the firmament, and they that turn many to righteousness, as the STARS, forever and ever." A sentiment of such transcendent beauty and consequence is not easily lost. This tribe, therefore, as above name, may they not have been of Jewish origin?

6. None of the American tribes have the striking, sharp, Jewish features, and physical conformation. [But other authors of equal celebrity have a contrary opinion.]

7. The American Indians eat hogs, hares, fish, and all forbidden animals of Moses, but each tribe abstains from their tutelar animals, (which, as they imagine, presides over their destinies,) or badges of families of some peculiar sort. But to this we reply, most certainly the Jews did use fish; as in all their history, even in the Bible, frequent reference is had to their use of fishes, and to their fish markets, where they were sold and bought.

8. The American customs of scalping, torturing prisoners, cannibalism, painting their bodies, and going naked, even in very cold climates, are totally unlike the Hebrew customs. Scalping, with several other customs of the sort, we have elsewhere in this work shown to be of Scythian origin; but does not, on that account, prove, nor in any way invalidate the other opinion, that some of the tribes are indeed of Jewish origin.

9. A multitude of languages exists in America, which may perhaps be reduced to twenty-five radical languages, and two thousand dialects. But they are often unlike the Hebrew, in roots, words, and grammar; they have, by far, says this author, more analogies with the Sanscrit, (the ancient Chinese,) Celtic, Bask, Pelasgian, Berber, (in Europe) Lybian, Egyptian (in Africa) Persian, Turan, etc. or in fact, all the primitive languages of mankind. This we believe.

10. The Americas cannot have sprung from a single nation, because, independently of the languages, their features and complexions are as various as in Africa and Asia. We find in America, white, tawny, brown, yellow, olive, copper, and even black nations as in Africa. Also, dwarfs and giants, handsome and ugly features, flat

and aquiline noses, thick and then lips, etc. (Also such variety is found among the Jews.)

BLOOD OF ISRAEL

It is now viewed by many that the early scholars of the day were very biased against the Indian people of America and noted in their works that they were idol worshipers, pagans; believed in polytheism, mythology, superstitions and human sacrifices. They were right on one point and that is the Native American Indian were not Jews, but rather from the pure blood of Israel. The Jews at the time of Josiah Priest's writings were and are imposters. The very word "Jew" was a name given to those who lived in Judea.

There are people today who call themselves "Jews" and who claim to be the Israelites of the Bible, yet they reject Christ YeHoWSHuWaH and constitute the greatest enemy of Christianity. The ancient Israelites of the Bible are not the "Jews" but rather the Anglo-Saxon and related peoples. How can these things be? Intriguingly, God, in His Word, warned His people about those who would one day lie, claiming to be Israelites, when in fact they are not. Certainly God would not warn the people if that were not true. [7]

God declared that He would cast Israel out of her land, and she would have a new home, mainly to the north and west, but also to every corner of the earth; she would have numerous kings and a perpetual monarchy (Genesis 17:16). She would constitute an immense multitude, and she would be a great nation and a company of nations and a people who would bless all the peoples of the earth. God declared that He would give Israel a new name and that the true Israelites would be lost to the world scene, for a time.

When Assyria conquered and deported Israel, the King of Assyria imported Canaanite tribes to people the vacant land. It was these people who fought against the remnant of the House of Judah when they returned from their deportation and captivity in Babylon; it was these people who tried to steal the inheritance of true Israel by claiming the land had been given to them by the king of Assyria—not by God (Ezekiel 11:125): and it was these people who later claimed to be Israelites in order to steal this inheritance. "And the King of Assyria [Shalmaneser (Pul)] brought men from Babylon and from Cuthah...from Ava...from

Hamath, and from Sephavaim and placed them in the cities of Samaria instead of the children of Israel" (II Kings 17:24).

Therefore, the Indians the first Europeans encountered were not Jews, but a pure blood people from the loins of Jacob. True as it may be, many of them did slide away from the truth and become loathsome much like so many of today's children of Israel have; leaving the truth to embrace a profound life of idol worshiping, self-gratification and paganisms. However there were tribes that did embrace truth and light as far as their intelligence would allow. They were clean, loved family, cared for the elderly and the sick, were friends to all who came to their towns and feared God.

Fig. 21. Beautiful cultivated fields and village of the Indians with the "six poles" to honor their chieftain.

NATIVE TRADITIONS

David Cusick was a native Tuscarora Indian born around 1780, and also a physician and painter and student of Iroquois oral tradition. He published the first edition of Sketches of Ancient History of the Six Nations as a 28-page pamphlet at Lewiston, NY, in 1826 or 1827. During his life, Cusick wrote extensively concerning his knowledge of the different tribes in eastern North America. One paper he wrote, titled "Ancient Chronology of the Onguys or Iroquois Indians," could be favorably compared with Fourth Nephi in the Book of Mormon. An extensive quote from this work states:

> Anterior to any date the Eagwehoewe, (pronounced Yaguyhohuy) meaning real people, dwelt north of the lakes, and formed only one nation. After many years a body of them settled on the river Kanawag, now the St. Lawrence, and after a long time a foreign people came by sea and settled south of the lake.
>
> 1st date. Towards 2500 winters before Columbus' discovery of America, or 1008 years before our era, total overthrow of the Towancus, nations of giants come from the north, by the king of the Onguys, Donhtonha and the hero Yatatan.
>
> 2nd. Three hundred winters after, or 708 before our era, the northern nations form a confederacy, appoint a king, who goes to visit the great Emperor of the Golden City, south of the Lakes; but afterwards quarrels arise, and a war of 100 years with this empire of the south, long civil wars in the north, etc. A body of people escapes in the mountain of Oswego, etc.
>
> 3rd. 1500 years before Columbus or in the year 8 of our era, Tarenyawagon, the first legislator leads his people out of the mountains to the river Yenonatateh, now Mohawk, where six tribes form an alliance called the Long-house, Agoneaseah. Afterwards reduced to five, the sixth spreading west and south. The Kautanoh since Tuscarora, came from this. Sone went as far as the Onauweyoka, now Mississippi.
>
> 4th. In 108, the Konearawyeneh, or Flying Heads, invade the Five Nations.
>
> 5th. In 242, the Shakanahih, or Stone Giants, a branch of the western tribe, become cannibals, return and desolate the country; but they are overthrown and driven north by Tarenyawagon II.
>
> 6th. Towards 350, Tarenyawagon III defeats other foes, called Snakes.
>
> 7th. In 492, Atorho I, king of the Onondagas, quells civil wars, begins a dynasty ruling over all the Five Nations, till Atotarho IX, who ruled yet in 1142. Events are since referred to their reigns.

Cusick speaks of a "Golden City" south of the "Lakes," meaning the Great Lakes. Where exactly was the Golden City located? I would suggest it was situated on the Mississippi where the Missouri joins to that river. It appears when Yatatan visited the Golden City, it was the occasion of a civil war of one hundred years, which ended in the ruin of the Golden City. A group of the citizens escaped to the east where they hid themselves along the shores of Lake Ontario, where they remained for several hundred years, until a great leader named Tarenyawagon led them to settle on the Mohawk just eight years after the birth of Christ. (See Book of Mormon, Mormon Chapter 1.)

The people of the Golden City became very numerous and strong and the Six Nations were formed, according to Josiah Priest:

Upon these, a nation called Flying Heads made war but was unsuccessful; also in 242 years after Christ, a nation called "Stone Giants" made an attempt to destroy them but failed. They were successful in other wars against the Snake Indians, a more western tribe.

Fig. 22 David Cusick's drawing of the "Stone Giants" attacking the people of the "Golden City"

MODERN DISCOVERIES

Many scholars have often voiced their opinion concerning the peopling of America and the notion that the land was once covered with forts, houses, and temple mounts as simple hogwash. However, the evidence is sure, and the history left by those ancient tribes, peoples, and travelers is without a doubt factual. To prove a single point I refer to a scientific experiment by the late David Allen Deal. Deal was an explorer and author, very knowledgeable in his field of study. He authored several books dealing with ancient history.

The following photos demonstrate how science has uncovered the secrets of ancient civilizations right beneath our feet. Scores of farms, buildings, roads and towns have been built on the same sites where anciently people lived and thrived. I quote from Deal's paper as he explains his discovery of one of these ancient cities in the state of Michigan:

Photo A.

"Photo A, is a USGS composite aerial or satellite view of Roland Center (township) Isabella County, Michigan where the solar eclipse tablet was found in 1893, reported elsewhere in *Ancient American Magazine*.

Quoting from Deal, we learn some very interesting details about this historical site:

It occurred to this author that this singular artifact must not have been found or created in a vacuum. It must have been associated with a Mound builder site or city of some kind. So the USGS was consulted and this amazing photograph resulted. The central rectangle is one square mile in area. The three interlocking 800 meter diameter breastworks may be seen distinctly, along with many redoubts and house foundations. Pony Creek winds around the northwest ring enclosure and descends to the south, almost as though it had been anciently rerouted around the city. This was a mound builder city, occupied on July 27 352 AD. This date is known because of the total solar eclipse tablet and the astronomical message it contained. Many ruins of buildings may be seen under farmer's fields. Not even 150 years of continual agriculture has been able to erase the cultural remains seen in this photograph. These ruins are most likely not visible to any great extent from the ground, but are completely visible from the air. It would be too much to ask the archaeologists from Michigan to work this site, as they probably deny its existence.

PHOTO B.

Photo B, is the same USGS (United States Geological Survey) view, but with an overlay depicting where each structure lay. The overlay was created by this author, on the Macintosh G4 computer, in Photoshop, after enlarging it to a one-meter resolution.

Continuing, Deal makes some astounding claims as reported in *Ancient American Magazine*, evidenced by the images he found in his research:

The picture [Photo B] enhances the ruins so that the extent of cultural development may be more easily understood. The artifact that brought attention to this place, and its contextual setting among thousands of similar artifacts with Egyptian, Coptic, Christian motifs and Hebrew writing, as well as Egyptian Hieroglyphic writing, found all over the state of Michigan from the 1850s to the 1920s positively indicate pre Columbian, old world connections. This great complex, overlooked in the past, is just one example of a vast culture, denied by the modern establishment archaeologists, historians and anthropologists, [a grand civilization] that was strongly embedded here in America from before the first century. This is known, because of other artifacts within this collection with writing styles that precede the first century, e.g., the infamous Ohio Decalogue found about 15 miles east of Columbus, Ohio, which is rendered in "monumental Hebrew," and the Bat Creek Stone found in Tennessee with Hebrew writing from before the first century B.C. Perhaps we will interest an archaeologist in this site that may be in the offing.

Continuing his treatise and argument, Deal explains our culpability in failing to preserve the remains of ancient artifacts:

Using Google Earth tool, I have spent hours scanning the American continent in search for similar sites like those above and to my surprise I discovered dozens of sites that I believe could be those of ancient cities, roadways, single family dwellings and more. Have we simply forgotten about ancient America only to plow it up, mow it down, dig it up and throw it in the landfills? We are guilty of a great crime against humanity by our neglect in preserving these ancient sites. There are simply too many to mention; too many to save but it's something we need to take a long hard look at before it's too late. Thank goodness that so many of the mound and temple sites have been preserved but how many more have been lost to the developer? Too many.

Michigan's classic mound builders are now identified as Hopewell. Described as "a riverine people" who set up villages and built ceremonial centers along the lower reaches of river systems. Around 500 BC, they settled in the Upper Great Lakes then in about 100 BC they settled in western Michigan. The Hopewell possessed a highly spiritual nature, and they continue to be regarded as the most gifted artisans ever to inhabit the Great Lakes regions.

Hopewell movement seems to have been religious rather than conquerors. They had skills and technologies that were not had in other cultures. The underlying Hopewellian theme was spiritual and their architecture was classical. As ambassadors of a new religious idea the Hopewell people erected burial mounds, known as tumuli, and impressive ritual precincts composed of earthworks and ceremonial roadways that reflect a sacred geometry as seen in the scene above; and other cemented/earthworks throughout the Mississippi drainages.

Deal concludes his essay with the call to preserve what remains while we can:

When the influx of European settles came west into the ancient land of the Hopewell they asked the local natives who constructed the mounds. The settlers claimed the [local] Indians had no idea who built the earthworks, [while] the Potawatomi continued to regard those areas with the greatest concentration of earthworks and tumuli as sacred. In the Treaty of 1812, the Potawatomi managed to have those sacred sites and lands incorporated into the Nottawaseppi Reservation.

And, so it went throughout the lands east of the Mississippi; Indians claiming sacred sites and telling of ancient peoples who inhabited the area, but for years the archaeologists discounted [the idea] that ancient white, yellow, black or giants ever inhabited the land in any great abundance. It has only been a short while that mainstream archaeologists have taken a second look at the evidence that is so abundant they can no longer ignore it. They have begun to involve projects such as "ethno-critical archaeology" and oral histories.

Who peopled America? Who indeed!

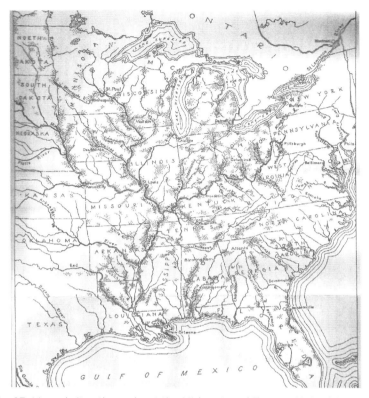

Fig. 23 Mound sites throughout the Midwest and Eastern United States

MOUNDS IN WESTERN UNITED STATES

Earthen Mounds are not features confined exclusively to the eastern and Midwestern parts of our country, because even in our western regions there are mounds. However, most of the mounds are not nearly as unique as those found along the Mississippi drainages. Nevertheless, many ancient rock walls, structures, dolmens and other features of ancient design are found in the western regions as well.

When visiting western states where a number of prehistoric ruins exist, many archaeologists immediately describe those ruins as of Pueblo origin or use the newer version of "Anasazi" origin. Most of the small earthen mounds excavated reveal fragments of burnt roofing clay, potsherds, worked stone, projectile points, etc. Skeletal remains have been identified as American Indian for the most part, but there have been

124

times when the remains found in mounds have revealed other cultures that inhabited the area such as Western European, Asian and African (North African).

Not far from the town of Willard, in Box Elder County, and within about a half mile of the shore of the Great Salt Lake, an excavation was conducted in ancient ruins. The ruins there consisted of a number of mounds; altogether there were fourteen then in evidence. Of these, seven were opened with a total of fifteen skeletons, a considerable amount of broken pottery, also a quantity of stonework, such as lance heads, arrowheads and steatite slickers used in polishing and straightening arrows. Also reported at the site were a number of Indian hand mills of superior make and size, made from granite, and hand stones of the same. On the floors of the rooms opened was discovered, in a charred condition, considerable quantities of beans, corn, corncobs, and also cloth fiber.

MOUNDS IN UTAH

Mr. Don Maguire of Ogden, Utah, conducted many such excavations on mound sites, before, during and after his employment with John Welsey Powell. During his excavations circa 1914, he mentioned artifacts discovered in mound including strange copper objects and bronze projectile points. Maguire was a consulting and mining engineer by profession but became interested in American archaeology during the course of vocational travels in Mexico and Central America. Between 1880 and 1905 he gathered a considerable private collection as result of excavations in prehistoric ruins, mostly around Utah.

Not only does Utah have many mound sites but so does just about every state in the west. Some are large while most are smaller and more subtle in appearance. The Fremont culture flourished in the Great Basin from circa 700 to 1300 AD, then seemed to vanish. Whether they were assimilated into local tribes, moved, died out or just what, will probably remain a mystery. There is still a debate as to who these people were. They seemed to be much different than most Western Indian cultures, in dress, architecture, arts, crafts, and traditions. The National Parks Service describes the Fremont thusly:

> The Fremont people lived throughout Utah and adjacent areas of
> Idaho, Colorado and Nevada from 700 to 1300 AD. The culture was
> named for the Fremont River and its valley in which many of the first

Fremont sties were discovered. The Fremont was a Puebloid group who had strong cultural affiliations with their better-known contemporaries, the Anasazi. While the Anasazi built cliff dwellings, the Fremont often lived in pit houses (dug into the ground and covered with a brush roof), wickiups (brush and log huts) and natural rock shelters. Their social structure was composed of small, loosely organized bands consisting of several families. They were closely tied to nature and were flexible, diverse and adaptive. The Fremont people often made changes in their lifestyles as social or environmental changes occurred.

The most unique and mysterious artifacts left by the Fremont people were clay figurines. The small figures resemble people, often showing intricate details such as ear bobs, necklaces, clothing, hair and facial decorations and sexual characteristics. The purpose of figurines is unknown, but it is believed they had magical or religious significance. Fremont figurines resemble Fremont rock art. Pictographs (painted) and petroglyphs (carved or pecked) are depictions of people, animals and other shapes and forms left on rock surfaces. Anthropomorphic (human-like) figures usually have trapezoidal shaped bodies with arms, legs and fingers.

The figures are often elaborately decorated with headdresses, ear bobs, necklaces, clothing items and facial expressions. A wide variety of zoomorphic (animal-like) figures include bighorn sheep, deer, dogs, birds, snakes and lizards. Abstract designs, geometric shapes and handprints are also common. The designs may have recorded religious or mythological events, migrations, hunting trips, resource locations, travel routes, celestial information and other important knowledge. Many believe rock art uses symbolic concepts that provide the observer with information and that it was important, not simply artistic expression or doodling.

Fremont rock art and archaeology sites can still be seen in numerous places in the southwest including Utah's Fremont Indian State Park, which protects the largest Fremont site ever excavated in Utah, including forty pit houses, twenty granaries and countless artifacts and rock panels. More can be seen at Zion, Capital Reef, and Arches National Parks and at the Dinosaur National Monument in Colorado.

By 1300 AD, the Fremont had abandoned their villages. Archaeologists can't quite agree on what happened, but several changes are generally blamed. First, climatic conditions favorable for farming seem to have changed during this period, forcing local groups to rely more and more on wild food resources and to adopt the increased mobility necessitated in collecting wild food.

At the same time, new groups of hunter-gatherers appear to have migrated into the Fremont area from the southwestern great Basin sometime after about 1,000 years ago. These full-time hunter gatherers were apparently the ancestors of the Numic-speaking Ute, Paiute and Shoshoni peoples who inhabited the region at historic contact, and perhaps they displaced, or assimilated the part-time Fremont hunter-gatherers.

Fig. 24 Fremont culture clay figurines

We now know there is much more to this story than has been told to us by the National Park Service and their archaeologists. It's hard to fathom a people with this much talent and knowledge living in mud and stick huts while the Ancestral Pueblo people lived in large rock edifices. The workmanship of tools and ornaments is not the work of an awkward and backward people but of a high caliber nation. This author believes that mainstream academia lacks the insight into the real truth of who these people were.

MCCONKIE RANCH

Sadie McConkie's Ranch sits along Dry Fork Creek northwest of Vernal, Utah. It wasn't until several years ago that the public was allowed to visit the ranch and its hidden secrets etched and painted on the high red and gray cliff faces east of the creek.

A fantastic pictorial of the Fremont people has never been equaled. Here we have a half mile of fantastic art work depicting the Fremont and Ute people (and possibly others). Many scholars have visited the site and commented—those who are die-hard mud and willow hut Fremont culturists, maintain this site is from a different group, perhaps one that was passing through. Religious groups, scholars and other researchers, however, see it much differently.

Fig. 25 Erroneously dubbed the "Three Kings" panel

A close up view of this panel reveals some clues as to who these people might have been, including their religion, workings, teachings and patriotism. According to Ute legend, these people flourished here thousands of years ago until they were wiped out.

Fig. 26. Photo Dr. Julian Fell, from replica after photo by Prof. Julian Steward. (Saga America, pg. 102, Berry Fell)

Fig. 27. Photos courtesy of Daniel Lowe

The photos above give us some idea of the magnificent and pains-taking work done by the artists. The paint is near gone but the messages are still here. Several scholars have attempted to translate the panels now referred to as Fremont.

Archaeologist and author Dr. Polly Schaafsma referred to this particu-lar panel as "Probably the most elaborately carved Fremont panel in exis-tence. The Classic Vernal Style petroglyphs are more wide spread than one realizes. They are not confined to Utah's northeast but spread throughout the Great Basin. It is very interesting to note the headdress on the central figure. There are few that match this rendition of a crown. The armor, shield, necklace and commanding posture is truly one of a kind. This cen-tral figure leaves no doubt that he was a chief or king among his people. Many other elaborately carved Fremont anthropomorphic figures have headdress and crowns but they would appear to be subordinate to this central figure. Their headdresses are not as pronounced or as detailed as his. It's important to note the detail in the crown or headdress. It is not unlike those worn by the ancient Persians and Libyans."

Fig. 28 Standing alongside the "King" is an anthropomorphic figure in bas-relief. It is believed this figure is denoting a "slave" or servant to the King. Other figures on this panel are depicting subordinate chiefs and a shaman. The Vernal/Ashley area of Utah has certainly the most exciting Fremont panels. Other sites throughout the Great Basin are not as elaborate.

The question that arises with this particular style and rendition of Classical Fremont figures is whether they are another culture apart from what we now believe to be Fremont. With the style of dress and the headdresses, it is possible these people are another race from afar that came to inhabit portions of the Great Basin.

In a cavern near this panel a Ute Indian by the name of Tom Riddley discovered an ancient sword. I was able to photograph it before Riddley took it back to the cave. The sword is depicted on yet another panel not a quarter mile from the main panel. Where these people Libyan or Persian? Did they conquer other races and cultures while there or were they themselves destroyed? It is our belief that the Fremont, and Ancestral Puebloans were separated because of race and status. The near-eastern people depicted here helped to change the landscape of human habitation in the region.

PORTRAITS OF EARLY AMERICANS

George Catlin, the great Western artist who captured many prominent Indian Chiefs on canvas, clearly demonstrated the physical differences between various tribes. In a publication titled *American Indians, The Art and Travels of Charles Bird King, George Catlin and Karl Bodmer* these differences become obvious, from their dress to hair styles to facial and physical characteristics. If we are to lend any credence to the works of men like Catlin and King we have to realize that the Indian as we know them had to have several different ancestral beginnings.

We pay close attention to those tribes that have a common denominator that connects them to near Eastern lineages. For example, those who wore turbans or bundles on their heads include: "Fork-luste-Hojo", Seminole, "Chief Chittee Yoholo", Seminole, "Asseola" a Seminole leader, "He Who Ties His Hair Before, Crow" a Hidatsa Chief. "Mon-Chnsia", A Kansas Chief. "Shau-Hau-Napo-Tinia", an Ioway Chief, "Chon-mon-I Case", an Otto Half Chief. "Pow-A-Sheek" a Fox Chief, "Kee-She-Waa" a Fox Warrior, "Nah-Et-Luc-Hopie" a Muskogee, "Timpoochee Barnard" an Ochee Warrior, "Tulcee-Mathla" a Seminole Chief. "Thayendanegea" was Captain of the Six Nations from the Mohawk tribe. Several more Chiefs and sub-chiefs in the Creek, Senaca, Cherokee, Shawanoe, Chippeway, Pottawatomie, Apache, Hopi and even Sioux wore such turbans. *

Their garments appeared as different as they themselves. Other people had shorn heads, Mohawk cuts, long hair, short hair, feathered headdresses and horned headdresses. Facial features differed as well—long noses, short noses, hooked noses, broad noses, thin noses, dark eyes, colored eyes. Many Indians were very tall, some short and stocky. It is within reason to suppose that not all North American Indians have come from one ancestral source, but from many!

Dr. James Harris Sr. of Orem, Utah, sees the "Three Kings" panel in yet another light. A scholar in ancient history, particularly that of the ancient Egyptians and the study of Hebrew writing found on rock art panels of the southwestern states of America, Harris wrote:

> It has never been and never will be desirable for Latter-day Saints or investigators of the Restoration to build their faith in the Church upon external evidences. But some investigators and members of the Church become so inhibited by anti-Mormon use of external evidence material that they are unable to give scriptural messages a fair or open-minded consideration. In many instances a little help from a knowledgeable believer could open their minds to the message of the restored scriptures.

Harris cited Dr. Polly Schaafsma's work on the Dry Fork panel in his book, *Southwestern American Indian Rock Art*, and went on to say that the heroic-size of the primary figure had sometimes been called the "Sun Carrier," identified by S. Herman Polock of Tropic and the Pratt brothers of Neola, Utah, as General Moroni in a most significant pose suggesting the text of Alma 46:12 - 13. Harris goes on to say that "... the possible relationship of this Book of Mormon text to the central figure on the Dry Fork Panel is sufficiently obvious not to require argument. It is also true that other interpretations are possible. Is the item on the end of the pole a medicine bag, a skull, a mask, a human head, or is it Moroni's banner ("title of liberty")? The figure certainly carries a shield and appears to be wearing a breastplate and head gear. If one takes the Book of Mormon seriously, one must take the Dry Fork Three Kings Panel seriously enough to consider it a reasonable possibility."

OTHER ETHNICITIES

More than likely ancient America saw scores of people from different ethnic backgrounds come and go that we have no record of whatsoever. Those that we do have knowledge of are somewhat ambiguous because of falsified or inaccurate data. Such is the case with the Mummy Cave discovered by Johnny Brewer in Sanpete County, Utah. A pencil sketch is all that is available of these mummies along with Brewer's description of the contents of the cave.

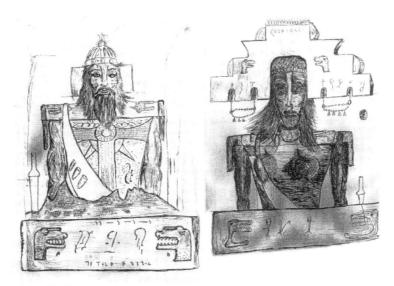

Fig. 29 The King   Fig. 30 The Queen

SANPETE COUNTY MUMMIES

Dr. John Heinerman, an anthropologist and nutritionist, claimed he was allowed in the cave to take hair and tissue samples. His conclusion was that these mummies were at least 1,000 years old. Heinerman described the male mummy:

The remarkable preserved remains of a Jaredite royal mummy (presumably a king) entombed in a stone sarcophagus in an ancient mountainous burial chamber in Sanpete County, Utah. This figure measured nine feet two inches tall. Note the decidedly proto-Mongoloid facial features which are typical of present-day Mongolians and other Oriental races. The hair and beard were a dull, rust-red color. Some of the original emigrants from the Tower, (including Jared and his brother and their extended families) may have looked this way.

The woman mummy he describes thusly: "The wonderfully intact remains of a Jaredite royal mummy (presumably a queen) enshrined in a large stone coffin in an ancient treasure cave located between the small Mormon communities of Manti and Ephraim in south central Utah. This particular individual measured eight feet eight inches. Observe the enormous headdress and dragon markings, so typical for women of royalty in some of China's earliest dynasties. Strands of mud-brown and ugly gray were intermingled with mostly straw-colored hair, giving the appearance of being "dish water" blonde. Radiocarbon testing of some hair and nail clipping and tissue samples dated this and her male companion to between 800 - 700 B.C. Some Jaredite women who emigrated from the Tower of Babel with their husbands may have had similar features, including the tall height."

In an interview with Johnny Brewer in the 1970s, he mentioned that the male mummy was seven feet tall and the woman near the same, a contradiction in terms from Heinerman's statement. However, since there are no actual photos of either the man or the woman, we have no way to substantiate their claims.

At first glance, the male mummy has a helmeted head that is near identical to the headdresses worn in battle by the Mongols during the Yuan Dynasty. The huge stone headdress of the woman is still a mystery.

Fig. 31. Copper head

One of the strangest artifacts taken from this Cave is the portrait of a man with curious signs and symbols etched into the headdress and face. The size of this particular piece fits in the palm of a hand. There was a larger rendition of this figure made from copper.

Inscriptions on this artifact and others discovered in the cave are perplexing to say the least. The characters resemble those found in the Kaweah Alphabet and seen on some of the Ancestral Puebloans petroglyphic panels in the Southwestern part of North America. The Kaweah language is akin to the Yokuts Language of Southern California. Kaweah actually means "Crow or Raven Cry".

While researching the Yokuts of California, I found a handbook of Yosemite National Park that gave this fragmented history of the Yokuts, to include the Gawia, Miwok, Ohlone, Maidu and Wintu tribes:

The origin of these Sierra Nevada tribes is not definitely known. There can, however, be no serious doubt that they form part of the generic American Indian race and that their ultimate origin must be sought wherever the source of this division of mankind may have lain. While no one is yet in a position to speak dogmatically on this matter, all indications point to the Indians having come at some time in the far past from Asia, probably by the Bering Strait and Alaska route. It is clear that in his bodily type the Indian more nearly resembles the Mongolian of Eastern Asia than any other variety of the human species. The long, straight, stiff hair, one of the most valuable marks in race classification, is alone sufficient to establish a strong presumption in this direction. As to when this migration of the first inhabitants of America out of Asia took place, there is growing up a fairly unanimous consensus among anthropologists that this movement must have occurred at about the time that the Old Stone Age was giving place to the New in Europe; that is to say, in the period at which chipped stone tools were being replaced by polished ones, and the ax, bow and arrow, textiles, agricultural implements, and domestic animals were becoming part of the heritage of the species. These steps in advance are believed to have occurred about ten thousand years ago. We may therefore say roughly that somewhere about 8,000 B.C.—with an allowance of a few thousand years either way as a margin for error, the American Indian became established on this continent and began his diffusion.

California was probably not very long in being reached; a mode of life adapted to local conditions was worked out, and with this the natives were apparently content, and their development progressed only slowly. They have left some traces of their occupancy in ancient village sites, shell mounds, and the like. Here the less perishable of their utensils, such as mortars, pestles, pipes, knives, arrow points, awls, beads, and other objects of stone, bone, and so forth, have been preserved. In one of the most favorable localities on the shores of San Francisco Bay careful computations have been made as to the age of these deposits, with the result that the lower levels of the shell mounds there have been estimated to date back at least 3,000 years. The implements at these lower levels are ruder by the modern Indians of the State, including the Miwok. We are therefore justified in assuming that native customs evolved very slowly in California, and that the ancestors of the Miwok and of the Yosemite Indians for a very long time past have lived very much in the manner and under the conditions in which they were discovered by the whites [over] seventy years ago" (brackets mine).

This is a typical governmental report when it comes to dating ancient American people or tribes. It is almost a generic report with only the names of the tribes, people or cultures changed. The old "*Bering Strait*" theory once again raises its obnoxious head! They use "definitely" and "probably" to describe the origin of the Indians of California. In reality they have no clue! These authors are so entrenched with popular theory they can't see any other course to pursue!

KAWEAH ALPHABET

As I noted above some of the characters on the Brewer's Cave artifacts resemble those of the Kaweah Alphabet. You may notice the similarities as you examine the charts.

KAWEAH ALPHABET

Fig 32 Example of Kaweah Alphabet

Fig. 33 Further Kaweah Characters

CHART I

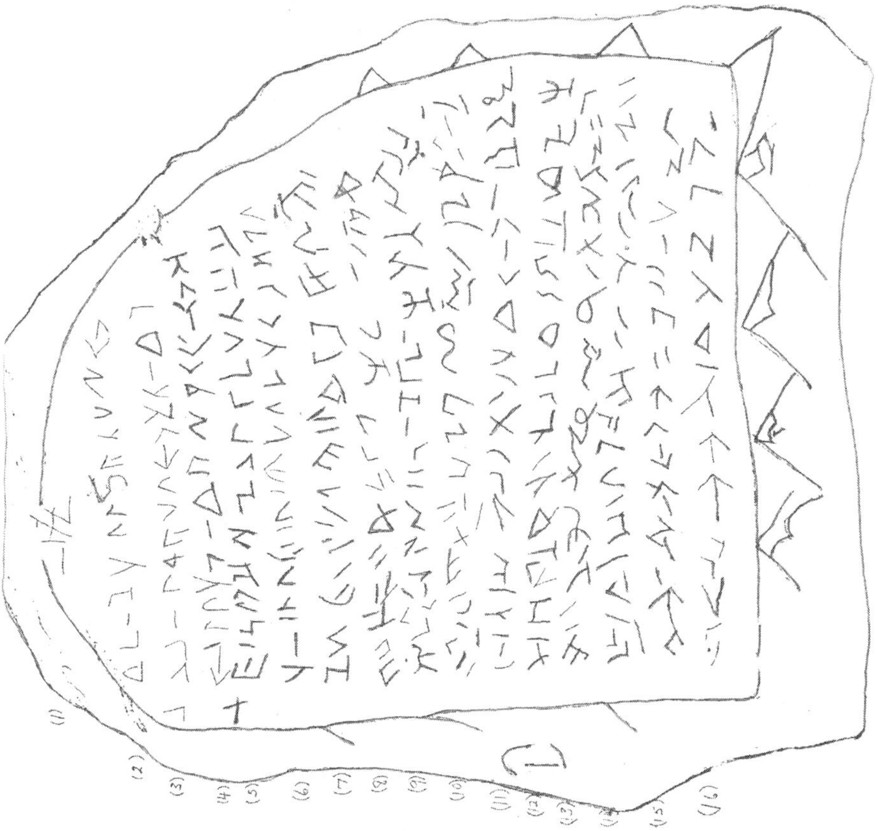

BYU 71-40.1 Obverse

Fig. 34

CHART 11

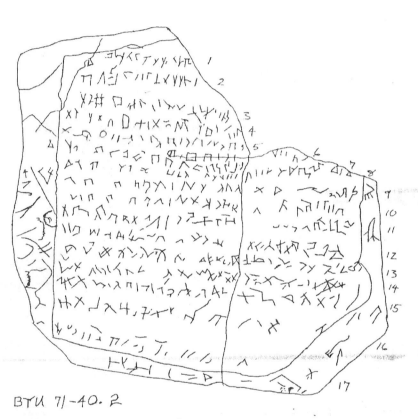

BYU 71-40.2

BYU 71-40.1 Obverse

Fig. 35

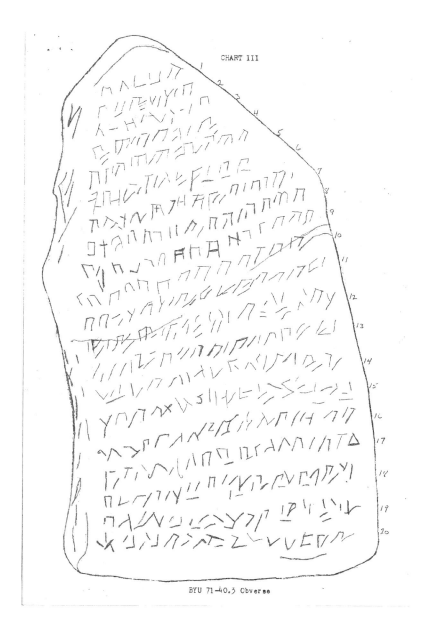

Fig. 36

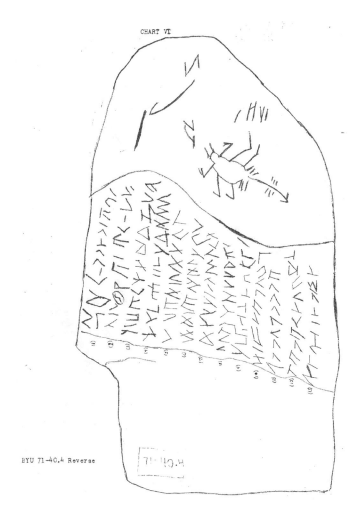

CHART VI

BYU 71-40.4 Reverse

Fig. 37

142

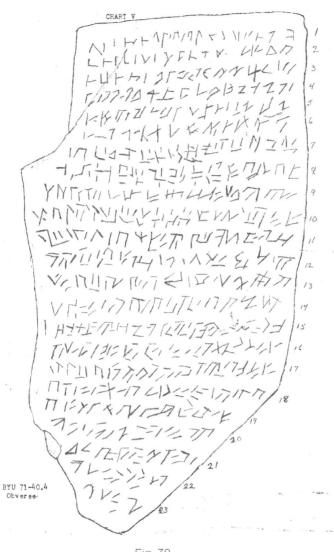

Fig. 38

The charts above are facsimiles of some of the lead artifacts taken from Brewer's Cave for examination by Brigham Young University. Open mindedness does not apply in this case. The idea that the cave of

143

records was a fraud was firmly etched in the minds of BYU's academic scholars long before these examinations began, so there was never any doubt that they would see the collection and the whole story as faked! Nevertheless, I present their findings in Appendix C. Keep in mind that the Kaweah Language was never even considered.[8]

Matheny and Adams dismissed the Manti Tablets as being fakes and that they were of far more recent origin. Did they ever stop to think the only reason why it had been so difficult to decipher them was because the people who wrote these strange characters had themselves developed a strange argot of their own? They looked for only known languages.

MULTIPLE MIGRATIONS

Over the centuries, different populations used bamboo rafts, reed boats, skin boats, and dugout canoes with woven reed sails, hide, and finally the planked ships to sail to the shores of western America. In Saga America, the late author Berry Fell alluded to the fact that pre-Columbian Europeans and North Africans crossed the Indian and Pacific Oceans as well as the Atlantic and settled in California and Nevada from the third century B.C. There is rich evidence of a Chinese as well as an early Arabic presence on the American continent. This may very well explain the Ogam script discovered in the western part of the nation, which we will discuss in a later chapter.

Indian legends tell of ancient races that came from the west. It is assumed they all spoke different tongues and as time marched on these races intermarried or became confederates with one another and began new slang languages much like we have in America today.

John Heckewelder had lived among the Delaware Indians, also known as the Lenni-Lenape in the latter part of the eighteenth century. During this time he gathered information concerning wars between the Delaware Indians and the Mound Builders of Ohio. His paper remained unpublished for many years until finally appearing in the first volume of the Transactions of the Historical & Literary Committee of the American Philosophical Society. He wrote:

> The Lenni Lenape (according to the traditions handed down to them by their ancestors) resided many hundred years ago in a very distant country in the western part of the American continent. For some reason which I do not find accounted for, they determined on migrating to the eastward, and accordingly set out together in a body.

After a very long journey and many nights' encampments by the way, they at length arrived on the Namaesi-Sipu [Mississippi] where they fell in with the Mengwe [Author Wayne May believes this tribe to be Iroquoi]), who had likewise emigrated from a distant country, and struck upon this river somewhat higher up. Their object was the same with that of the Delawares; they were proceeding on to the eastward, until they should find a country that pleased them. The spies which the Lenape had sent forward for the purpose of reconnoitering, had long before their arrival discovered that the country east of the Mississippi was inhabited by a very powerful nation who had many large towns built on the great rivers flowing through their land. Those people (as I was told) called themselves Talligew or Tallegewi. Colonel John Gibson, however, a gentleman who has a thorough knowledge of the Indians, and speaks several of their languages, is of opinion that they were not called Tallegewi, but Alligewi, and it would seem that he is right, from the traces of their name, which still remain in the country, the Allegheny river and mountains having indubitable been named after them.

The Delawares still call the former Alligewi Sipu, the River of the Alligewi. Many wonderful things are told of this famous people. They are said to have been remarkably tall and stout, and there is a tradition that there were giants among them, people of a much larger size than the tallest of the Lenape. It is related that they had built to themselves regular fortifications or entrenchments, from whence they would sally out, but were generally repulsed.

I have seen many of the fortifications said to have been built by them, two of which, in particular, were remarkable.

One of them was near the month of the river Huron, which empties itself into the Lake St. Clair, on the north side of the lake, at the distance of about 20 miles northeast of Detroit. This spot of ground was, in the year 1776, owned and occupied by a Mr. Tucker. The other works, properly entrenchments, being walls or banks of earth regularly thrown up, with a deep ditch on the outside, were on the Huron River, east of the Sandusky, about six or eight miles from Lake Erie [named after the "Cat" Indians]. Outside of the gateway of each of these two entrenchments, which lay within a mile of each other, were a number of large flat mounds in which, the Indian pilot said, were buried hundreds of these slain Alligewi, whom I shall hereafter, with Colonel Gibson, call Alligewi. When the Lenape arrived on the banks of the Mississippi they sent a message to the Alligewi to request permission to settle themselves in their neighborhood. This was refused them, but they obtained leave to pass through the country and seek a settlement farther eastward.

They accordingly began to cross the Namaesi-Sipu, when the Alligewi, seeing that their numbers were so very great, and in fact they consisted of many thousands, made a furious attack upon those who had crossed, threatening them all with destruction, if they dared to persist in coming over to their side of the river. Fired at the treachery of these people, and the great loss of men they had sustained, and besides, not being prepared for a conflict, the Lenape consulted on what was to be done; whether to retreat in the best manner they could, or to try their strength, and let the enemy see that they were not cowards, but men, and too high minded to suffer themselves to be driven off before they had made a trial of their strength and were convinced that the enemy was too powerful for them.

The Mengwe, who had hitherto been satisfied with being spectators from a distance, offered to join them, on condition that, after conquering the country, they should be entitled to share it with them; their proposal was accepted, and the resolution was taken by the two nations, to conquer or die.

Having thus united their forces the Lenape and Mengwe declared war against the Alligewi, and great battles were fought in which many warriors fell on both sides. The enemy fortified their large towns and erected fortifications, especially large rivers and near lakes, where they were successfully attacked and sometimes stormed by the allies. An engagement took place in which hundreds fell, who were afterwards buried in holes or laid together in heaps and covered over with earth. No quarter was given, so that the Alligewi at last, finding that their destruction was inevitable if they persisted in their obstinacy, abandoned the country to the conquerors and fled down the Mississippi River, from whence they never returned.

The war which was carried on with this nation lasted many years, during which the Lenape lost a great number of their warriors, while the Mengwe would always hang back in the rear leaving them to face the enemy. In the end the conquerors divided the country between themselves. The Mengwe made choice of the lands in the vicinity of the great lakes and on their tributary streams, and the Lenape took possession of the country to the south (Silverberg. 1968, pp. 54-56: parts included Mercer. 1885; see also Donehoo, 1998, pp 2-3). [10]

Fig. 39 A gray slate slab depicting warring nations. Could this be the war between the Lenape and the Alligewi?

147

DOCUMENTATION OF BATTLES, FAMINE, RELIGION, ASTRONOMY

The above slab is one of thousands discovered in mounds, burials and plowed fields in the Mississippi Valley. Scenes of war, famine, religion, astronomy and more are depicted on these slabs of stone. How else would the history of these ancient peoples be known other than by oral traditions over time. These nations were not so barbaric as to not have a written language. There are numerous historical references to the Talligewi or Alligewi. These histories were actually written in hieroglyphics in ancient times. The following is an English translated portion of a hieroglyphic panel:

> The Great River divided the land, and being tired, they tarried there. Yagawanend (hut-makers) was next Sakima, and then the Tallegwi were found possessing the east. Followed Chitanitis (Strongfriend), who longed for the rich east land. Some went to the east, but the Tallegwi killed a portion. Then all of one mind exclaimed: War, war! The talamatan (not of themselves) and the Nitilowan all go united (to the war). Kinehepend (Sharp-looking) was their leader, and they went over the river. And they took all that was there, and despoiled and slew the Tallegwi. Piniokhaszewi (Stirring-about) was next chief, and then the Tallegwi were much too strong. Teuchekensit (Open-path) followed, and many towns were given up to him. Paganchihilla was chief and the Tallegwi all went southward. Haltanwulaton (the Possessor) was Sakima, and all the people were pleased. South of the lakes they settled their council-fire, and north of the lakes were their friends the Talamatan (Mercer, 1885).

We will discuss this topic at greater depth further on in the book.

FURTHER RESEARCH

It is most likely those strange beings in the Manti cave and those depicted on sandstone cliff faces at Dry Fork, Utah, as well as those buried alive in Lovelock Cave, Nevada, were cultures that sailed to our shores via the Pacific Ocean. Chinese and Libyans more than likely crossbred to get the Mongolian looking features of some of those races that tried to conquer the tribes in the Mississippi valley. There is no certain timeline as to when these cultures landed on the western coast but we do know that the Chinese landed in San Francisco Bay 200 years before Columbus. There are written fragments as well as artifacts scattered from Quebec down the coast of California and a few at sites along many of the western river systems.

After the U. S. Bureau of Ethnology was established in 1879, an investigation of western tribes of Indians began. The anthropologists of the day noticed unusual features of the Zuni and Hopi tribes and it got the attention of Professor J. Walter Fewkes and of James Stevenson. Not only their physical appearance was different from what the two scientists had been used to, but their vocabulary soon made it plain that the Zuni language was related to no other Amerindian family of tongues.

While examining Pueblo materials in the Peabody Museum of Archeology , Dr. Barry Fell's attention was focused on a white leather sun-disk that, according its label had been brought from New Mexico and once belonged to the Zuni. On it was painted Libyan letters T-M, a formula adopted in Egypt as the phonetic rendering of Atum, the primeval sun god of North Africa. He noted:

> The Libyan language, as I have shown elsewhere, is basically Egyptian combined with Anatolian roots introduced by the Sea Peoples who invaded Libya, while the written form of the language is like that of the Phoenicians, alphabetic but using only consonants.

The western part of the American continent has many sites that give clues of ancient races that once inhabited it. Not only petroglyphic and hieroglyphic sites, but artifacts that have been unearthed that seem to be totally out of context with what we think we should discover in the west.

One such find came by way of Richfield, Utah, when some men were digging a well not too far off the Sevier River. The discovery was related to me by an associate who asked that I do research on the item. I sent the item to Mr. Wayne May, editor and Publisher of *Ancient American Magazine*. He along with Frank Joseph wrote an article that appeared in Volume 16, Issue No. 97: [11]

LADY ELCHE OF THE WEST

To introduce the artifact, publisher May provides a comprehensive description of the find and what it may represent:

> *This issue's Ancient American cover is the never-before-published photograph of an item said to have been found in Utah some time during the early or middle 20th century. It measures approximately six inches in diameter and appears to have been made from copper alloy.*

Circumstances surrounding its discovery are very uncertain, having been allegedly recovered from six feet six inches beneath the surface of the state's geographical center in the Sanpete Valley. An alternative version describes anonymous family members digging a well somewhere along the Sevier River outside Richfield, in south-central Utah, where they accidentally unearthed the object, again at about six feet down. After having been told by a nearby historian that "it must have belonged to local Indians," the unconvinced discoverers passed their find along through three generations and into the possession of a grandchild. If such paltry background information has robbed the piece of whatever artifactual provenance it may have once had, it stands on its own as something curiously convincing. Everything about it argues against fakery—from the fine workmanship to its lack of comparison with anything similarly known in the modern world, to say nothing of its arcane details.

Figure 40 Richfield, Utah Artifact

The article continues, focusing on the inscriptions:

At first glance, it nonetheless seems like an impossible mish-mash of disparate cultures. The typically "Egyptian" figure, hair style, profile, eye, necklace, and lotus appear contradicted by uncharacteristic discs on either side of the head and an inscription of cuneiform...not hieroglyphs...at the top. In truth, the Phoenicians are known to have been a mosaic people, borrowing and incorporating the cultural elements of other folk, particularly the Egyptians.

The Phoenicians created their own written language, of course. But according to Omniglot, the online encyclopedia of writing systems and languages, "The Phoenician alphabet developed from a proto-Canaanite alphabet during the 15th century B.C. Before then, the Phoenicians wrote with a cuneiform script. The earliest known inscriptions in the Phoenician alphabet come from Byblos [in Lebanon], and date back to 1000 B. C." (http://www.omniglot.com/writing/phoenician.htm). Hence, if Phoenicians inscribed the Utah plate with cuneiform, they could only have done so before the 15th century B.C.

Archaeologist May then speculates on how the artifact found its way to Utah:

At that time, they were strictly confined to the Levant, in the Near East, by the predominance of other more powerful kingdoms. Only with the collapse of these late Bronze Age civilizations around the turn of the 12th century B.C. were the Phoenicians free to become the far-sailing merchants renowned throughout the Archaic and Early Classical Periods. Perhaps the Utah plate was already five hundred or more years old and a particularly revered object, when it was carried by Phoenicians to our continents eastern seaboard. They may not have gone on to actually reach the location of its modern discovery in the American Southwest, where it could have arrived and been deliberately buried as a precious commercial good handled by aboriginal traders.

Then editor May makes a remarkable synopsis of what the artifact tells us:

In any case, those strange discs at either side of the woman's head identify her Iberian origins. A similar otherwise unique accoutrement appears on the Lady of Elche, the 4th-century B.C. stone bust of a Carthaginian priestess to the Phoenician lunar goddess, Tanit, found outside Valencia. In fact, double headdress discs depicted on the Utah profile and Spain's Lady of Elche both feature some tell-tale details—rectangular sets of small triple knobs running around the edge.

As Carthaginians, the Phoenicians built several major cities in Iberia, such as Cartagena and Gadir, today's Cadiz. The Utah image appears related to one of these urban centers. Gadir was founded in 1104 B.C., the earliest possible date for the metallic plate's arrival in North America. Its most recent date would have coincide with Roman conquest of all Carthaginian cites in Spain by the early 13th century B.C.

Fig. 41 The enigmatic Lady of is a once polychrome stone bust

While insufficiently known circumstances of discovery obscure the object's possible archaeological genuineness, its own beauty, high craftsmanship, and internal details suggest an ancient authenticity beyond the loss of provenance. As such, it is potential powerful evidence for the arrival on our shores of Phoenician visitor from Carthaginian Spain 2,200 to 3,100 years ago.

ANITA MEYER RESPONSE

Anita Meyers, originally trained in criminology, has been studying languages and the origins of ancient scriptures, gave her impressions of seeing this Utah artifact, called Lady Elche of the West.

My first impression of the artifact is that of a calendar, compass, or sundial. You will notice that the same design that looks like a tambourine over the ear (in front) is also repeated again in the picture behind the (person's) head. This tells me that it is a calendar. The second clue rests with (the person) "looking" to the West as if the sundial or compass was looking in his/her point of view.

Also notice that there are 3 round notches for each one of the 12 segments. Now when you overlay this design with the Hindu calendar, you can now see how the 3 segments fit into the 12 sections (Zodiac). However, the same concept ensues with other calendars.

Cuneiform script can be seen on the outside edge of this artifact and can be interpreted. Unfortunately, our linguist can only clearly read the

right side for now. The left side is not clear enough, but we are pursuing another photo to examine.

Using the Semitic cuneiform structure we have translation. The letters on the left are blurry, but the ones on the right are clear as day and spell the word "MAZZAROTH," which is the Hebrew word that the patriarch Job used for the calendar seasons known as the Zodiac, (Job 38:31-33) "Canst thou bind the sweet influences of Pleiades, or loose the bands of Orion? Canst thou bring forth Mazzaroth in his season? Or canst thou guide Arcturus with his sons? Knowest thou the ordinances of heaven? Canst thou set the dominion thereof in the earth?

The term "cuneiform" is very deceptive in that it tricks people into thinking that it's some type of writing system. The truth is that cuneiform denotes not one but several kinds of writing systems, including logo syllabic, syllabic, and alphabetic scripts. In fact, "cuneiform" came from Latin "cuneus," which means "wedge." Therefore, any script can be called cuneiform as long as individual signs are composed of wedges.

Many languages including Semitic, Indo-European, and isolates are written in cuneiform as the following list shows: Sumerian, Eastern Semitic, Assyrian, Babylonian, Elamite, Hittite, and a few others.

ANOTHER LADY ELCHE FROM FRANCE

Fig. 42 Lady Elche Medallion from France

This "Lady Elche" Medallion was one of seven brought back from France. It seems there was an old antique shop closing its doors when the seven medallions were found there. It is strange that these medallions are only found in Europe with the exception of the one found here in America, and at a depth of six feet!

An observation was made concerning the hair style of Hopi maidens. The photo below bears a strong resemblance to our Lady Elche. Is

Fig. 43 A Hopi Indian Maiden

there a connection, or is it just a co-incidence?

In the next chapter, we will explore ancient artifacts, petroglyphic and hieroglyphic panels and their association with Ancient America.

5

ARTIFACTS & PROVENANCE

"The wilderness of the people! Probably another country which would be to them another wilderness in which they were tested as to whether they would hear."
—*E. W. Bullinger*

STORIES, LEGENDS, CAMPFIRE TALES AND even rock art are not enough to prove or disprove that any particular people, culture or their influence ever had a presence in a given region. On the other hand, the discovery of artifacts would help in identifying certain peoples or cultures that may have either inhabited a region and if the local people were somehow influenced by them.

There have been literally millions of artifacts extracted from the earth that can never be proven to be authentic simply because they lack provenance. Yes, an authority on certain artifacts can assume the item is authentic looking and yes, at times radio-carbon testing will confirm an approximate age; however, a definitive "*Yes*" can hardly be used because we don't know where it came from, and unless extracted properly, we can only use certain tools to bring it into compliance.

The greatest hope for all investigators of Ancient America is to have a find be authenticated. Most investigators fear that if they tell anyone of their discovery it will be taken from them, or they won't get the credit for the discovery. Most discoveries are made by novices, amateur archaeologists, rock-hounds, prospectors and those just messing around in the hills for the weekend.

CONTEXT/PROVENANCE

An important concept in archaeology, and one that isn't given a lot of public attention until things go awry, is that of context. Context, to an archaeologist, means the place where an artifact is found. Not just *the* place, but the soil, site type, and the layer(s) the artifact come from, and what else was in that same layer. The overall importance of where a certain artifact is found is very important; the site needs to be properly excavated to tell us about those that lived, worked, ate, and to the extent possible, their customs and whether they had an organized society. The whole of human existence and its past is tied up in archaeological remnants; it is only considered viable when the entire package of any given site is properly and scientifically excavated.

Archaeologists and those who are true historical investigators of human ancestors get very upset when a site is *looted*! For instance, when an artifact is brought to an archaeologist out of context and without provenance they are naturally very skeptical of its authenticity.

To explain more fully the context concept, including how crucial it is to our understanding of the past, how easily it is lost when we glorify an object, and why artists and archaeologists don't always agree, we cite an article by Prof. Romeo Hristov and Santiago Genovés in the journal *Ancient Mesoamerica*. In 1933, a Mexican archaeologist, Jose Garcia Payon, was excavating near Toluca, Mexico, at a site continuously occupied beginning somewhere between 1300-800 B.C. until 1510 A.D. when the settlement was destroyed by the Aztec emperor Moctecuhzoma Xocoyotzin. The site, according to Payon, had been abandoned since that date, although some active farming was still being practiced nearby. At one of the burials located at the site that was excavated by Payon, he found a terracotta figurine head of Roman manufacture about two inches long by about one-half inch across. Most noted terracotta historians believe the figurine head as having been manufactured about 200 A.D. Thermoluminescence dating of the object provided a date of 1780 plus or minus 400 B.P. which supported the historian's theory. Now, what does this all mean? The artifact was deemed by our modern archaeologists as a fake! Why? Although the artifact was excavated by a professional, it was removed from its location without verifying and documenting the *in situ* context.

When such artifacts are presented to professionals the first question is "How" or how was this obtained? The Roman head was found in Mexico without provenance or context. How many artifacts are brought to us this way? I can name dozens that I've inspected. When you ask the question they usually respond, *"What difference does it make?"* They think that by giving the origin of the items it is sufficient.

Any artifact has a maker. The maker has an idea, then the maker or someone else designs the artifact, thereby creating the three steps re-

quired to make any object: idea, design and creation. In previous chapters I show artifacts taken out of context, such as the Lady Elche Medallion and more. In this chapter will we explore artifacts taken with both context and provenance and those that lack this vital information. Unfortunately, some of the most significant and staggering discoveries come to us with no provenance. It's a shame too! However, we must realize that before radio-carbon dating and the science of recovery was the standard tool, people gathered artifacts haphazardly not knowing what they were doing.

Figure 44 The Tecaxic-Calixtahuaca Head

Such was the case with many of the artifacts gleaned from the mounds of the Midwest and the surrounding areas. However, we are fortunate that in some cases, photos were taken of the artifacts while they were still "in place."

Figure 45 Copper Head Piece

Hopewell style copper head dress and cheek guards excavated in Ohio. The two wings actually are cheek and ear guards. There would have been a cloth or buckskin bonnet that would be used to tie the head dress to the wearer. [12]

Fig. 46 A Hopewell grave where examples of copper head dress and breast plate were discovered.

Fig. 47 Note the copper head dress on the right skeleton. Also note the size difference between this one and the one shown above. [13]

MISTAKEN INTERPRETATIONS

The Adena People was originally published in *The University of Kentucky Reports in Anthropology and Archaeology,* Volume VI, 1945, in which the authors William S. Webb and Charles Snow note discoveries of isolated decapitated heads with burials. They categorize these discoveries as an archaeological "problem of the trophy skulls." It seems both the Adena and the Hopewell cultures practiced the ritual of the "Severed Head Society." Many heads appeared to have been painted with red ochre and drilled so they could be suspended with a cord to be hung up either on a pole or even around the neck of the owner. Web and Snow noted that another strange discovery had been made in the Hopewell group of mounds in Ohio. Many implements and ornaments were strewn about near skeletons and on a detached skull of what they deemed "a young male" had been placed a "curved, helmet-like copper plate" or described as a copper head plate.

Breast plates were also discovered and photographed, as well as bronze spears and arrow points, leggings and arm bands. Many artifacts were taken without ever gathering needed organic material, simply because there was no need at that time. However modern technology has allowed us to get a pretty good idea of the age of the metal artifacts and with the photos it helps all the more.

Fig. 48 Hopewell style breastplate used for protection against spears, arrows

More than likely most copper artifacts were removed from sites before archaeologists could make a determination. Still today, copper artifacts are being discovered in America's heartland by amateurs and professionals alike. One item that brings a lot of scrutiny is the copper hand axe and hatchet. Even some bronze arrow and spear points have been discovered as far west as Utah. Utah? You ask! Right, even Utah, and to make that statement even more remarkable is that those items came from, yes, Sanpete Valley and very near Manti, Utah.

In a book written in 1930 by Henry Clyde Shetrone, *The Mound-builders: A Reconstruction of the Life of a Prehistoric American Race, Through Exploration and Interpretation of Their Earth Mounds, Their Burials, and Their Cultural Remains,* provides insight into the mindset of those early historical pioneers. They perceived the North American Indian was so backward he did not have the intellect to make certain copper artifacts. I quote from Shetrone's book:

> *Although the highly developed Mayas, Aztecs, and Incas of Middle and South America had learned the secret of smelting metals and therefore had passed over into the so-called Age of Metals, the mound-building peoples remained altogether in the Stone Age. In using copper and other metals they treated them as malleable stone, hammering them into form and finishing prospective artifacts by grinding and polishing. By constantly annealing copper they were able to pound it into thin sheets from which their remarkable artistic scroll and repoussé ornaments were made. Annealing, it may be explained, consists in heating a metal and allowing it to cool slowly, by which process it is softened. Under the hammer, copper tends to harden and split apart, and experiment has shown that the native metal cannot be pounded into thin sheets without this repeated heating and gradual cooling.*
>
> *Since the Mound-builders had not learned to melt any metal, it is clear that the old and widespread belief that they possessed a long-lost secret process of hardening copper is unwarranted.*

Really? Is that why so many copper artifacts were haphazardly excavated because of the unwarranted belief that they were not the ones who smelted and created the copper artifacts? Who cares about context or provenance? It was a huge mistake on the part of those early pioneers of archaeology.

Shetrone was one of many who thought the Indians were nothing but a barbaric left-over from an earlier culture and in some ways they were right. The Indians had lost much of the knowledge their ancestors possessed but they still retained enough to know how to make certain instruments. Near the source of copper supplies, as in the Hopewell culture of Ohio and the upper middle Mississippi region, the mound people utilized copper for implements, ornaments and warfare. Farther south, the Cumberland-Tennessee area and in the area bordering the Gulf, the metal was too precious to be used for utility purposes and was treasured solely for ornament. The utility forms made from copper com-

Figure 49 Copper Ingot with Handles

prise the adze, axe blades, spuds, knives, spear points, mauls and some minor artifacts. Many of these artifacts were found in private collections, small museums and in some cases a person's stocking drawer!

Not all axes are the same. Each manufacturer had a certain style and method of achieving his goal. The same goes for tablets and plates. The photo below is of two copper tablets discovered in the West (whereabouts unknown) that were taken out of a small earthen mound. The whereabouts of the mound was kept secret so there was no way to verify their authenticity. Again, we see how important information has been lost forever.

Fig. 50-51 Types of axes discovered in Hopewell Mounds

Fig. 52 Copper Tablets

BURROWS CAVE

The story of Burrows Cave is well known among Ancient American investigators. I will summarize the story here for readers who have never heard of Burrows or his discovery in southern Illinois. Here is a prime example of artifacts being pulled out of a site with absolutely no provenance. Hence many of the artifacts were dubbed fraudulent, and to make things even worse, Burrows' was accused of manufacturing some of them for monetary gain.

Russell Burrows discovered an underground cavern on April 2, 1982. Burrows was a novice "*caver.*" While walking along the edge of a slab or rock he suddenly dropped through a crumbling cover that dropped him several feet below the surface. After he got his senses back and his eyes adjusted to the darkness he noticed that during his fall he had dislodged a large stone that covered the pit. Had this large stone fallen on him he would have either been killed or seriously injured. The underside of the stone was covered in strange carvings and what appeared to him as lettering. In the pit he discovered more carved stones and this was the beginning of a long love-hate affair between the cave and Burrows.

Over the space of many years, Russell Burrows, removed hundreds of stones with all types of inscriptions and reliefs on them. He removed many thousands of dollars' worth of gold coinage as well, only to melt it down, selling it for the gold content. To my knowledge there are no coins or gold artifacts left.

The following photos are of some of the Burrows Cave stones and artifacts removed from his cave. Are they authentic? Or were they of recent manufacture? It's a question that has haunted archaeologists and investigators from the beginning. [14]

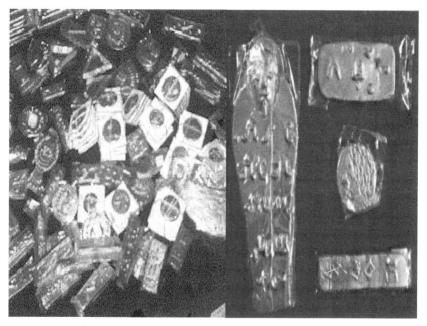

Fig. 53   Gold from Burrows' cave   Fig. 54   Gold medallions

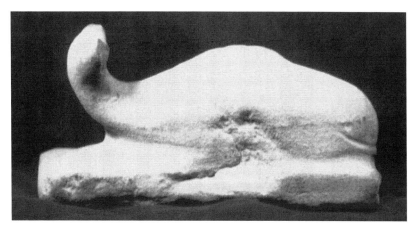

Fig. 55 Carved Whale

Fig. 56 Image in gold (See Fig. 24)

Fig. 57 Burrows' Cave coinage

Fig. 58 Golden tablet with inscriptions

165

Fig. 59 Obverse side

Fig. 60 Golden eagle effigy

Fig. 61 Golden tablet depicting the Egyptian God "Anubis"

Fig. 62 Gold tablet with a type of Ogam inscriptions

Fig. 63 An "all seeing eye" Medallion

Fig. 64 Rock with what appears to be Ogam writing with three pyramids.

168

Fig. 65 A Mohawk warrior

Fig. 66 Small Rock with Effigy

Fig. 67 Stylized Gorget

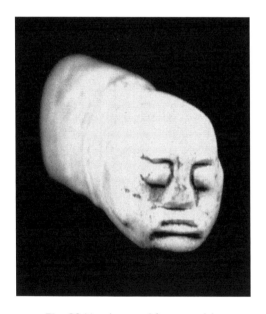

Fig. 68 Head carved from marble.

Fig. 69 Egyptian Warrior

The shame is that we'll never know what's left in the Burrows cave because he has refused admission to anyone. Many believe Burrows discovered the greatest archaeological find of the 20th century in North America. Regardless of the controversy, what is left of these artifacts deserve the most serious if not most painstaking and deliberate study by all available experts possible. The same importance should be placed on the Michigan tablets as well.

Unfortunately for Burrows and his companions, the idea of fabricating artifacts put a damper on authenticating any of them.

FORENSIC ANALYSIS

Mr. Scott Wolter, a forensic geologist who coined the phrase *archaeopetrography*, conducted a study on a few of the stones extracted from Burrows' lair. One of the stones was referred to as *"Isis"* a marble piece. Wolters concluded that this particular stone appeared to have been made from an old weathered tombstone most likely in the early to mid-1980s. Wolter stated that "Further, the ten white marble artifacts tested to date that contain identical silt were likely created at the same time." So, those artifacts shown above may be fakes! [For an example of a complete forensic analysis, see the study performed on the famous Bat

Creek stone at http://www.ampetrographic.com/files/BatCreekStone. pdf.]

On August 2 of 2012, renowned archaeologist of Biblical Lands in Israel, Dr. Babriel Barkay described ten key points related to determining the authenticity of artifacts. These key points are critical in the great debate to answer the question of how ancient America was settled— was it entirely by illiterate hunter-gathers or did literate cultures who may have traversed the oceans in ships colonize this land. This talk by Dr. Barkay was aimed primarily at those archaeologists hanging on to the old worn out Bering Strait migration theory. Following are his ten points:

1. Expertise, knowledge, and experience of the person presenting, translating, or interpreting an artifact are important.
2. The humanities: epigraphy, languages, philology, anthropology, archaeology, and history are of primary importance.
3. Fixing the authenticity of objects and artifacts is a matter of time.
4. No committee of scholars or court of law should decide the authenticity of any artifact.
5. The "Too Good To Be True" principle used by many to condemn an artifact, historical concept, or translation is too common and not an acceptable method to determine the truth about an artifact.
6. The importance of context and controlled excavations: some artifacts are planted, yet we should not reject an object if it comes without provenance.
7. Linguistic or paleographic variations or anomalies should not automatically bring condemnation on an inscription.
8. We must assume that all scholars dealing with publishing information about ancient inscriptions and artifacts have integrity.
9. The scholarly community should agree that all researchers and scholars are generally honest people until proven otherwise.
10. The time factor: It is important to let scholarship mature over time before scholars can draw certain conclusions.

A CASE STUDY

Figure. 70 The author inspects a copper bowl from the Negev Desert.

As seen here, I am inspecting a bowl that came to us from a woman living in Willard, Utah. She was present at an Ancient American Forum I was involved in several years ago. After the presentations Mrs. Connie Udell came forward with this bowl wrapped in a cloth. She asked if I had time to hear her story. Of course I did. She said that years ago her father was working down in the Four Corners area (Where Utah, Arizona, Colorado and New Mexico meet) when he saw a young Navajo boy playing in the sand, digging with this bowl. When her father asked the lad if he could see it, the little fellow readily agreed.

He could see it had strange inscriptions that didn't look like anything he had ever seen. Wanting to somehow acquire the bowl, he asked the lad what he would trade for it. The boy had been eyeing this little dog that Mrs. Utley's father had so knowing that was what he wanted, the exchange was made.

The bowl was kept in the family for some time. A friend of the family, Mr. John Hutchings of Lehi, Utah, a collector of all sorts of things and well known throughout the community for his knowledge in ancient cultures, was asked to take a look at it. Hutchings told his friends that he had no idea what the writing was or where the bowl came from. So, it sat on a shelf for years, until Mrs. Udell heard of the Ancient American

Forum being held in Provo, Utah. With us at the presentation was Dr. James Harris who was fluent in Hebrew and Egyptian languages. I asked him to take a look at it. After a while, he told us that the inscription was most likely old Hebrew writing from the Negev Desert.

I asked him for a paper on it so we could keep it with the artifact. Dr. Harris said he would send me the paper and I could deliver it to Mrs. Udell.

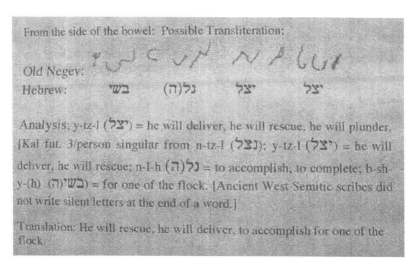

Fig. 71 Dr. James Harris Possible Transliteration of the inscription.

Fig. 72 Note the inscription just below the ornate rim of the bowl.

We noted that the bowl was copper but had been over-laid with silver. Dr. Harris estimated the bowl was manufactured around 300 AD, which raises questions related to when, where, by whom, how and why. Since we have no provenance on the bowl we can only make an educated guess.

WORTHY OF STUDY

Earlier we discussed the Michigan tablets as well as the Manti tablets and other significant finds. Even though most of these artifacts are without provenance, they are worthy of study for other compelling reasons.

Fig. 73 Ten Commandments on Copper Tablet

Many people have heard of the *Michigan Tablets* with the label "fraudulent" attached to them. Most of those who believe this to be true, probably have not really studied the history or the relics themselves. The

Michigan artifacts first gained public awareness in 1879 when an article was published in the local newspaper. Many folks thought the finds were some kind of hoax and made fun of the so-called discoveries, while others were fascinated by them. Artifacts such as these have been shown to be evidence of an ancient race of people with knowledge and great understanding, who lived their lives out in this part of the country.

There are still some with many questions: who were the people that buried these artifacts; are the artifacts genuinely ancient; are some deliberate fakes? By what criteria are we to judge the authenticity of such articles?

Many artifacts are authentic—their ancient origin cannot be questioned—but certain others are held in great doubt. Between 1890 and 1920, hundreds if not thousands of artifacts were extracted from countless mounds throughout the Midwest and the state of Michigan. Since most of all the artifacts have similar markings, including what we refer to as the "Mystic Symbol," they are classified as "Michigan Tablets and Artifacts." Now, they are often described as the "Soper-Savage Collections," named after two of the men prominent in their discovery. Many people have become involved with the Soper/Savage artifacts, either in their discovery or their study and research. However, there are essentially just two camps—those who vouch for their absolute authenticity or those who declare them absolutely fraudulent.

Some discard them for the simple belief that there were no "elephants" in America at that time. However, we know that is not true. Another reason they were deemed fakes was because of the scientific knowledge of the time. Nevertheless, the word "fake" is still heard among many scholars.

It seems that these ancient people who lived throughout the states of Michigan and Ohio were great in number and as we know left thousands of mounds as mute evidence of their historical past. In 1911, Mr. John A. Russell in a pamphlet entitled Prehistoric Discoveries in Wayne County, Michigan, penned:

> Since the year 1907 certain definite and orderly lines of investigation have been pursued in Wayne County, Michigan, having for their purpose the uncovering and preservation of the remnants of a prehistoric civilization which apparently flourished in this territory and in that immediately contiguous to it.

The beginning of these investigations was the result of an accidental discovery. While exploring a wood lot in the neighborhood of Palmer Park, [Detroit's northernmost playground], Daniel E. Soper, a citizen of Detroit, [who was a retired journalist and a former secretary of state for Michigan], was attracted to the debris thrown out of an excavation made by some burrowing animal. Examination of the debris developed that it contained some broken pieces of burnt clay pottery. An excavation following the burrow led to the discovery of several objects of natique character, which appear to have been the first of their class taken out in Wayne County by any of the group of investigators who have since become associated with the exploration. He continued:

One area which has been most productive in results lies directly north of the city of Detroit, in the village of Highland Park. In this 40 acre wood-lot there appear to be upward of 1,200 mounds, of which something more than 400 have been opened.

To provide some perspective on these discoveries, Dr. Paul Cheesman of Brigham Young University, once wrote:

By the time modern Americans became interested in these mounds and began their work of excavations, many of the mounds, no doubt, had become parts of farming lands and thereby had become obscure. Thus, the principle mounds excavated in Michigan have been those that were covered with dense vegetation and even with heavy timber. *Our most reliable and best information regarding these ancient mounds comes from the men who excavated them.* He went on to say that the two best authorities were the Reverend James Savage and Mr. Daniel E. Soper, both of Detroit, Michigan. They excavated over 500 mounds between the year of 1907 and the time Father Savage published a small book on the Michigan Mound Builders in 1911.

Perhaps no man assisted in opening more mounds than did the Reverend James Savage, a Pastor of the Roman Catholic Church in Detroit. His descriptions have been viewed by many as very accurate and of great value. He described these mounds and their hidden treasures as follows:

The Silvan Club owns two forty-acre tracks (minus two acres) on the Ausable River, Crawford County, Michigan. On the west forty acres we found only one group of mounds. This group contained eleven mounds.

On the east forty acres we found three groups of mounds—one of three another of seven, and another group which covered an acre or more of ground. In this group some were close together, others from forty to sixty feet apart. We opened every grave we found on this group, and found but one specimen. It was a large, well-made chilled copper spear point. In the group of seven mounds, were found two tablets—one of copper, the other of stone; one copper knife, and one medal of sandstone. In the group of three, we found only one specimen, a beautiful medallion of dark stone. In the group of eleven mounds, on the west forty acres, were found six specimens, two slate tablets, three copper spear points and one very handsomely worked ceremonial. We found groups and lowly graves along Ausable as we explored. Some of these groups were half a mile or more back from the river" (Prehistoric Discoveries in Michigan, pp. 11-12).

The following account is a continuation of James Savage's description of the mounds he encountered:

On the mound in which one copper tablet was found there stood the decayed stoup of a large pine tree. This mound was eighteen feet by nine, of oval shape, and stood in height three feet. When we came to the roots of the tree the man in the pit remarked, "We can't dig any farther here 'til we get an axe; that hand axe is not heavy enough to cut these roots."

I jumped into the pit and directed him to clear away the earth from the end of the root most exposed. When he did so, I got hold of the root. It was so decayed we tore it out and threw it onto the bank. I noticed that the roots of the tree had perforated the basin-shaped stria of charcoal and ashes on the sides of the mounds. Directly beneath the stump there were ten to twelve inches of sand between the lower center of the stump and the stria of charcoal and ashes at the bottom of the mound. There lay this copper tablet, directly beneath the stump on the stria of charcoal and ashes. I was the first who saw tablet 14 and 15 of booklet as it lay in its ancient bed. It alone was left to tell the story of the manner of its master's death, whose bones had long since mingled with the ashes that covered the bottom of his grave. The mound in which this tablet was found was nearly round, ten feet across and flat, and more than eighteen inches in height. On the side of the mound to the northeast stood a tree. One of the roots of this tree had grown across the tablet as the tree was strong and vigorous. This mound was one of a group of eleven mounds. In this group we found six specimens (Prehistoric Discoveries in Michigan, p. 12.)

Fig. 74 Copper vessel with inscriptions

Fig. 75 One of the Kings Crowns

179

Fig. 76 Copper Egyptian profile

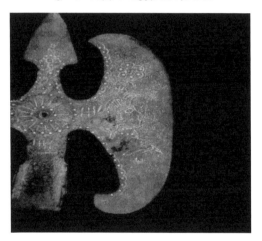

Fig. 77 ceremonial battle axe.

Mr. John Russell also wrote in his book that thousands of ancient artifacts which had been dug from the mounds throughout the state of Michigan were similar to each other in the various locations found. He described their provenance, which dispels any sense of forgery or fraud regarding same:

....composed of hardened copper, slate, sandstone, and limestone; that these objects are recovered from timber areas containing trees from ten to two hundred years old; that to follow the ash strata of the opened graves has called for the chopping away of tree roots representing many years of growth; that these objects are ornamented with drawings, fluting and decorations quite out of touch with the culture of the American Indian; and that they carry in great quantity hieroglyphic writings which their finders cannot read and which they have so far found nobody capable of interpreting. This statement represents the sum of all the claims made regarding the discoveries.

The earliest discoveries of any artifacts in association with the Michigan Mounds can be traced back to 1877 when a farmer plowed up artifacts. However, some say it was earlier, around 1858. It stands to reason many more had been exposed from the time man began plowing the ground in those areas, but the finders considering those items pagan, most likely discarded them.

A newspaper article from 1892 in which a Mr. M. E. Cornell cites a newspaper article published in Genesee County, Michigan as follows:

An interesting product of one of the lost arts has just been discovered in this vicinity. Mr. Robert Hon, while plowing on his farm a few miles south of this village, unearthed a perfectly formed and well preserved copper dagger. The blade is nine and one half inches in length, one and one fourth inches broad at the hilt, double-edged, tapering to a fine point, and bearing unmistakable evidence of great skill and efficiency in its maker. No smith or artist of this or any other period of science can show evidence of higher attainment. It is wrought of pure copper, and is as hard to-day as the finest still.

From what people this wonderful relic came, or at what remote age they inhabited this country, and to what plane of civilization they attained, are but matters of conjecture and speculation. Mr. Dean Hawley, of this village, is possessor of this interesting souvenir. Hundreds have called to examine it.

Fig. 78 Copper spear and arrow points

In a paper written in 1892 by W. K. Moorehead titled "The Hopewell Mounds," he elaborated on several very exciting discoveries. Of two skeletons unearthed, indicated only by fragmentary bones, he says:

I think that these were in the original center of the mound, and were the first interments made. The small mound erected over them evidently permitted water to collect about the remains. One of the dome-shaped structures, such as have been described, surrounded them, the earth was very loose and the structure appeared to have been larger than that built around any other skeleton. Both skeletons lay with their heads to the west. (Face to the east for the resurrection). The sheet copper had been found ten feet south of them. Right over the skeletons were sixty-six copper hatchets, ranging from four ounces to thirty-eight pounds in weight; twenty-three plates, several dozen broken plates, many thousand pearl and shell beads, perforated teeth and bear tusks, fragments of wood, fragments of meteoric iron, three or four meteoric iron celts, two eagle effigies (badly oxidized), fragments of carved bones, a stone celt, a broken shell and several copper figures of unknown form and use.

It is no exaggeration to state that the entire person [whose skeleton is marked 248] glittered with mica, pearl, shell and copper. All that the ancients could give him were showered upon his remains. About the legs were numerous beads and fragments of copper plates. On the chest and under the back were several copper plates of large size. Perhaps a thousand beads, many of them pearl, were strewn everywhere about him. Bear teeth, cut and sawed into fantastic shapes, were also found with the remains. There were copper spool-shaped ornaments and panther teeth among the ribs. Upon the copper there was a perfect imprint of cloth, and many of the beads had been sewed to the cloth. As near as I could judge, a cloth or skirt had extended to the knees of the skeleton. At its right shoulder was a large platform pipe and an agate spear head. Over the cranium had been placed a cap or helmet of copper. (footnote) This was corroded and could only be taken out in fragments. From the crown of the head there extended wooden antlers, covered with thin rolls of sheet copper. They were fifteen by twenty inches, with four prongs on each side. The imitation was admirable. These antlers were exceedingly frail. They could only be removed by taking out the entire mass of earth enclosing them.

List of sheet copper found in one place (in a mound); a long mass of copper covered with wood on one side, squares and circles, patterns, etc., on the other. Eighteen copper rings and bracelets (some double rings). Two sets of anklets joined together by oxidation, three in one and two in the other. Five saucer-shaped disks. Two swastika crosses, a saw pattern, a large grotesque arrow head and several unknown forms stuck together. One wheel or circular pattern with straight and curved lines and bars running across it. Small discs, wheels, etc. One shole fish (evidently a sucker), one fragmentary fish. Two diamond shaped stencils, four spool-shaped ornaments, four comb-shaped objects, one St. Andrew's cross, fifty-one various pieces resembling washers, etc. Ten small circles and other fragments. No bones were near this singular copper find. It occupied a space of three by four feet, and had somewhat discolored the surrounding earth. No burnt earth, ashes, charcoal, etc., accompanied the sheets. They seem to have been intentionally thrown down (as an offering), when the mound was partially complete.

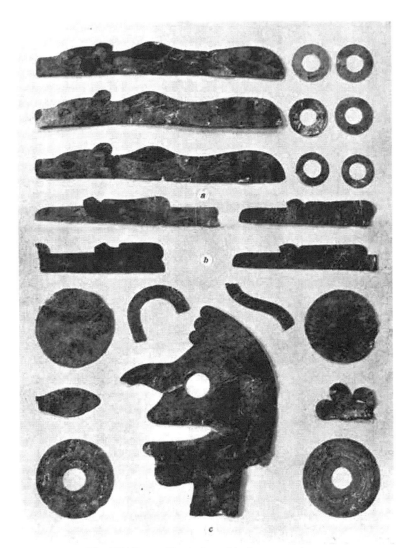

Fig. 79 Mica artifacts found in the mound.

Fig. 80 strange pattern   Fig. 81   Bronze axe

Moorehead continued excavating mounds throughout the group including one of the smaller ones in the northest corner. He reported:

. . . as many as 3,000 sheets of mica varying in size and thickness were taken. I remember shipping a barrel and a soap box from this structure, filled with nothing but mica. Many fine bone needles, mostly broken and damaged by heat, a rude altar full of bones and ashes, two or three hatchets and some spools of copper, ornaments, shark's teeth, and about 200 pounds of galean showing no marks of heat were taken from the structure.

From the northeast corner Moorehead moved to the southeast corner where he once again excavated a mound.

Thirty-nine skeletons lay upon the base line, most of which were accompanied by singular and unique specimens. The eastern portion of the mound was covered on the bottom with small stones. Several post holes were observed in different portions of the mound. These may have contained timbers 8 to 10 inches in diameter, which were the supports for a building of some description erected over the hard burnt floor of the mound where gravel and clay intermixed seemed to have been subjected to heat sufficiently intense to form a cement of equal toughness to that of an ordinary cellar floor. Among the finds were various forms of copper, including an axe weighing 17 pounds; large shells; pearls; human jawbones, both upper and lower, carved into ornaments; animal teeth, set with pearls and smaller teeth; piples of different patterns, and a bowl, fourteen and half inches in diameter, cut quite accurately from a piece of limestone.

Moorehead gives us accurate information and we can picture in our minds the events as they unfolded as he excavated those numerous mounds. It is very obvious that a knowledgeable and civilized culture once lived here. In those days not much was thought about provenance or context since archaeology was still in its infancy.

Fig. 82   Black slate gorgets or charms from the mounds

In spite of this vast collection being the butt of jokes and labeled fraud, it is nonetheless on the lips of every investigator and historian searching for truth. So it is with many other artifacts from other discoveries. The next five photographs are from the collection of Milton R. Hunter and are in possession of the author.

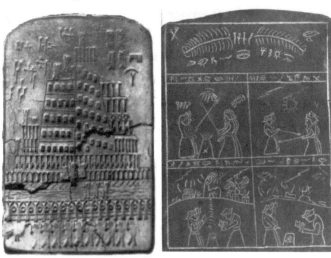

Fig. 83 The Tower of Babel   Fig. 84 Death and Destruction

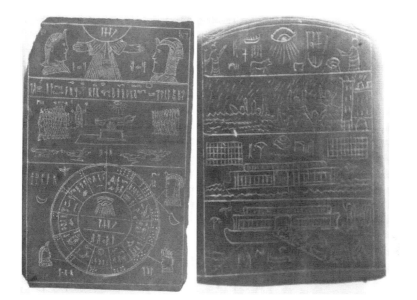

Fig. 85 War and Peace   Fig. 86 Noah's Flood [15]

The photos below caused major controversy because of their content. The photo on the left is depicting what many say is Jesus and those same naysayers believe that the inhabitants of the Americas did not know about Jesus until the Spanish brought word of Him. The photo at right is depicting the Crucifixion. One thing that stands out is the nail prints in the hand and the "Sure Sign of the Nail" in the wrist.

Fig. 87   Is this Jesus?   Fig. 88 The Crucifixion.

It has been said that because of the Michigan discoveries, Burrows came up with the idea of a "new discovery." He wanted and needed recognition. So, he devised a scheme to make himself look important by bringing to light a famously rich cave of ancient travelers from Egypt. Although we may never know for sure, many believe that in order for such a scheme to be successful, the perpetrator would require extensive knowledge in epigraphy and history. In my opinion, it's highly unlikely that was the case with Burrows. I share several photos of Burrows Cave Stones that are from my own collection. I believe Burrows did have a cave but I also believe he got greedy and his methods caused the investigation and research to suffer.

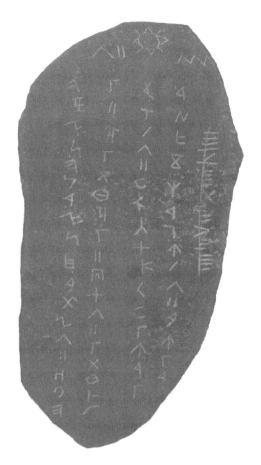

Fig. 89 Note the Ogam Script.

Fig. 90   Several characters appear to resemble Phœnician.

Fig. 91 A type of Charm.   Fig. 92   Ancient Algonquin?

190

Fig. 93 Negroid featured man with rays of light shining on him.
Perhaps to show favoritism.

Fig. 94   Known as the Chaldean Portrait Stone. [16]

THE DAVENPORT CALENDAR STONES

After their discovery in 1877, another set of stones and tablets that have been dubbed fakes made news. They are referred to as the Davenport Calendar Stones. Reverend Jacob Gass was digging in a mound in a well-known archaeological site called Cook's Farm. After their discovery the news spread quickly and the story was published far and wide. Much speculation circulated of their origin ranging from the Lost Ten Tribes of Israel to the burial of the stones by the Latter-day Saints when they moved west.

By studying the photographs of these stones and other stones discovered during that same time period, the Smithsonian Institution declared the entire group fake, publishing their pronouncement in the Second Annual Report of the U. S. Bureau of Ethnology. Charles E. Putnam, a former Academy president and prominent Davenport Attorney, came to the defense of Reverend Gass, the Academy and the authenticity of the artifacts. The argument was debated in scientific journals of the time. Because of the fact that "Mormons" might be involved it was noted that two members were expelled from membership for declaring that the stones and pipes had been made in the basement of the building by members and planted in the mounds.

In 1970, Dr. Marshall McKusick, then State Archeologist of Iowa, conducted an exhaustive search of the Museum's archives with the expressed purpose of publishing the complete, true and documented story about the stones. His conclusions were originally published in 1970 as The Davenport Conspiracy. He rewrote the book for a more general audience with the title: *The Davenport Conspiracy Revisited,* published in 1991 by Iowa State University Press.

Fig. 95 Obverse side of the Davenport Stone Tablet 1.

McKusick discovered enough documentation to come to the conclusion that the three stones and the pipes were indeed made in the Academy basement. He also concluded that the expulsion of the members was done in the heat of emotion without due regard to the facts. The final explanation was that a few academy members salted the mounds with the artifacts so that Reverend Gass would discover them and make claims about them and then become very embarrassed when they would be shown to be fakes.

In 1976, Dr. Barry Fell, author of several books including *Saga America* and *America B.C.,* took the stance that the stones were authentic. Even though The Smithsonian and Harvard institutions had declared the group fakes, Fell was determined to get to the bottom of the controversy. Under the drawing of the Davenport Tablet, Fell penned the following:

> The Davenport Calendar stele, found in a burial mound in Iowa in 1874 by the Reverend M. Gass, together with numerous other artifacts of North African and Iberian origin or relationship. This inscription is written in three languages, Egyptian hieroglyphs at the top, then Iberian-Punic from right to left along the upper arc, and

Libyan from right to left along the lower arc. The Libyan and Iberian-Punic inscriptions say the same thing, namely that the upper hieroglyphs contain the secret of how to regulate the calendar. The hieroglyphs give this information by indicating that a ray of light falls upon a stone called the "Watcher" at the moment of sunrise on New Year's Day, which is defined as the spring equinox in March, when the sun passes the first point of Aries. This stele, for long condemned as a meaningless forgery, is in fact one of the most important steles every discovered, for it is the only one on which occurs a trilingual text in the Egyptian, Iberian-Punic, and Libyan languages. It is in the Putnam Museum, Davenport, Iowa, the repository of other priceless national treasures found by Gass.

Fig. 96 Davenport Stone Tablet 2

Other artifacts that came without provenance, as stated earlier, are the Manti Tablets and artifacts. Shown below are a selected few that will give the reader an idea as to the content of the collection. And as noted earlier the language found on these tablets as well as most of Burrows and the Michigan artifacts are not found anywhere else in the world.

Fig. 97 Note the scorpion.   Fig. 98 strange designs.

Fig. 99 Brewer's cave artifact with sea serpent similar to a Petroglyph of an aquatic cryptid known as the Sea Grizzly found in Alaska.[17]

Fig. 100 A strange medallion.   Fig. 101 An elaborate design

Fig.102 Could these pieces represent a form of currency?

Fig.103 Amulet.   Fig.104 Other artifacts

Besides script and geometric designs, many artifacts from caves and graves are accompanied by other kinds of artifacts such as the ones shown below. The usages of these particular pieces are subject to debate. However, they do show signs of age, the lead being heavily oxidized and of an inferior material; possibly from a native deposit. This may be the only thing that keeps investigators actively seeking more evidence of their authenticity.

Many question the authenticity of the copper artifacts discovered throughout America as being made by non-literate Indians, since in their biased view the creators had no knowledge of metallurgy or the science needed to be so creative. One only has to look north to Michigan and Royal Island for an astounding wealth of artifacts.

THE PADILLA PLATES

Another great discovery that lacks provenance is known as the Padilla Plates. The discoverer was Dr. Jesus Padilla Orozco and companions who reportedly found a tomb in Mexico sometime between 1952 and 1956. During the excavation of the tomb, Padilla discovered many artifacts made of gold including twelve plates with writing on them. This discovery was dubbed a fake almost as soon as it was made public. Five of the twelve tablets or plates were given to Jose Davila.

In January 1971, Dr. Padilla was contacted by Brigham Young University Prof. Dr. Paul Cheesman, who asked to view the tablets. Padilla proudly displayed some of the plates and other artifacts including jade beads, short tube-like objects, jewelry of all kinds and designs, and a larger gold piece with the likeness of an elephant on it. Other artifacts of less importance were lip ornaments, pottery, arrow and spear points, and funerary objects. It was thought this discovery was of the Post Classic Period A.D. 900-1200. As far as Cheesman was concerned, it supported Padilla's claim that the artifacts taken from a tomb in Mexico were indeed authentic.

Dr. Ray T. Matheny studied the Padilla Plates as well and wrote a report titled "An Analysis of the Padilla Gold Plates." After noting the size and layout of them he noted that they were done with "…*remarkable accuracy of layout and precision*". He went on to say that the plates …"*are bright gold in color, but the smaller ones in Davila's possession show a slight copperish hue when turned to different angles in the light.*" Another point of concern was that the five plates examined …"*has a hinge attached on one edge so that the plates fit together like a bracelet when strung by wire or thread.*" Matheny questioned the authenticity again when he noted: "*The question of how these gold plates were scribed out and cut is an important one to explore because it will also tell us something about the tools available to the maker. I know of nothing made in antiquity, either in the Old or New Worlds that approaches the rectangularity achieved by the maker of the Padilla Plates.*"

The tests conducted by Matheny and others suggested that by using their sophisticated measurements they were dealing with gold sheet that had been manufactured by the most precise means known, stating "*The plates were cut of a gold sheet stock that gives every indication of having been manufactured on a metal roller press and not by any known hand method. (The sheet metal roller press was invented by Leonardo da Vinci in the six-*

teenth century and was not generally used in Europe until the nineteenth century.)"

The metallurgical tests conducted on the plates indicated that the gold is considerably more pure than the gold of most New World artifacts; for example, even gold foil found in the Andes and thought to be pure gold was subjected to atomic absorption testing method, and showed the samples to be about 47% gold, 29% silver, 23% copper, with small amounts of zinc and iron. Script and engraving analysis suggested it was most likely engraved using a magnifying glass; further analysis concluded that the hinges were attached to the plates by a soft solder. According to studies of pre-Columbian America, no use of solder has ever been found on copper or gold artifacts. In conclusion Matheny wrote: *"It is my opinion that the Padilla Plates are not authentic because of any one of the major technological anachronisms given above. But given all of the factors considered, the case against the authenticity of the Padilla Plates should be closed once and for all."*

Fig. 105 Padilla gold plates and ornamental piece.

Unfortunately, the whereabouts of the alleged tomb was not given and only a few of Padilla's close friends claimed they knew of its location.

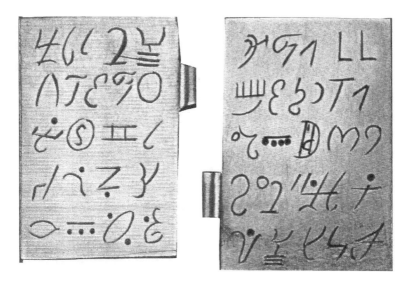

Fig. 106 Obverse side.   Fig. 107 Reverse side.

Fig. 108 Obverse side.   Fig. 109 Reverse side.

All of the tablets were inscribed on both sides. It seems to this author that even though there is evidence to prove this as a fraudulent discovery, it raises the question of knowledge of a strange and perhaps lost art. There have been many such discoveries throughout time that cannot be explained, yet we are quick to discount anything that does not meet our political, scientific. social, religious and personal agendas.

THE DAVILA TRANSLATION

Such was the case with Jose Davila. He was a convert to The Church of Jesus Christ of Latter-day Saints and he would do almost anything to prove the authenticity of the Book of Mormon. This was not a bad idea, but the way he went about it was very unorthodox. As it was with his dealings in Fillmore, Utah and the alleged Moroni Site, his enthusiasm would get the best of him.

Even after an artifact has been dismissed as fake there are still many who will go to extreme lengths to prove otherwise. By using the *character guide*, Jose Davila attempted to "translate" the plates. I am not belittling the LDS faith or those who are faithful members, but simply showing how overzealous people can take anything of antiquity and turn it into whatever they like. Giving him the benefit of doubt, I decided to give the reader Davila's full translation of the Padilla plates. The translation can be found in Appendix B of this volume.

It is very interesting as to how Davila came to such conclusions from these few tablets and figures. Once this so-called translation came to be published, it furthered the idea that the tablets were absolutely

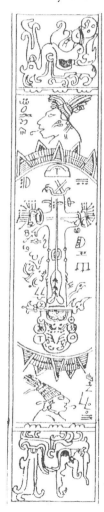

Fig. 110 Character Guide

faked! However, some will not just pass them off as fakes but will continue to study and learn from them. It is not a dead case such as some have indicated.

After the report by Paul Cheesman, Ray Matheny and Bruce Louthan was published in January of 1973, Mr. J. Golden Barton of Bountiful, Utah, read the report and then wrote a rebuttal to Cheesman, et. al. In an unpublished manuscript, Barton, as a student of the Book of Mormon, writer, and researcher of truth, defends the authenticity of the Padilla Tablets. In his 22-page paper he set out to prove the tablets were from a sacred source and should be thought of as such. At the end of his paper Barton concluded that:

> The writer has made an honest attempt to evaluate the paper in the light of his own research. He would ask the reader to forgive his own bias which surely must show thru [sic]. Nevertheless, he leaves his conclusion in the status quo. Too much remains to be done. Perhaps further information will eliminate his own bias.
>
> He does not believe the paper has accomplished the stated purpose [that] "the obligations as scholars to seek the unvarnished truth." Many of the scholarly contributions would bring into view serious conflicts with the Joseph Smith account of the original Gold Plates. This is particularly true of the Limited Tehuantepec Theory, which the writer strongly supports.
>
> The writer has clearly shown the authors have not thoroughly investigated the facts nor interviewed all the people involved in the story. Their reliance on third party reports is unacceptable. There is left to the imagination too many unanswered questions. There is an abundance of obvious bias underlining the entire report. The writer has demonstrated that the reader can easily draw opposite conclusions on many important points, than those represented by the paper.
>
> The report is untimely. Too much remains to be concluded on almost every detail of this subject. The writer would suggest the paper should be withheld, recalled and re-written based on further study, investigation and evaluation.

THE DODGE CANYON TABLETS

The story surrounding the Dodge Canyon Tablets is a most interesting one. This story began with a phone call from a young man by the name of Dave Hall living in Manti, Utah. Mr. Hall was quite pleased when we arrived at his home in Manti. He took us to the back of his home to inspect the pit and the site of the strange rectangular slabs of stone. I was surprised by the size of the slabs and equally surprised by the size and depth of the hole that he described as an old cesspool. He showed my colleague and me why he thought the pit was an ancient burial tomb of some type. I couldn't deny that he was wrong because of its strange construction. The pit was circular, approximately eight feet across and about twelve feet deep. The entire structure was built with very evenly placed round river rock about the size of a child's head. In one side of the pit a hole was seen; it was explained to me that the old sewer from the old home fed into it. The city had required him to now tie-in to the city sewer system which was the reason for this discovery. The next thing Mr. Hall showed us were the strange markings he discovered while turning over one of the large slabs. At first I thought perhaps the markings were caused by the teeth on his backhoe, but upon further examination I concluded that the dotted line marks were too small to have been made by the backhoe; furthermore, it was picked up with a sling rather than with the bucket of the backhoe. I asked Mr. Hall how the slab was situated above the pit. He then demonstrated exactly how the stone was positioned. This gave us the idea that the markings on the stone may perhaps be a *pointer* to a site off to the west.

Fig. 111 The Dodge Canyon Tablets

Fig. 112 Chisel marks in slab

Fig. 113 Slab that covered the pit with highlighted markings

By focusing on the direction I thought the carved stone was pointing, I made plans to venture west, but first took a bearing with my military lensatic compass to establish a course of travel from the slab to a point west across Sanpete Valley.

Weeks later, my older brother Marty and I decided to make the trek across the valley to a point I had ascertained by the use of the compass that might be the area indicated by the marks on the slab. In this area was a rocked up tunnel entrance that I had investigated years before. I had always assumed it was much older than the time of the Mormon entry into the valley. It bears a strong resemblance to a Roman style archway. [18]

Fig. 114 Roman style Arch with Key Stone

Above this archway and up the canyon my brother discovered what appeared to be a rock foundation jutting out from the hillside but hidden from view by brush. He called my attention to the site; I was convinced that it was part of a building or rock wall of sorts, and may have been connected to the tunnel farther around the hillside. I made plans to return with equipment to find out if any metallic objects were near the rock foundation or near the archway.

In August 1998, I drove back down to Dodge Canyon which lies about 7.5 miles west of Manti. I was there for the sole purpose of investigating the rock wall my brother had discovered. As soon as I appeared on the scene I was greeted with dozens of red location flags stuck in the ground in no particular order. After some investigation of the site I determined that BYU archaeologists had been there. I noticed blue flags as well, and those were very close to my rocked up foundation. I soon located the site and began scanning with a metal detector owned by a colleague of mine, Mr. Brad Etachel, who with his father Wes, accompanied me that day. Brad worked for the LDS Church in the mapping department and was responsible for making any new boundary changes that affect wards, stakes, and missions throughout the world.

Fig. 115 Rock Foundation at Dodge Canyon

Brad and I took turns with the metal detector and as we neared the rocked up foundation we got a very sharp "beep." Working the instrument back and forth along the bottom of the foundation we lost the sound but in the center of the foundation we got a beep. I took the metal detector and panned it across the face of the foundation; the machine emitted a steady beep-beep indicating the presence of metal somewhere beneath one particular cornerstone. Once we got the stone removed, I noticed a cavity or hollow depression off to one side. I got down on my knees and gingerly stuck my hand into the hole, hoping and praying all the while that there was no rattlesnake curled up inside.

As I probed deeper into the dirt I felt two hard objects, so I took hold of them and pulled them out of the hole. To our surprise, there in my hand were two small metal plates. Once I cleaned the surface dirt off, we could see what we believed to be ancient hieroglyphics inscribed on their surfaces. I was astonished by the similarity that these characters bore to those on the Brewer Plates. Gathering material from the hole and taking many photographs we left the area, but first I returned the corner stone back to where it was and cleaned up the site.

Once back home I contacted Mr. Cary Krog and Mr. Ken Slater. Krog was educated by the "Sons of Moses" in the Jewish Quarter at Jerusalem; Slater was an educator at the Utah Valley Community College (UVCC), now the Utah Valley University (UVU) at Orem, Utah.

Besides these two professionals, I had several geologists and an epigraphic specialist examine the plates, without disclosing the location or how they were obtained, as I did not want to influence their position regarding the plates. A spectrographic analysis showed the plates to be primarily composed of galena alloy, a lead/silver mix in combination with a few other trace elements. Our inscription authority was a past president of the Utah State Epigraphic Society. He brought along some documents from his own archives that showed a variation of ancient language characters from Celtic, Iberic, Phœnician and old Libyan to use as reference and comparison materials. He believed that though he never got any kind of interpretation from this as to the plates' messages, he felt that these other languages could have been influenced by the ancient Jaredites through possible contact in some way. [19]

Tablet A   Tablet B

Fig. 116 Artist's Sketch of Both Tablets and Inscriptions

I have included this personal experience because even though the discovery is not without provenance, it was still deemed fraudulent by mainstream academics and not even a good "fake," and if they were "real," they would be considered ooparts, or out of place artifacts and most likely "planted." It seems strange for the artifacts to be summarily dismissed as fraudulent, despite having been led to the site by a potential "map rock" and subsequently discovered in a rock foundation that had never been excavated before!

PARIETTE DRAW TABLETS

Another set of lead type tablets came out of Eastern Utah. The circumstances surrounding this discovery began first with the discovery of a petroglyphic panel in Pariette Draw just west of the Green River and southeast of present day Myton, Utah.

A member of the Ute Indian Tribe took me out beyond this site to where a small earthen mound was located. He claimed that the symbols carved on the rock face were an actual guide to this mound; the trail led right up to it as shown as the two vertical lines beneath the half moon fighter to the right of my head.

Fig 117 Inscription in Pariette Draw

My friend (who shall remain anonymous) began digging into the mound at the point where the sloping "trail" seemed to disappear into the side of the mound. Suddenly his shovel hit a flat upright stone slab of rock. It was then I began removing dirt very carefully until we had exposed what appeared to be a four-sided rock vessel with a slab of sandstone covering the top. All sides and top were free from each other; no cement or any material joining them was used. They were simply laid up together to form a protective cover for the vessel.

My friend took the top cover off and peered in the vessel and then reaching in, withdrew four small lead tablets. He was afraid! He was sure that he had opened a sacred tomb of sorts and wanted to destroy the tablets. I told him that we shouldn't destroy them. Rather, we should cover the box and leave it as was, but retain the lead tablets. He then wiped them off with his tee-shirt and handed them to me.

We had compromised the site, and since it was on private property (we later found out), it was decided that we should not tell the land owner that we had made the discovery. My friend was concerned about the consequences that would follow should this discovery be revealed at this time.

Knowing that we had taken these tablets out of context and without provenance, the chances of them being found authentic would be close to zero!

Fig. 118 Tablet A   Fig. 119 Tablet B

Fig. 120 Tablet C Obverse side   Fig. 121 Tablet C Reverse side

I was surprised to say the least when I saw the cuneiform script on three of the four tablets and further intrigued by the strange characters on the tablets shown above. This particular tablet was rolled up into a scroll and had to be warmed up before we could unroll it because we feared it would break or crumble.

This "underlined" tablet seemed to be of some importance to its creator; almost like an "Introduction" or "Table of Contents," but whatever it was intended to be, we most likely will never know and that is simply because this particular cuneiform script is unknown. I enlisted professionals in ancient scripts and was told the find was fraudulent and not even worth their time and effort to continue examining the tablets.

Later, when I first began researching the Michigan Tablets, I discovered that Tablet "C" had some of the same style script on it as those tablets. This revelation made me all the more determined to get to the bottom of it.

Fig 122 Tablet D Underlined Script

THE THRUSTON TABLET OF TENNESSEE

In a book titled *Picture-Writing of the American Indians* by Garrick Mallery, 1894, he gives an account by Gen. G. P. Thruston concerning this discovery:

> There has been discovered in Sumner County, Tennessee, near the stone graves and mounds of Castalian Springs, a valuable pictograph, the ancient engraved stone which we have taken the liberty to entitle a group of Tennessee Mound Builders.
>
> This engraved stone, the property of the Tennessee Historical Society, is a flat irregular slab of hard limestone, about 19 inches long and 15 inches wide. It bears every evidence of very great age. The stone was found on Rocky Creek, in Sumner County, and was presented with other relics, to the Tennessee Historical Society about twelve years ago.

It is evidently an ideograph of significance, graven with a steady and skillful hand, for a specific purpose, and probably records or commemorates some important treaty or public or tribal event. Indian chiefs fully equipped with the insignia of office, are arrayed in fine apparel. Two leading characters are vigorously shaking hands in a confirmatory way. The banner or shield, ornamented with the double serpent emblem and other symbols, is, doubtless, an important feature of the occasion.

Among the historic Indians, no treaty was made without the presence or presentation of the belt of wampum. This, the well-dressed female of the group appears to grasp in her hand, perhaps as a pledge of the contract. The dressing of the hair, the remarkable scalloped skirts, the implements used, the waistbands, the wristlets, the garters, the Indian leggings and moccasins, the necklace and breast-plates, the two banners, the serpent emblem, the tattoo stripes, the ancient pipe, all invest this pictograph with unusual interest.

The double serpent emblem or ornament upon the banner may have been the badge or totem of the tribe, clan, or family that occupied the extensive earthworks at Castalian Springs in Sumner County, near where the stone was found. The serpent was a favorite emblem or totem of the Stone Grave race of Tennessee, and is one of the common devices engraved on the shell gorgets taken from the ancient cemeteries. The circles or sun symbol ornaments on the banners and dresses are the figures most frequently graven on the shell gorgets found near Nashville.

Fig 123
The Thruston
Tablet

Like so many other artifacts, the Thruston Tablet immediately came under fire as a "fake" because there was no record of its removal and because it "appeared to be faked." However, in the *American Anthropologist*, 1891, W. H. Holmes commented on the stone thusly:

The slab upon which this remarkable example of aboriginal delineation is engraved is of gray fossiliferous limestone of silurian age, derived, no doubt, from the formations of the locality in which it was found. According to Gen. Gates P. Thruston, by whom it was first described in his work on the *Antiquities of Tennessee*, this stone was found on or near the surface of the ground on Rocky Creek, in Sumner County, and was presented, with other relics, to the Tennessee Historical Society about the year 1878. It is 19 inches long, 15 [inches] wide, and about one inch thick, although varying in considerable in the latter dimension on account of the unevenly weathered surfaces. The shape is unsymmetrical and the outlines uneven, portions having been broken away in recent times. Both sides have been well covered with engravings, but the reverse side has been subjected to more active weathering and retains but imperfect traces of the devices.

The figures were engraved, for the most part, with sharp points, which were handled with considerable freedom, yet not with great certainty or grace. Certain portions of the design are filled in with rudely scratched lines, while others, such as the ornaments and parts of the costume, have been rubbed down with a blunt point and still retain a considerable degree of polish. In a few cases parts of the costume were painted red, the color being now barely traceable. The engraving appears to have been done at somewhat distinct periods, as indicated by differences in the degree of weathering of lines within the same space. The more recently executed figures have been drawn over the earlier, resulting in places in great confusion.

Fig. 124 The Thruston Tablet sketched

The delineations consist principally of human figures placed in a variety of attitudes and comprise three or four groups, more or less independent of each other. As a matter of record the pictures should be described separately and in considerable detail. General Thruston has contented himself with brief references to the leading figures.

The principal group consists of four full-length standing figures, which extend along the greater length of the tablet. They are about six inches in height and are arranged in pairs at a convenient distance for shaking hands or cracking heads. A question may fairly be raised as to the significance of the attitudes depicted. General Thruston infers that a friendly salutation is intended; but it may also be suggested that the encounter is warlike in nature, or that a mock contest, such as are introduced into dances, is represented. The first personage on the left extends the left hand so that it touches or passes behind the shield held by the second individual, while the right hand brandishes what may represent a rattle, but which strongly suggests a war-club or hatchet.

The second figure faces the first and holds a spear in the right hand, while with the left he supports a large square shield, bordered with scroll devices and crossed obliquely by a serrate band. The right arm and shoulders are seen above the shield, and the legs from the knees down appear below it. The third and fourth members of the group face each other in close juxtaposition. That on the left holds what may be likened to a bundle of strands, a belt of wampum, a sling, or similar article. The left arm has been drawn twice, giving a confused result. One hand seems raised to meet the right hand of the opposing figure, while the other touches that figure at the belt. The right arm of the second figure of this pair has also been drawn in two positions. One hand rests upon the shoulder of the opposing personage, while the other grasps his hand. The left arm of the fourth figure is obscure; some lines appear to make it cross the body to meet the lower left hand of the opposing figure, and others seem to carry it behind the body, where it is probably intended to grasp an object, a weapon or rattle, very obscurely seen in the drawing.

The very extensive analysis of the Thruston Stone by Holmes continues:

General Thruston believes that the third figure probably represents a female, as the hair is dressed differently from the others and there is an absence of tattooing and of plumes or elaborate head-gear. In physical characters and dress there is a close resemblance in all the figures. The costumes are notable, not only as records of the habits of the aborigines of the period, but as illustrations of the graphic acquirements and skills of the sylvan artist.

The head-dresses are in most cases rather elaborate, combining the knotted hair, the plumes and the lofty crests of ordinary aboriginal forms. The skirt or shirt fastened at the waist with a wide girdle, is worn in most cases. The skirts are plain, scalloped, or fringed, and are decorated over the surface with circles or scroll-work. The wrists, knees, and ankles are encircled by lines representing ornaments or fastenings, and a necklace in each case supports a more or less elaborate gorget. Moccasins are worn in all cases. The skirt and moccasins of the third figure were painted red and still retain portions of the color. The tattoo-marks upon the faces are of the same general type in all cases, and consist of a group of parallel lines running from the nose downward across the cheek to the back of the neck. The third figure is without these marks. The shield held by the second figure is large and square and is bordered by a band of scroll-work. A serrate band extends obliquely across the shield, giving it the appearance of a totemic banner. As to the significance of the various devices upon the costumes and weapons, it is perhaps useless to speculate. Scrolls are associated with three of the figures and groups of concentric circles with the other three.

Above the principal group of figures and partly behind or across the head of the second personage are some small, rather indefinite devices, arranged in horizontal rows and apparently separated by strong horizontal lines, which, however, from the degree of weathering, seem to be newer than the associated devices. The arrangement of the obscure figures suggests an alphabetic record or rows of pictographic devices. A close examination makes apparent a strong resemblance to human heads. Each roundish figure has a suggestion of plumes, and in two cases the face, eye, neck, and upper part of the body may be made out. To the right of these devices and over the head of the third figure of the main group is a conventional delineation of the sun, which may pertain to the landscape setting of the principal group, or which may be a totemic device belonging to one of the personages, or which again may be independent of the other parts of this engraving.

Below the main line of figures are two groups of particular interest. That beneath the second figure of the line and occupying the lower angle of the slab is very much confused, there being traces of at least five figures occupying parts of the space in common. The principal personage, however, can be clearly made out. He is seated within a square frame-work or enclosure and is smoking a long-stemmed pipe of the form quite common in Tennessee. The drawing of this figure is interesting on account of its resemblance to ancient Mexican work in its conception and treatment. The figure drawn in profile sits upon what may be a mat, which, as in Mexican work, stands upon edge, the figure resting upon the upper margin. The enclosing rectangle resembles the shield held by the standing warrior above, but it possibly represents the house or chamber in which the smoker sits, after the Mexican manner of delineation. The American tribes had no conception of perspective.

To the right of the sitting figure is a full-length figure, placed at such an angle in relation to the others as to be nearly prostrate. This personage grasps an object of problematic nature—a weapon, perhaps—which is held after the manner of a gun and from the outer end of which appears to issue smoke. The end of this object next (to) the shoulder does not turn down as does the stock of a gun, but bends upward in front of the face and terminates in a heavy barbed point like that of a spear. Pendant from the horizontal shaft are two rectangular tassel-like figures, more appropriate to a pipe than to a gun. In costume the figure agrees pretty closely with the first and fourth figures of the main group above, but the head-dress is of a distinct type.

The space near the acute angle of the slab and to the right of the main line of figures is nearly covered with confused and partly obliterated figures and parts of figures. The most recent of these is a leg on a scale twice that of the other designs and drawn in an inverted position. Less distinct are portions of heads and figures with obscure indications of regalia, weapons, or ceremonial objects.

On the reverse side of the slab are traces of similar figures. On the left hand is a warrior holding a bow and arrow in the extended left hand, the right hand resting against the body. In front of him is a personage seated within a square enclosure bordered with scrolls; he holds a weapon, rattle, or wand in the left hand.

Whether the principal groups of figures of the obverse belong together or are separate conceptions cannot be determined, and the significance, if there is any significance, of all or of any one must remain obscure. The action in contest or in mock contest, dance, or other ceremony would be the same. The differences in costume and markings are pronounced, but not so pronounced that all may not have pertained to one tribe. Some of the devices may be clan or personal totems.

These delineations correspond somewhat closely to the best work on shell and copper, but are inferior to many in conception and execution. The age is not great. The newer drawing retains a freshness of line and a polish of surface that could not endure through many centuries, whether embedded in the soil or exposed upon the surface.

This specimen forms an important addition to the interesting family of engraved tablets. Its authenticity has not been questioned and most careful scrutiny does not develop any trace of the white man's touch or thought. The introduction of a gun, if susceptible of verification, would confirm the impression given by the fresh appearance of the engraving that the work is not of very great antiquity.

A great deal of information regarding the Thruston Tablet can be found in a paper entitled "*The Thruston Tablet, Deciphering the Iconography of an Ancient Twins Cycle.*" Although the author is unknown, the work is interesting and exhaustive. Since the Thruston Tablet somehow went missing from the Tennessee Historical Museum there is no way to test it or really scrutinize it with all of our modern scientific equipment. Until it resurfaces we'll just have to guess as to its authenticity.

THE ANCIENT TABLET OF COTTONWOOD CANYON

Dozens of artifacts have been unearthed without provenances. I have shown a few, but one additional story needs to be shared. Although it can be found online, not many people know what to look for or how to find it.

The artifacts in question have mysteriously disappeared and it seems no one knows who has them or where they went. We do know that State Archaeologists were called to the site to excavate further and the story was published in a Salt Lake City, Utah, newspaper. As far as we know, there were only drawings or sketches of the discoveries. If there are photos, they have disappeared as well.

This discovery was dubbed "The Indian Copper Mine Workings" by those involved, and brought instant attention to the canyon. The frame of mind in those early days had little to do with reality or what was true—it was much more politically motivated, saving face and saturated with religious undertones. Oh, wait! That sounds like today.

All kidding aside, the discovery of a cave in Cottonwood Canyon, Utah, was extensively described in a Salt Lake City newspaper *The Telegram,* with many people weighing in on the items discovered there. On November 8, 1911, the heading on the newspaper read: "Mysterious Tablet is Uncovered in Cottonwood. Archaeologists Explore Workings of Ancients."

The story tells of two miners, who while driving a drift in one of the canyons of Upper Cottonwood, broke into a small cave and upon closer examination found it to be not only a cave but a passageway. After several days of cleaning and removing debris, a complex series of subterranean passages and chambers were exposed. From the number and length of the old workings they figured they must have been mined *". . . upon an extensive scale and throughout a considerable period of time. It would take some time to thoroughly explore the labyrinthic passages to find out if they would disclose archaeological data of any great value."*

It was first thought that they had uncovered one of Utah's legendary Lost Spanish Mines such as the Lost Josephine or the Lost Rhoades Mines. However, after more explorations those thoughts soon diminished. Instead, a large number of Indian artifacts such as flints, arrow points, tools, hammered iron, and more importantly a remarkable collection of decorated potteries were discovered.

Fig. 125 Ceramic A   Fig. 126 Ceramic B

Fig. 127 Ceramic C   Fig. 128 Ceramic D

218

The newspaper account continues:

The walls of many of the tunnels and chambers are decorated with sculptured reliefs and hieroglyphic inscriptions, but by far the most interesting relic found so far is a smooth discolored marble tablet which stood at the entrance of one of the larger chambers. It is completely covered with remarkable sculptured reliefs and hieroglyphic inscriptions.

Fig. 129   Marble Tablet Found in Mine Entrance

This discovery of the marble tablet was considered one of the most important archaeological discoveries of recent years. The article went on to explain:

The discovery is all the more remarkable in that heretofore no hieroglyphic inscriptions have ever been found north of Mexico. Everything points to the great antiquity of these workings and their contents. The inscriptions are uncolored and appear to have been incised and picked into the receiving the stone by quartz and flint implements, some of which have been preserved. A noteworthy feature of the marble tablet is the combination of pictographs and alphabetic writing. As pictographs are generally conceded to have preceded and to have originated the graphic systems, this tablet would appear to date from a period of transition from the pictographic to the hieroglyphic art. As noted above, none of the records

*ever found north of Mexico have contained hieroglyphics. This tablet,
therefore, may chronicle an amalgamation of inscriptive expression between North America and Mexican tribes; or it may record the progress
of civilization of an American tribe, probably the Utes. Although it is
possible that other tribes may have come from great distances to obtain the
highly prized red metal.*

Here's a little background regarding this particular site of such significant and remarkable ancient artifact discoveries. The area between
Big and Little Cottonwood Canyons is an extensive wilderness of rocky,
steep mountains, deep valleys, lakes and streams and populated with
fish, deer, elk, moose, mountain lions, bears and wolves.

The beginnings of commercial mining in Utah are traced to Colonel
Patrick E. Connor and his California and Nevada Volunteers who arrived in the Salt Lake Valley in October of 1862. Many of these soldiers
were experienced prospectors and, with Connor's blessing and prompt-
ing, they searched the nearby Wasatch and Oquirrh mountains for gold
and silver. In 1863, the first formal claims were located in the Bingham
Canyon area, and this spurred further exploration.

Discoveries soon followed in Tooele County and in Little Cottonwood Canyon (1864). With the development of the transcontinental
railroad in 1869, came the transportation network necessary to elevate
Utah's mining efforts from small-scale activity to larger commercial en-
terprises. Other early mining areas included the Big Cottonwood, Park
City, and Tintic districts, along with the West Mountain District, which
encompassed the entire Oquirrh mountain range. Mining activity in
these regions grew through the 1850s, but, as surface deposits dwindled,
the need to mine for mineral sources at depths far beneath the surface
necessitated larger amounts of capital, and individual efforts generally
gave way to corporate interests. Between 1871 and 1873 the British
invested heavily in Utah mining ventures, the most noted being the
Emma Mine in Little Cottonwood Canyon, which was rocked with
scandal involving unscrupulous mining promotion.

It was while hunting new copper deposits that the miners discovered
these ancient caves and passageways. The narrative continues:

*An interesting mineralogical feature to be noted is that throughout
these ancient workings, which are at no great distance below the surface,
native copper abounds, in some places being scattered through the vein
rock in small fragments, in others occurring as chunks of metallic copper,*

weighing from a pound or two up to eighty or one hundred pounds. Or-
dinarily, such a discovery of copper would create considerable excitement,
but the wall writings and relics are of such absorbing interest that the cop-
per has been, for a time, relegated to the back-ground. It is puzzling how
these Indians, with their primitive tools, were able to break up and extract
the exceedingly tough chunks of copper. A number of copper implements
and ornaments, hammered and incised, have been gathered, as well as
diggers, scrapers, hoes, arrow heads and pounding stones.

Various receptacles for food and drink, as well as for earth and ore,
were uncovered, they being all made of pottery and decorated with geo-
metric figures, or with picturegraphs or hieroglyphics. (Figures 126 - 129)
This pottery is now being carefully studied as it is ornamented with sym-
bols and characters which may aid in the deciphering of the stone records.
The light gray or black coloring of all the pottery as well as its crude form
would tend to indicate its very early origin. In fact, everything connected
with the find evidences great antiquity, and the mine apparently was
worked at least many centuries before the appearance of the Spaniards in
this region. So far, no key to the decipherment is known, but the various
inscriptions are being carefully scrutinized and compared, in the hopes
that one may be detected. In this search, collaboration is invited, and
should this picture reach the eye of anyone familiar with Indian symbols
and records, the investigators would be pleased to have their opinions and
suggestions regarding its translation.

It has long been known that Utah is a veritable treasure house
of archaeological records, *but it is claimed by scientists who have exam-*
ined this stone [Figure 130] *that it is the most important archaeological*
find ever chronicled in Utah's history! Owing to the intense interest man-
ifested in these discoveries it was thought best to keep their location secret,
at least until such time as they could be thoroughly explored and proper
precautions taken to adequately protect them.

In regards to the ceramics discovered in the old mine workings,
many scholars attempted to translate them with what knowledge they
claimed to have on the subject. In another article in *The Telegram* these
men opened up to the press what they knew.

A Professor V. Reyas was invited to the site from out of state. He was
a noted archaeologist and was asked to join in the discussion concerning

the inscribed artifacts to determine the meanings of the characters on them. He was taken to the site where the artifacts were kept, and we learn from his disparaging remarks that prejudice, bias and bigotry were alive and well even then:

A discussion immediately arose amongst a number of archaeological friends, as to the meaning of the pictographs and hieroglyphics, and I was amazed to find that some of your (speaking to the editor of the Telegram) learned professors seemed anxious to read into the simple story told by three crude pictures, some extraordinary mystical stories that might do credit to some of our present day writers of fiction. They seem to forget that the aboriginal did not possess the brain capacity of the ten-year-old children of today. Their thoughts were simple and expressed in such a way that even our children can readily understand them. *Any normal person, spending a few minutes studying these simple pictures, can easily piece together the interesting story.*

How absurd! Storytelling was a precise art form because of the nature of Indian languages. Some tribal languages had as many as twenty words or signs to describe snow, rain, wind, water, etc. They used these ideograms to describe various states of human emotion, the intensity of human physical efforts and the serenity of the lands they lived on.

We read further what our pompous and simplistic Professor Reyas had to say:

In translating these old pictographs and hieroglyphics, always remember the first impression that each picture produces in the mind, and never try to make them difficult, always keeping in mind that the simple thought that first inspired the picture did not originate in the brain of a Harvard student.

Further, our learned professor decided he would translate the ceramics so his audience could see that he was superior to the minds of them who sent for him. Said he:

Here we find a squaw left alone at home and night approaching, *as evidences the moon and stars.* Next morning, sun arising and still no husband. Terror seizes the unhappy woman, as evidences the tears and up-lifted hands. Determination to seek the lost one. On the way, accident, fall over a rock. Discovery of murdered loved one, over which his companion is weeping. Burial in rock hewn tomb. Weeping widow. Empty home.

Just a simple every-day story in the life or our dear old ancestors. I understand no human remains have been discovered which may point to the fact that after a short sojourn here, this wandering tribe moved on and possibly we shall soon hear of discoveries of a similar nature. Perhaps thousands of miles away.

During this same period of time the editor of *The Telegram* newspaper received this communiqué from an unnamed person who wrote in part:

The remarkable discoveries recently made in our mountains will probably awaken a tremendous public interest in these interesting archaeological studies. Your interesting description of these relics of the past awaken pleasant memories of that part of my life spent in Berlin. With several friends we took up the study of the progress of the human race, as depicted in stone and metal, and found ample material housed in that noble edifice known as the "New Museum," a branch of the Royal Museum, located in the Unter-den-Linden, which was founded by Frederick William III, in 1824. Here is located one of the world's greatest collection of Egyptian relics.

In studying the pictographs in the recent Cottonwood find I notice a remarkable similarity to some of the stones and metals of ancient Egypt. My memory leads to a large stone in the Royal Museum on which are figures of an ancient priestess, who sacrificed herself evidently to appease the wrathful Great Spirit, which was recognized in the shape of a cat.

The figure in these old Egyptian stones was clothed in the robes of a priestess, which are remarkably like the apparel of the figure on the Cottonwood stone; and again, I find that where the Great Spirit on the Egyptians stone was in the shape of a cat, that the Great Spirit in the Cottonwood stone is in the shape of a tortoise.

The Egyptian stone must be at least 100,000 years old, whereas the Cottonwood stone cannot possibly be more than 10,000 years old.

It can be said that many scholars thought the Indian to be inferior; with a smaller cranial capacity and intelligence than any other race save it were the black race. And, the Indian petroglyphic writing or art was always cast aside as a superstition, precluding Indians from having an acceptable status as human beings, and reducing them in the eyes of most so called "educated people" to be subhuman with a level of pure ignorance.

Fig. 130 Engraved slab of pure copper taken from the old tunnels

The following article was penned by the editor of *The Telegram* in regards to the copper tablet seen above.

These pictographs had as their main purpose the permanent visible recording of thoughts and ideas for which purpose a material object was chosen and depicted in such a way as not to be simply a reproduction of that object, but figurative of some other object or person. In some instances, too, the picture was used to denote a symbol of some quality or characteristic. These basic facts should be borne in mind in an attempt to decipher the accompanying picturegraph.

It is believed that these picturegraphs generally record some event of importance, such as fire, flood, pestilence, famine, a feast, a battle, a hunting festival, a religious ceremony or dance, etc. In the present instance the inscription upon the wall possibly commemorates a hunting trip or a memorable journey of some kind.

Probably the most interesting feature of this pictured rock is an ingot of virgin copper and driven into the rock about the center of the picturegraph, which might indicate that all of the objects pictured centered about this copper filling or possibly that the scene depicted took place upon the

journey to the copper rock, or copper mine, in which this picturegraph was discovered. (Photo not available)

Or, again, it may be a chart starting with the discovery of the copper mine as the basic date, and calendaring the subsequent years by means of important events which distinguished them from commonplace years. [See Ether 10: 21, 23, 27 for additional insights and possible interpretations.]

Various birds and animals are depicted upon this rock, among them being the deer, elk, beaver, bear, weasel, lynx, wolf, wild horse, mountain goat, lizard, crow, tec., and several unknown animals, one of which closely resembles the great dinosaur of prehistoric times. If this is in reality the picture of a dinosaur, it would place the birth of this engraving in remote antiquity. Various stone weapons near the dinosaur are implied to indicate that it required, in addition to the bow and arrow, many ponderous stone weapons to slay the giant dinosaur, and the designation of a river with arrows pointing in opposite directions apparently record that after being wounded, the dinosaur crossed and re-crossed the river before he was finally slain.

What amazes me is the way these "experts" so calmly and deliberately deciphered these stones, copper and ceramic artifacts with no regard for the intelligence of their authors. They had the nerve to blaspheme the sacredness of these ancient items by *assuming* they had all the answers; but certainly far from the reality of the true meanings and representations inscribed thereon. It is a constant reminder of how this act of *knowing* has grown in today's circles of *know it all* societies—specialists, experts, academicians, special interest groups, scholars, universities and others. The ignorance continues unabated today as much as it did a hundred or two hundred years ago.

But amazingly enough, the story continues with "Letters to the Editor" as follows:

Medicine Man Show

Indians with bows and arrows, as well as medicine men, are depicted in their picture, and it should be noted that it is not so deeply engraven in the rock as were the characters of the marble tablet. In fact, many of the pictures are so lightly graven upon the rock that they do not show in the photograph.

One of the Indians pictured might be described as "heap hunger hunter used heap lots bows," the lines on his body indicating pain or hunger.

That the discovery of the hieroglyphics in the copper mine is attracting wide-spread attention is indicated by the numerous letters received by this newspaper.

Editor of The Telegram:

Have read your articles on the Cottonwood copper mine, and the stone writings found in it. I am satisfied that these inscriptions were made by Mexican Indians and that the Mexican Indians were at a very early date quite skilled in the working of copper.

Yours truly, Fred G. Johnson.

Editor of The Telegram:

Having read with interest the report of the finding of the prehistoric tablets in a Cottonwood canyon mine, we would suppose that an explanation from a clam eater from the East is not out of order.

We note that some of the learned men of the day, who have traveled from East to West, have given a deciphered story of the translation of the pictographs and hieroglyphics, but we would suppose that the pictographs and hieroglyphics depicted a common or garden variety of everyday family life, as seen in the year 1916, and such as has happened regularly since the year 1. The male species of this animal, as it appears on the tablet, which we believe is supposed to represent a human being, arises the morning after the night before and is troubled with dark brown tastes in his mouth, owing to the fact that the firewater consumed by him has affected him like the kick of a full grown mule, said firewater being probably known in those days as chain lighting brand—which same brand is utilized by all Indians throughout the world.

The brave evidently has a head on him like a tack, for, as you know, the only feeling that a tack has is manifest when someone hits it on the head and then the sparks fly, and the brave's head has been hit a mighty hard blow by his squaw the said morning after, as, according to the pictographs, he is seeing shooting stars, caused by his squaw refusing to give him bromo-seltzer, or whatever concoction they used for this distemper in those pre-historic days.

Then we notice that the chase is on and that the brave and the charmer are hitting the high spots, and the squaw is disconsolate, but continues searching for the brave, and finally finds his footprints, which look like elephant tracks but are caused by the brave having what is known as a 'still-on'. Said 'still-on' has been handed down to us from prehistoric times, and we meet many of there prehistoric 'still-ons' frequently.

There are many beautiful and pastoral scenes depicted on said tablet, and we noticed particularly the bird floating up-side down—or is it standing on its tail. Then the lone succulent turtles were worldly wise in the prehistorical days, even as they are today, and though this one is rather large appearing on the tablet, we must remember that it was necessary to have large turtles in those days, for their shells were in great demand for the shell game, which humans do fall for daily.

The remainder of the article is cut off, but this much suffices to show the disdain of the author. It is merely signed *Yours, Historically.*

Here we have a case where very important artifacts were discovered that could potentially unlock some greater truth in the historical record of North American cultures. Nevertheless, as the reader can plainly see, these as well as many similar discoveries have been lost, ridiculed, stolen, destroyed or just plain hidden from us.

This is not the end of the story concerning the Old Indian Copper Mine. It seems that soon after the discovery, an accidental blast from a poorly placed dynamite package (or, maybe even intentional placement) brought a mass of debris into the corridors of the old mine, sealing it forever. Was it an accident? Or did someone not want this information going out; perhaps they were anti-Mormons and the last thing they might have wanted was to give an upper hand to further the cause and practice of Mormonism.

The important thing here, regardless of beliefs or customs, is a major discovery was made and the accompanying artifacts are now gone. What we could have learned from those few items alone would most likely fill volumes.

ANCIENT AMERICAN COPPER CULTURE

As we know, copper artifacts have been discovered across the American continent as well as in South America. It was, and is to an extent, believed that the Copper Culture or Bronze Age began in Europe. I've included numerous photos of copper artifacts that have been dated from the mid- 18th century to as far back as 6,000 B.C., and perhaps even beyond.

Large deposits of pure copper are known to exist along the north shore of Lake Superior, Royal Isle, the Keweenaw Peninsula of Michigan, and other deposits in the upper Midwest around Minnesota and Wisconsin. Reports of huge copper deposits were heard of by early explorers to the Great Lakes Region. It was reported that Samuel de Champlain in 1608, received a foot-long specimen of native copper from an Algonquin Indian chief that he in turn sent to King Henry IV of France. Copper was a coveted commodity in those early days because the supplies were limited. The early explorers relied on the Indians to help them in procuring ample supplies of the mineral.

By early 1840, mines were opened up on the Keweenaw Peninsula, and it was then miners began to find traces of earlier mining activity in the area. As the miners penetrated deeper into the earth they began to uncover ancient pits and tunnels that revealed ancient tools and huge nuggets of pure native copper. Tons of grooved and un-grooved copper hammer-stones were discovered along with many finished and unfinished copper artifacts such as awls, knives, spear and arrow points, spuds, and amulets. The cry went, "Who mined these pits of copper?"

Many theories over the course of time have suggested that early travelers from Europe came to collect the copper for themselves—Berbers, Phoenicians or even Egyptians. Carbon-14 testing of the organic materials found within the old copper pits and with artifacts removed from them, has established the shaky date of around 6,000 years ago.

There has always existed a disagreement among archaeologists as to the time period ascribed to the Old Copper Culture. Dates are all over the place from 7,000 years to 2,500 years and those arguments stem from Carbon-14 dating. I doubt very sincerely if all artifacts discovered in any given area will produce the same timeline! Because of the variations in available carbon in the atmosphere over time, Carbon-14 dating only get us "close" to a given timeline, sometimes varying many centuries in its reliability.

Many scholars would discount early Indians working copper pits or mines. They would claim that would be impossible since they didn't have the knowledge to be miners at this magnitude. If there was not an extensive ancient mining technology, then how did so many copper artifacts find their way into thousands of mounds, let alone spanning the country and the world?

These pits and mines were opened up and dug by hand by a people with a wonderful knowledge of mining and metallurgy. They dug pits as deep as 30 feet and then timbers were set under huge copper nuggets that weighed many tons. They fashioned copper hammers by hardening them using a now lost art to cut or knock off other chunks of copper to be worked into weapons, ornaments and items of utilitarian usage. Who indeed were these people? Perhaps a clue can be found in the Book of Ether:

> And they did work in all manner of ore, and they did make gold, and silver, and iron, and brass, and all manner of metals, and they did dig it out of the earth; wherefore they did cast up mighty heaps of earth to get ore, of gold, and of silver, and of iron, and of copper. And they did work all manner of fine work.

Wayne May wrote in his magazine *THIS LAND: Zarahemla and the Nephite Nation:*

> One scholar writes this to us, "Most of the Mound Builders were too primitive (they didn't build a temple like Solomon's), and their period of greatest expansion and growth was several hundred years after the Book of Mormon. Also, there is no evidence of more than one group of people being among them (Nephites, Mulekites, Jaredites)."

Mr. May then went on discuss the copper and temple issue, referring to 2 Nephi 5: 15-16:

> And I did teach my people to build buildings, and to work in all manner of wood, and of iron, and of **copper**, and of brass, and of steel, and of gold, and of silver, and of precious ores, which were in great abundance.

As hard as they may try, those who fail to acknowledge any groups coming to the New World before the Spaniards with superior knowledge of metallurgy, mining of ores and constructing vast cities, have lost the battle as far as this writer is concerned. There are just too many facts to prove otherwise.

In 2008, the late C. Fred Rydholm sent me an autographed copy of his book *Michigan Copper, A History of Discovery: The Untold Story.* From the very first page, I knew Fred was authentic and that the read was going to be awesome! Here's a sample:

There are two basic methods of learning almost anything. One is to get the general (overall) picture and then go to the specifics. The other is to get very specific and then piece the specifics together.

In nearly everything I can think of, the first method is most logical. You learn to dog paddle before you learn to crawl or backstroke; you learn carpentry before you start cabinet making. You learn arithmetic before physics or you learn to sew before you learn petit-point.

It appears to me when looking over all the clues, ancient skeletons, gene studies, Clovis point arguments, ancient cities, etc., etc., that we are going at things backward.

So, the question still remains, where did all that copper go? We have evidence that Michigan Copper mined by ancient people, including more than one culture, was shipped to many parts of the world. How do we figure that to be the case? It is obviously apparent by the fact that over 99% of the copper mined in Michigan, some of the purist strains on earth, has never been accounted for. Only about 1% of all the copper mined in that region (which would be nearly 50,000 pounds) is found in museums, private collections and probably much more still buried in mounds or other places. There was so much copper taken from the pits and mines in the Michigan area, especially on Lake Superior's Isle Royale and Michigan's Keweenaw Peninsula, that it would have taken 10,000 men 1,000 years working with little more than fire, hammer-stones and pure brute strength to achieve this feat. It appears that over five million metric tons of copper was mined. That is a staggering amount! So, where did it go?

There are many conflicting arguments that this copper ended up in Europe, Asia and Africa in ancient times. This concept, however, increasingly held by more and more scholars and investigators, is gaining support based on evidence of Michigan copper in the Middle East and elsewhere. Although isolationists still believe or hold to the concept that few or no groups of people preceded Columbus, (except maybe the Norseman), others of us, called *diffusionists,* hold that unknown ancient cultures extensively transported copper and other treasures across the seas of the world.

Fig. 131 Copper gorget   Fig. 132 Copper amulet

How did the copper found in America's west come to be? Was it shipped from Michigan to the Rockies or was it mined on site? We read of the copper mines in Utah's Cottonwood Canyon and we've read about the copper discovered in tombs and in other places as well. It is obvious that copper is plentiful in the west but it doesn't mean that some of it didn't come from the East. A little copper hammer was discovered that immediately caught the attention of the scientific community. Right away it was deemed a fraud! Why? Because it "looks too modern." End of story! Is that it? Because it *looks too modern*?

Really! Did not the people of old learn how to make amazing tools, weapons of superior design, incredible jewelry, unique implements for farming, many of which we are unable to duplicate today? In a speech given on the occasion of receiving the Nobel Peace Prize for 2001, United Nations Secretary General Kofi Annan stated, "The idea that there is one people in possession of the truth, one answer to the world's ills, or one solution to humanity's needs, has done untold harm throughout history."

This view seems to hold true in law, medicine, politics and all the branches of science. When a belief holds unchangeably firm in an individual's mind, regardless of what or how much proof is presented against it, then it has become idolatrous. It is something one believes, no matter what the circumstances, evidences or arguments.

Fig. 133 Copper Hammer.

EVOLUTION AND DEGRADATION OF INTERPRETED PETROGLYPHIC PANELS

Fig. 134 The Dighton Rock.

The interpretation of petroglyphic panels is a science. Not everyone or just anyone successfully accomplishes it. It takes years of research with hands on experience, and it helps if one has the aid of a local tribal member if they are working on Indian petroglyphic panels. The Dighton Rock is a prime example of the degradation of a panel. Seen here in Fig. 135, is a later rendition of the panel. To quote a little history I turn to a book by Garrick Mallery titled, *Picture-Writing of the American Indians,* an extract from the Tenth Annual Report of the Bureau of Ethnology, 1894.

In this connection some allusion must be made to the learned discussions upon the Dighton rock before mentioned, p. 86. The original Algonquian characters were translated by a Scandinavian antiquary as an account of the party of Thorfinn, the Hopeful. A distinguished Orientalist made out clearly the word "melek" (king). Another scholar triumphantly established the characters to be Scythian, and still another identified them as Phoenician. But this inscription has been so manipulated that it is difficult now to determine the original details.

An official report made in 1830 by the Rhode Island Historical Society and published by the Royal Society of Northern Antiquaries, in Antiquitates Americanæ. by C.C. Rafn, presents the best account known concerning the Dighton rock and gives copies made from time to time of the inscription, which are here reproduced. Pl. LIV. The text is condensed as follows, but in quoting it the statement that the work was not done by Indians is without approval.

It is situated about 6 1/2 miles south of Taunton, on the east side of Taunton River, a few feet from the shore, and on the west side of Assonet neck, in the town of Berkley, county of Bristol, and commonwealth of Massachusetts; although probably from the fact of being generally visited from the opposite side of the river, which is in Dighton, it has always been known by the name of the Dighton Writing Rock. It faces northwest toward the bed of the river, and is covered by the water 2 to 3 feet at the highest, and is left 10 or 12 feet from it at the lowest tides; it is also completely immersed twice in twenty-four hours. The rock does not occur in site, but shows indubitable evidence of having occupied the spot where it now rests since the period of that great and extrusive disruption which was followed by the transportation of immense boulders to, and a deposit of them in, places at a vast distance from their original beds. It is a mass of well characterized, fine grained graywacke. Its true color, as exhibited by a fresh fracture, is a bluish gray. There is no rock in the immediate neighborhood that would at all answer as a substitute for the purpose for which the one bearing the inscription was selected, as they are aggregates of the large conglomerate variety. It's face, measured at the base is 11 1/2 feet, and in height it is a little rising 5 feet. The upper surface forms with the horizon an inclined plane of about 60 degrees. The whole of the face is covered to within a few inches of the ground with unknown hieroglyphics. There appears little or no method in the arrangement of them. The lines are from half an inch to an inch in width; and in depth, sometimes one-third of an inch, though generally very superficial. They were, inferring from the rounded elevations and intervening depressions, pecked in upon the rock and not chiseled or smoothly cut out. The marks of human power and manual labor are indelibly stamped upon it. No one who examines attentively the workmanship will believe it to have been done by the Indians. Moreover, it is a well attested fact that nowhere throughout our wide-spread domain is a single instance of their recording or having recorded their deeds or history on stone.

Mallery goes on to explain how the committee examined the various drawings that had been made over time of the inscriptions and what they came up with. He likened the Dighton Rock inscriptions to those on the Pennsylvania "Indian God Rock" stating that "the characters are very similar in appearance."

The first known drawings of the Dighton Rock, and thought at the time to be "a faithful and accurate representation of the inscriptions; was taken by Dr. Danforth in 1680."

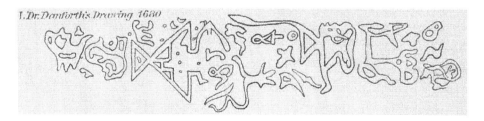

Fig. 135 Dr. Danforth's 1680 Drawing.

The committee didn't really consider Danforth's drawing but why they didn't is not revealed to us. They considered the very first rendition of the petroglyphic characters to be made by Cotton Mather as early as 1712; and may be found in N. 338, vol. 28, of the Philosophical Transactions, pp. 70 and 71; also in vol. 5, Jones's abridgment, under article fourth.

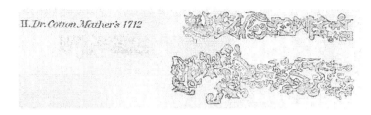

Fig. 136 Dr. Cotton Mather's 1712 Drawing.

In 1630, a new band of religious immigrants arrived on the shores of Massachusetts. They survived cold harsh winters, bouts with phenomena, and all kinds of afflictions besieging them. These were the obvious physical problems; adding to those problems were spiritual and political crises as well. As those people lived out their daily struggles, they observed many strange and exciting sites such as strange carvings and ancient writings on boulders and rock walls. One such rock was our Dighton stone. As show above (Fig.136), a single drawing was made depicting those characters on the rock. It wasn't until around 1730 that people began to seek someone with knowledge to interpret the strange inscriptions on the rock.

Many of the strange designs looked more comical than of a serious nature but be as it were, they still wanted answers. The people called upon the Reverend Cotton Mather who resided in Boston, Massachusetts, and who was revered as a great preacher, scholar, and scientist. When the opportunity presented itself, Dr. Mather painstakingly copied the inscriptions and figures, and then sent them off to the Royal Society in London for their opinion.

Since the time of Dr. Mather, countless scholars have attempted to decipher the stone. As the reader will see, not only did the craze bring on a host of would be interpretations, it would also add more mystery to the origin of the characters on the Dighton stone.

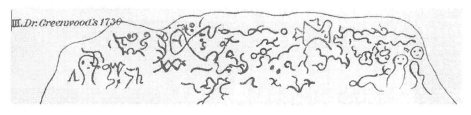

Fig. 137 Dr. Isaac Greenwood's 1730 Drawing.

Dr. Isaac Greenwood exhibited a drawing of the inscription before the Society of Antiquarians of London bearing the date of 1730.

The following drawings show us the absolute degradation of the stone over time. It is a prime example of what happens to inscriptions when allowed to be chalked or cleaned in order to read the script, petroglyphic or hieroglyphic panel more clearly.

Fig. 138 Mr. Stephen Sewell's 1768 Drawing

Fig. 139 Mr. James Winthrop's 1788 Drawing

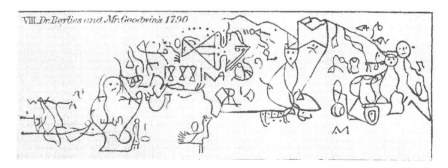

Fig. 140 Dr. Baylies and Mr. Goodwin's 1790 Drawing

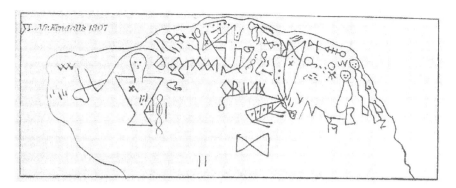

Fig. 141 Mr. Kendall's 1807 Drawing

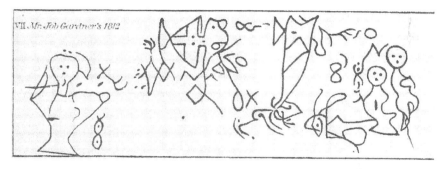

Fig. 142 Mr. Job Bardner's 1812 Drawing

And lastly, the drawing accepted as the only authentic rendition of the Dighton Stone, as approved by the Rhode Island Historical Society of 1830.

Fig. 143

237

Now we come to the modern version of the inscriptions and the supposed translation or interpretation. Modern scholars tell us that the rock represents prominent constellations and stars by which Phoenicians from Spain sailed across the Atlantic Ocean to the shores of New England some 2,000 years ago. The consensus is that they (the Phoenicians) carved these constellations on the rock. So, why did they do that? Our experts claim it was a navigation chart for others to steer back across the Atlantic to their own lands. Sounds preposterous to me, since they found their way to America, why wouldn't they be able to find their way back home? Our experts claim there are 13 bright stars contained within the scribbling on the Dighton Rock including Polaris and Sirius. According to one scholar, Mr. John Gallagher:

> The Dighton Rock is one of the oldest star charts in the Americas. Long before the Maya of Central America lifted their heads towards the stars and inscribed them on their Codices, the Dighton Rock was already centuries old.

He claims that a rebus form of a young horse with Iberian-Punic letters across its upraised leg appears on the left hand side of the rock and translates as Equuleus. "On the hind legs of the young horse are the Iberian-Punic letters F-L-S, which when translated means "Foal." The second from is a rebus spelling out the letters b-d-c-u, which translates as "serve or (worship) Cetu the constellation Cetus, the Whale." The constellation "Equulleus the Foal" appears between the Eastern and Southeastern sky in the month of August, next to the constellation Pegasus and directly above Aquarius. These are the last two forms on the Dighton Rock."

Fig. 144 Amherst College Archives.

John Gallagher's work on interpreting the Dighton Rock is admirable and the work involved had to have been intense, however, because of the many changes—the chalking or rubbings that have taken place since the 15th century—we really have no idea how the stone looked the first time it was seen by Europeans. The question remains, why weren't the local Indians brought forth to explain their thoughts on it? Below is a chart compiled by Mr. Gallagher.

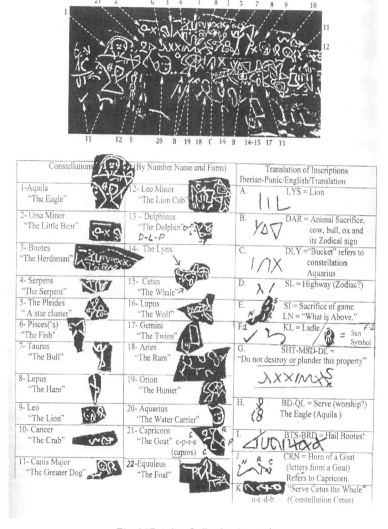

Fig. 145 John Gallagher's work

239

Mr. Garrick Mallery concluded by stating:

From considerations mentioned elsewhere, and others that are obvious, any inscriptions purporting to be pre-Columbian, showing apparent use of alphabetic characters, signs of the Zodiac, or other evidences of a culture higher than that known among the North American Indians, must be received with caution, but the pictographs may be altogether genuine, their erroneous interpretation may be the sole ground for discrediting them.

THE GRAVE CREEK STONE

Rock inscriptions or rock art usually consists of anthropomorphic, zoomorphic and miscellaneous incised lines to form shapes and figures. Many rock art sites contain clearly recognizable motifs whose styles have been documented correctly. Many so called Indian Rock Art sites are of inscriptions and lost languages, etc. The worst thing that can happen to an incised panel is to have it compromised by chalking, tracing, scrubbing or removal. This causes degradation to the inscriptions that is not at the normal rate caused by natural weathering and age. Also, "evolution" in the opposite direction can do apprehensible damage, causing an ever changing idea of thought or of interpretation as seen in the above example.

The Grave Creek Stone is an example of both. It has been so manipulated that it is now considered a "fake."

Fig. 146 Grave Creek Stone.

Even if this stone is authentic, it will not stand the test of time because of "evolution" and "degradation."

Garrick Mallery explained it thusly:

A mere collocation of letters from various alphabets is not an alphabet. Words cannot be formed or ideas communicated by that artifice. When a people adopts the alphabetical signs of another it adopts the general style of the characters and more often the characters in detail. Such signs had already an arrangement into syllables and words which had a vocalic validity as well as known significance. A jumble of letters from a variety of alphabets bears internal evidence that the manipulator did not have an intelligent meaning to convey by them, and did not comprehend the languages from which the letters were selected. In the case of the Grave Creek inscription the futile attempts to extract a meaning from it on the theory that it belongs to an intelligent alphabetic system show that it holds no such place. If it is genuine it must be treated as pictorial and ideographic, unless, indeed, it is cryptographic, which is not indicated."

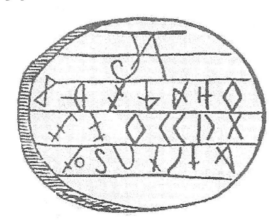

Fig. 147 Faked Grave Creek Stone?

From what we have seen it is very apparent that a great many of the historical panels and artifacts discovered have been so sorely manipulated that it is near impossible to come to any intelligent conclusion as to its authenticity.

Fig. 148 Author's daughter Shellie and husband Allen with Hopewell Artifacts

6

FACTS: WRITTEN IN STONE

"Artifact (arte, by skill, plus facere, to do): A usually simple object (such as a tool or ornament) showing human workmanship or modification."
—Webster's Dictionary

TWO OF THE MOST TALKED about *stone* artifacts dealing with a written language are the Kensington Rune Stone and the Los Lunas Ten Commandment Stone. Much has been written either to "authenticate" or to "disprove" these two stones—far more than any other artifacts known.

LOS LUNAS TEN COMMANDMENTS STONE

The Ten Commandments Stone is located on Hidden Mountain, New Mexico, not far from the town of Los Lunas. Dr. Robert Pfeiffer of the Harvard University Semitic Language Department, was the first to recognize what was then referred to as *Inscription Rock,* to be a copy of the Hebrew Ten Commandments. The translation was made in the late 1940s.

The late David Deal observed that "letters of the inscription cut deeply and accurately in very hard, flinty igneous rock, are by no means a mystery. They are clearly and unequivocally a form of Paleo-Hebrew. A comparison of alphabets easily proves this point."

Several hundred yards uphill is what appears to be the remains of an ancient fortification. Deal went on to add: "surprisingly similar to finds in the Middle East and of course unlike anything we normally see here in the West and Southwestern U.S."

Fig. 149 Ten Commandments Stone

In his book, *America B.C.,* Berry Fell comments on these stones:

This remarkable version of the Hebrew Decalogue or Ten Commandments, located on Hidden Mountain, near Albuquerque, New
Mexico, became the main focus of attention during the Epigraphic
Congress sponsored by the Western Chapter of the Epigraphic Society in 1984. The inscription, written in ancient Hebrew letters of the
style of the Moab stone, about 1000 B.C., was not translated until
1949, when Professor Robert Pfeiffer of Harvard University recognized it as a short version of the Ten Commandments as given in the
twentieth chapter of Exodus. For long it was thought to be a modern engraving until the examination carried out in 1984 disclosed
anomalous features that may imply antiquity. The geologist George F.
Morehouse, reporting in *ESOP* [*Epigraphic Society Occasional Papers*]
volume 13 (1985), found patina indicative of an age of from 500-
2,000 years, and Fell, reporting in the same volume, noted that the
punctuation matched that of ancient Greek manuscripts, such as the
Codex Sinaiticus of the fourth century A.D. [Brackets author's]

A full account of the Los Lunas Ten Commandments stone with transcription, transliteration to modern Hebrew characters and translation, is given in *ESOP* Vol. 10, part 1 1982.

According to some sources, the first recorded mention of the Los Lunas Ten Commandment Stone was in 1933, when Professor Frank Hibben (1910-2002), an archaeologist with the University of New Mexico investigated it. He was convinced the inscription was ancient and therefore "authentic." The first time Hibben saw the script it was covered in desert lichen and a deep dark patina making the inscriptions hard to see.

Some folks had a hard time with Hibben's theory since he had been accused of manufacturing testimony regarding his archaeological data supporting his pre-Clovis migration theory. Some argue the inscriptions on the stone are not as old as one might theorize because of the apparent usage of Modern Hebrew punctuation. How does one explain patina, lichen and what is colloquially called desert varnish if various inscriptions are of recent origin? I myself, have seen mammoths, brontosaurs, and men riding on bulls near Blanding, Utah. They are coated with the patina of centuries if not millennia. I have also seen the damage done by recent carvings into the same stone and the difference is unmistakable.

Archaeo-linguist Cyrus Gordon proposed that the stone Decalogue is in fact a Samaritan mezuzah. The familiar Jewish mezuzah is a tiny scroll placed in a small container mounted by the entrance to a house. The ancient rock slab is at the gateway to a property or synagogue, and bearing an abridged version of the Decalogue. The Samaritan alphabet is a direct descendant of the Paleo-Hebrew alphabet. He regarded the Byzantine period as most likely for the inscription.

According to archaeologist Kenneth Feder, the stone is a fake. He pointed out that the flat face of the stone shows a very sharp, crisp inscription and that it lacked any archaeological context.

Dr. Feder argued that to get to the location of the stone would have required whoever inscribed it to have "*stopped along the way, encamped, eaten food, broken things, disposed of trash, performed rituals, and so on. And those actions should have left a trail of physical archaeological evidence across the greater American Southwest, the discovery of which would undeniably prove the existence of foreigners in New Mexico in antiquity with a demonstrably ancient Hebrew material culture.*" He further stated, "*There* are no pre-Columbian ancient Hebrew settlements, no sites containing the everyday detritus of a band of ancient Hebrews, nothing that even a cursory knowledge of how the archaeological record forms would demand there would be. From an archaeological standpoint, that's plainly impossible."

There have been a host of investigators, writers, archaeologists, and curiosity seekers that seem to just "know" what the stone is all about. One writer penned:

> The stone preserves an abbreviated form of the Ten Commandments as written in Exodus 20, which is very exciting, but what makes this stone an enigma is the fact that the writing is clearly Semitic in origin. The ancient Hebrew inscriptions were once thought to be a combination of Greek, Hebrew and Phoenician characters but now are clearly seen as a form of Hebrew writing dating to approximately 1000 B.C.! The Greeks borrowed from the Phoenician [?] alphabet so the characters would be familiar. The Hebrews and the Phoenicians were neighbors which, in their trading environment, shared the same language and alphabet. The style of the characters is strikingly similar, almost identical, to that used on the Moabite Stone in the days of the Israelite Kings Omri and Ahab. The Moabite stone was engraved by captive Israelites for the Moabite King, Mescha, as per its own inscription. After examining the Los Lunas site, the geologist George Morehouse, estimated the placement of this Decalogue inscription up to 3000 years ago, which would, again, date it around 1000 B.C. Just how were historians to explain how a seventy ton boulder with Hebrew inscription appeared on the mountain landscape in North America around 1000 B.C.?

As I have noted, we know that over 2000 years before Columbus set sail for the New World there were people of Semitic origin already in what is now New Mexico, and it is obvious that expeditions were launched from the Old World financed by men who heard of a strange land to the west that was rich beyond anyone's imagination. These explorers brought with them their religious beliefs and rituals. The Phoenician ships carried all sorts of people, regardless of religion or ethnicity.

They needed warm bodies to do the work needed once they reached this new land.

History was written by those who possessed that knowledge and by what they saw and heard. The Greeks told one story, the Phoenicians another story and so on, but we get the general idea. The question we must ask is why did a particular people use their form of writing to be etched on stone?

One translation of the Los Lunas Stone was published by a local Epigraphic Society:

I Jehovah Eloah who brought you out of the land of Mitsrayim out of the house of bondages. You shall not have other gods in place of me. You shall not make for yourself molded idols. You shall not lift up your voice to connect the name of Jehovah in hate. Remember your Sabbath to make it holy. Honor your father and your mother to make long your existence upon the land which Jehovah Eloah gave to you. You shall not murder. You shall not commit adultery. You shall not steal. You shall not bear witness against your neighbor, testimony for a bribe. You shall not covet wife of your neighbor and all which belongs to your neighbor.

One argument against the stone's antiquity is its apparent use of Modern Hebrew punctuation. But epigrapher D. Barry Fell argued that the punctuation is consistent with antiquity. Other researchers and linguists have pointed out that because of numerous stylistic and grammatical errors that appear in the inscriptions they dismiss the whole of it.

Juergen Neuhoff, a computer graphics designer, and Stan Fox using Interlinear translation came up with the following report with notes added:

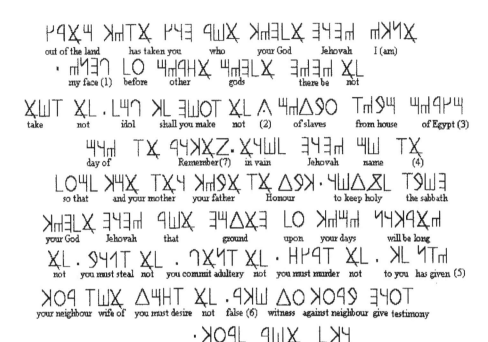

Notes: (1) normal Hebrew spelling is without the HE character
(2) probably an insertion mark for an additional line (the 2nd one from top)
(3) right 3 characters (RES,SADE,MEM) are broken off
(4) right character (ALEPH) is broken off
(5) right character (YOD) is corrupted due to surface crack
(6) normal Hebrew spelling uses QOPH instead of KAPH
(7) normal Hebrew spelling is without the ALEPH character

Fig. 150 Ten Commandments Translated?

In an article written in *Ancient American Magazine* Vol. 15, Issue No. 93 we read:

> *Another copy of the Ten Commandments in pre-modern Hebrew appears on a boulder outside Los Lunas, New Mexico. According to archaeologist Dr. Gunnar Thompson, Geologist George Morehouse reports that a heavy patina on the stone is indicative of an age between 500 to 2,000 years... Barry Fell (1917 - 1994, professor of inverte-*

brate zoology at the Harvard Museum of Comparative zoology) identified linguistic peculiarities in the text that are characteristic of 4th century [BCE] *Hebrew manuscripts; and Cyrus Gordon noted linguistic peculiarities similar to texts in the Jerusalem Museum, dating between the 3rd and 4th centuries A. D.*

In 1992, David Deal confirmed the existence of a 2nd Century zodiac at Los Lunas. Unfortunately, much damage has occurred at the Los Lunas Ten Commandment site since it became a novelty in the public eye and therefore the damage is done!

Fig. 151 Damaged characters

THE KENSINGTON RUNE STONE

Not many discoveries have gone through the test of time as the Kensington Rune Stone. It had previously been authenticated, but then no sooner had it been accepted, it was once again debunked as a fraud.

In 1898, the Kensington Rune Stone was discovered on a Minnesota farm owned by Olof Ohman. A Swedish immigrant, Ohman came to America in 1879, and purchased a farm from another Scandinavian some ten years later. According to Ohman, the stone was discovered partially buried on a small wood covered knoll and was tangled up in roots of brush and trees. The first thing Ohman noticed was the curious inscriptions that covered much of the stone's surface.

When Ohman publicized his discovery it was taken to Northwestern University where Professor G.O. Curme examined it. Curme came to the conclusion that the message on the stone was a modern Swedish inscription with a rude style of runes incorporated in it. He also made the comment that the cuts looked fresh, and that they lacked the patina on its face unlike the rest of the stone. Therefore, Professor Curme dismissed the stone as a poor fake and sent in back to Olof Ohman. But before doing so he commented that it was very unlikely such a stone would have been shipped to the site in question or even chiseled there by ancient Scandinavians in the first place.

It was further discovered that Mr. Ohman was a mason [Freemason?] and knew some of the runic signs, and even owned a few books on runes and knew how to read and write them. The runic inscription contained on the face and edge of the stone read:

> 8 Goths and 22 Norwegians on an exploration journey from Vinland to the west. We had camp by 2 skerries one days' journey north from this stone. We were to fish one day. After we came home found 10 men red of blood and dead. AVM. We have 10 men by the sea to look after our ships 14 days' travel from this island. Year 1362.

Ohman never admitted to having carved the stone but the evidence pointed to him as its author. The stone would have been likely forgotten about if it had not been for the keen interest of amateur historian Hjalmar Holand. It was some years later after the discovery that Holand set out to prove to the world that the stone was indeed authentic. He held to that belief until his dying day.

Following Holand's death, two researchers, O.G. Landsverk and Alf Monge came forward with the idea that the runes contained on the stone held some sort of cryptic message. However, the stone brought all kinds of free thinkers out of the woodwork with their ideas of origin and messages. Fast forward to Aug. 2, 2012 from a talk given by Dr. Gabriel Barkay, renowned Archaeologist of Biblical Lands in Israel, who cited a paper entitled "The Kensington Rune Stone," by John D. Bengtson:

> The KRS was given new life recently when the Larson Papers were found and it was shown that the nine aberrant runes were identical or similar to those in a runic alphabet used in Denmark in the 13th century A.D. just prior to the date of 1362 inscribed on the KRS itself. Historical

anthropologist and linguist John D. Bengtson points out that there are many different runic alphabets used during the history of the Norse and that there was no standard runic alphabet, rather variations from time to time and place to place. This hugely important artifact seems now to be a deep anchor in the record of pre-Columbian Norse contact in North America.

Fig. 152   Kensington Rune Stone.

The late great epigrapher Gloria Farley, who contributed so much to the science of epigraphy and published a great work titled *In Plain Sight,* investigated the Kensington Rune Stone at length. Even though many scholars don't agree with her insight, they still regard her as an expert in her field and respect her opinions.

Mrs. Farley not only spent time with the Kensington stone but was instrumental in authenticating the Heavener Runestone. She claimed

Fig. 153 Gloria Farley

that the white settlers in the Heavener area were illiterate and incapable of carving runic inscriptions. This we find to be false as many Europeans wrote extensively of their explorations in North America during the 17th and 18th centuries. Dr. J.D. Hanes noted that:

The proponents of the Viking origins for the runestones have employed virtually every form of flawed reasoning, including appeal to myth, shifting the burden of proof, argument by authority, irrefutable hypotheses, and others. These are common [practices] of pseudoscience favored by proponents of myths and hoaxes.

In a testament to the unending quest for the tourist dollar, both the Kensington and Heavener Stones are the centerpieces of State Parks. This, despite the numerous doubts that have been cast on the Viking hypothesis. The myth of the Vikings in the Midwest will persist as long as verifiable scientific fact and logical reasoning are absent from the beliefs of the proponents.

Editors of major publications parrot the party-line of no-foreigners-before-Columbus for public consumption, a case in point being journalistic reaction to Nielsen's announcement confirming the Kensington Runestone's medieval authenticity. Instead of welcoming the news as an important scientific discovery, Laura Billings wrote in her front-page story for the *Saint Paul Pioneer Press* that "*it might be easier to prove that Santa Claus lives at the North Pole.*"

Her flippant remark was preceded in an earlier issue (December 12) of the same newspaper by Jim Ragsdale, who suggested that the Kensington Runestone was being used as a commercial ploy to hook gullible tourists. Both reporters treated Nielsen's proofs as equivocal at best—leaving readers with the distinct impression that only a handful of odd-ball amateurs support the artifact's Norse provenance against amused professionals, who know better. In the same spirit that prejudiced Olof

Ohman's Swedish background, Ragsdale emphasized Nielsen's Scandinavian ancestry.

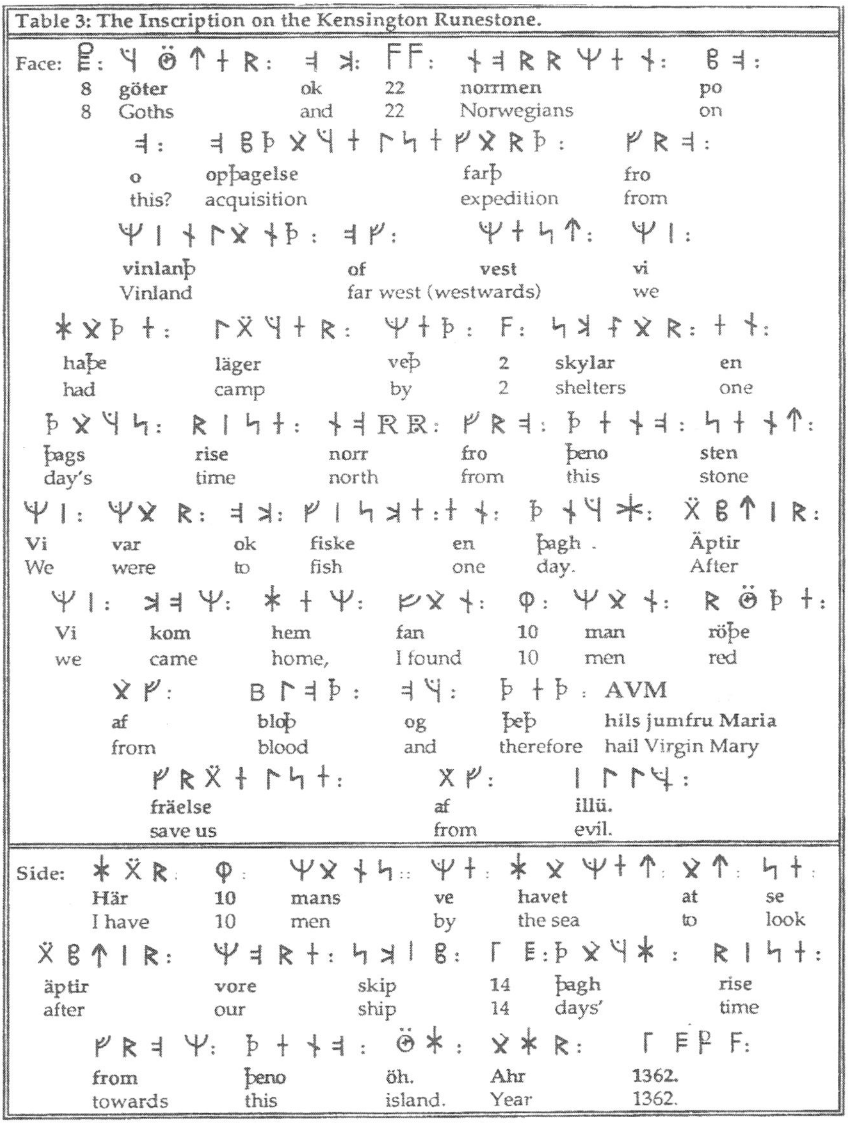

Table 3: The Inscription on the Kensington Runestone.

Face:					
8	göter	ok	22	norrmen	po
8	Goths	and	22	Norwegians	on
o	oppagelse		farp	fro	
this?	acquisition		expedition	from	
vinlanp		of	vest	vi	
Vinland		far west (westwards)		we	
hape	läger	vep	2	skylar	en
had	camp	by	2	shelters	one
pags	rise	norr	fro	peno	sten
day's	time	north	from	this	stone
Vi	var	ok	fiske	en	pagh .	Äptir
We	were	to	fish	one	day.	After
Vi	kom	hem	fan	10	man	röpe
we	came	home,	I found	10	men	red
af	blop	og	pep	hils jumfru Maria		AVM
from	blood	and	therefore	hail Virgin Mary		
fräelse	af	illü.			
save us	from	evil.			

Side:	Här	10	mans	ve	havet	at	se
	I have	10	men	by	the sea	to	look
	äptir	vore	skip	14	pagh	rise	
	after	our	ship	14	days'	time	
	from	peno	öh.	Ahr	1362.		
	towards	this	island.	Year	1362.		

Fig. 154 Courtesy, the Epigraphic Society

Hired by the directors of Alexandria's Runestone Museum, Saint Paul forensic geologist Scott Wolter studied weathering of grooves in the carving and found they were made many centuries ago. His examination revealed that most if not all of the artifact's runes had been individually "gone over" with a modern tool sometime after the object's discovery at the close of the 19th century, probably to make the weathered letters more easily discernible.

This tampering caused skeptics to declare that the inscription had been newly created. But Wolter's microscopic scrutiny of the runes showed that the modern scratches were made on top of the original runes carved centuries earlier, as indicated by oxidation residue surrounding each of the written characters. Comparing variously weathered areas of the stone's exterior likewise suggested a date for its inscription anterior to the 1898 discovery by at least two hundred years. In order for Ohman to have faked the runestone, he would have had to induce "*mineralization within the carved-out runes after they were carved,*" Wolter said, and "*induced mica degradation on the split side of the stone to match a five-hundred-year effect.*"

Is this the end of the scrutiny? I seriously doubt it. Other runes have been discovered as recently as five years ago. Near Kansas City, a man by the name of Rolf Rosendahl discovered a hidden panel on a 45-acre ranch that revealed Runes carved deep into a brownish rock face. In a letter to me with the photo he stated:

A few years ago I found a Runestone within the Kansas City, Missouri, City limits on a 45-acre ranch. Yesterday I got a high-definition photograph and you can compare this one to any others with Elder Futhark inscription. There is evidence of a settlement at this site and the writing is about 900-1000 A.D. I simply attached the photo and if you think some drunken Irish guy carved it, I suggest it took weeks or months to carve this into granite rock a half-inch deep.

Many folks simply won't come forward when new discoveries are made because they don't want to be scrutinized or demoralized, so they stay quiet. Our friend Mr. Rosendahl was heavily demoralized and accused of manufacturing the runes himself. At the time of his letter to me he was a History Major at UMKC and had researched and examined all the variations of Elder Futhark and the Anglo-Saxon variations called "Futhorc," and further commented that he believed the Knights Templar either funded or supported the Viking expansion into the New

World. Elder Futhark & Futhorc runes are thought to be the oldest versions of the Runic alphabet.

Fig. 155 Kansas City Runestone

A ROMANTIC HOAX

Mr. Rosendahl informed me that he had contacted a Professor Henrik Williams at Uppsala University. Williams spotted the word "Arthur" as having a modern "th" in the Anglo Saxon runes used in England. Soon several scholars began taking a long hard look at the runes and it was discovered that these runes were a modern version, so a new focus using Anglo-Saxon transliteration began. Once these runes were identified as Anglo-Saxon, the origin of these particular rune forms was begun. The words "Cyrus Arthur Slater Hannah Y" appeared giving the new name of this site the "Cyrus Arthur Salter Rune Stone". A further transliteration of the runic inscription yielded the following.
Cyrus Arthur Salter - Hanna Yearsley Wed (Y?) 1888. Day: Third (N?)

ᛃᛢᛗᚱᚾᛋ ᚠᚱᛏᚺᚢᚱ ᛋᛏᚠᛏᛁᚱ - ᚺᚠ�ᛏᛗᚻ ᚫ

| 1 | 2 3 4 5 | 6 7 8 9 10 11 | 12 13 14 15 16 17 | 18 19 20 21 22 23 24 | 25 |

C y r u s   A r t h u r   S l a t e͡r   H a n n e͡h   Y

Fig. 156

Census records indicated that Cyrus Arthur Slater was alive and well between 1859 and 1941 and had knowledge and information enough to carve the inscriptions. He had access to *Ruthwell and Bewcastle Runes* published by George Stephens in 1866 -1867.

However, even after a full report on this Rune Stone conducted by Dr. Richard Nielsen, there are still those who look for other factors to disprove what has been determined authentic. As of February 2012, this Rune Stone was registered as an archaeological site with the Missouri Department of Natural Resources, State Historical Preservation Office. The official name is: The Kansas City Slater Rune Stone.

ELEPHANTS IN AMERICA

Elephants have been a subject of controversy since the very first time a European explorer found one depicted on rock. Elephant? How quaint; but how come? At first it was thought that it was used as a form of an ancient deity or god of some kind. How could these illiterate In-

Fig. 157 The Elephant of Rainbow Rocks

dians know anything about elephants? Pennsylvania's Elephant Petroglyph on the Allegheny River was one of these rocks depicting an elephant.

This rock facsimile features the carvings of snakes, bird tracks, anthropomorphic, quadruped, etc. While these images are common in rock art designs and very typical across much of the continent the elephant is not, but it is found here depicted on the face of a large rock standing near the Rainbow Rock.

James Swauger, who was recognized as an expert on petroglyphic panels throughout the Ohio Valley, examined the elephant etched in the rock surface. "*It is obvious at this time that the figure was carved recently by persons using metal tools, and that it has no relationship to the undoubted American Indian petroglyphs of the site.*" He therefore declared the head a forgery.

Quoting from *Ancient America* Volume 13 Issue No. 88, Thomas Anderson noted:

> While Swauger and company are correct in pointing out that pre-Columbian Indians used stone tools, their assumption that the Rainbow pachyderm must be, ipso facto, a modern fake, because it was carved with a metal utensil, is only an assumption. Large numbers of ancient arrowheads, spear-points and related items of hardened copper have been found especially in Upper Michigan since the early 19th Century. They comprise a great body of physical evidence on behalf of metal tools used by the prehistoric residents of our continent. Of course, Swauger was far more disturbed by the representation of an elephant, a creature mainstream academics such as himself insist was totally unknown to the pre-modern inhabitants of North America.

In their hasty decision to label the Rainbow Rock elephant a forgery, mainstream archaeologists have and still do condemn valuable insight into North American prehistory.

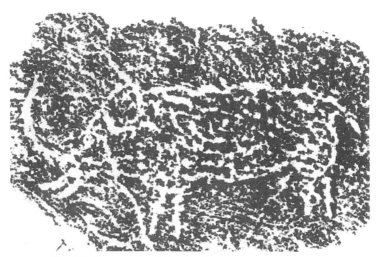

Fig. 158 Barnesville, Ohio Elephant Petroglyph Sketch

Here's an insight offered courtesy of the Midwestern Epigraphy Society regarding the Barnesville, Ohio elephant:

This petroglyph is so old and weathered that one can walk right by
without noticing it, this is, unless the sun is shining just right. We are
told that it stands out sharp in early morning or late afternoon sun-
light. Evidently the lower angled rays of the sun produce better high-
lights and shadows on opposite walls of the peckings and enhance
legibility. Unfortunately, our visit occurred about noon and even the
photographs we took are hard to read. They proved to be unsuitable
for reproduction but a rubbing taken on stiffener cloth with a black
crayon was obviously an instant success. The original rubbing renders
a petroglyph that is 18-inches wide.

How the memory of this animal came to the Track Rocks, we do
not know. Either the engraving is so old that the artist was recording a
mastodon or, more reasonably, it dates to a later period associated with
ancient colonists from the Mediterranean who were familiar with the
elephant.

Going along with the last assumption, it is interesting to note that
the 1975 radio carbon dating of core samples from the Grave Creek
Mound (less than 25 miles from the Track Rocks) gave a date of 200
BC for its construction. This corresponds well with the time period for

the use of the Iberian-Punic script found on the tablet removed from the mound. The script also identifies people who were familiar with elephants and Carthaginians.

Not long before the construction of the Grave Creek Mound, the Carthaginian General Hannibal utilized this enormous animal as a kind of shock weapon in warfare from Spain to Italy. It was the counterpart of our modern day tanks.

Another factor confirming this first millennium date for pecking the elephant petroglyph is the Track Rocks Goddess Symbol. This symbol carries a brief Ogam script which also dates to the Carthaginian period or, at least, within easy memory of it.

This Track Rocks Petroglyph is not the first rendering of an elephant in America. There were many of reports of tablets, steles, petroglyphs, and sculptures depicting elephants. Wisconsin even records an enormous elephant effigy earthwork. Many of these were reported in the early 1800s, long before it was fashionable to deny the presence of ancient mariners on this continent prior to the coming of Christopher Columbus.

If we look at many of the Michigan Tablets and the Burrows Cave stones we find numerous depictions of elephants. Not only do we find them on these artifacts but we can find them on southwestern petroglyphic panels and even into Mexico and South America as well. In the Book of Mormon we find references to them as elephants and also as *cummoms* and *cureloms,* perhaps referencing mastodons and mammoths. Others believe these creatures to be of some ancient large now extinct species. Be as it may, the fact remains that elephants played an important role in prehistoric America.

Fig. 159 Michigan knife artifact with elephant

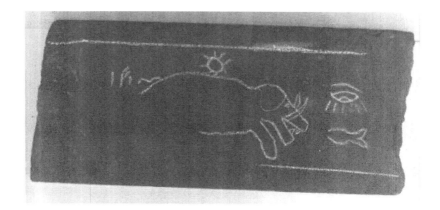

Fig. 160 Michigan tablet with elephant, fish, sun and all Seeing Eye

Some believe this to be a boar pig and not an elephant.

Conventional looking elephants are what we would normally look for, but in a work published by John Ruskamp, a scientific investigator of some of the world's most enduring enigmas among other things; he shows us compelling evidence of Chinese influence within our Southwestern Petroglyphic panels. In his books *Asiatic Echoes* and *Asiatic Echoes Addendum 2012,* he introduced the idea of Chinese using ancient signs generally thought of as "Indian Petroglyphic" *jargon* to a new level. I have to admit that when John first introduced me to the science referred to as "Jaccard's Index of Similarity," I was skeptical, but after reading his work and then reading it again and again I began to understand what he was conveying. He showed me Chinese elephant glyphs that I had no idea existed in southwestern petroglyphic rock art. The Chinese showed with their rock writing skills that elephants were part of ancient life not only in China but the Americas as well.

ELEPHANT REMAINS IN MEXICO

In an article published in 1903 in the prestigious *American Antiquarian* (25:395-397, 1903) we read of elephant remains in Mexico:

From the City of Mexico comes a statement bearing the signature of Dr. Nicholas Leon, archaeologist of the National Museum of Mexico. The signature would justify the belief that proper investigation of the facts related has been made. The one great fact is that an ancient city, which was located near the present town of Paredon, in the state of Coahuila, some 500 miles north of the City of Mexico, was suddenly destroyed in some past age by an overflow of water and mud, and that its remains are still existent on the spot. Many massive walls have been found, but they are covered with a mass of deposited earth, sixty feet in thickness. And mingled in this earth are human skeletons, the tusks of elephants, etc., distributed in a way which indicates that the overflow of water and mud was sudden, giving no time for escape... According to the estimates of the scientists under whose directions the excavations are now being made, the city in question had a population of least 50, 000.

The destruction which was brought by the flood was complete. All the inhabitants of the cities were killed, as well as all the animals. Skeletons of the human inhabitants of the cities and of the animals are strewn all through the debris, from a depth of three feet from the surface to a depth of sixty feet, showing that all the debris was deposited almost at once. Measurements show that the debris is on an average, sixty feet deep where the largest of the cities stood.

Most remarkable of the minor finds that have been made at Paredon is that of the remains of elephants. Never before in the history of Mexico has it been ascertained positively that elephants were ever in the service of the ancient inhabitants. The remains of the elephants that have been found in Paredon show plainly that the inhabitants of the buried cities made elephants work for them. Elephants were as much in evidence in cities as horses. Upon many of the tusks that have been found were rings of silver. Most of the tusks encountered so far have an average length for grown elephants, of three feet, and an average diameter at the roots of six inches. Judging from the remains of the elephants so far unearthed, the animals were about ten feet in height and sixteen to eighteen feet in length, differing very little from those at present in existence.

The idea of elephants in the Americas in antiquity is quickly labeled *intrusive*, which is a favorite concept for some scientists who find that the data do not conform to theory. When evidence is discovered contrary to accepted dogma, some archaeologists will dig and worm their way into the soil until they come up with the discrepancies they want, and then explain away evidence that would conflict with his or her theory, using a spurious argument phrased in customary scientific phrases.

We can see how many of these scientists come to the conclusions they do and that is in part because of fraudulent artifacts that have become so popular. Such is the case with some of the Burrows Cave artifacts. Fig. 161 is more than likely such a fake. It does not conform to the time line of other elephant artifacts brought forth over the past century or as seen on age old rock panels. It's obviously a modern rendition. This would make any archaeologist cringe at the sight!

Fig. 161 Burrows Cave Elephant

Fig. 162 Father Crespi Collection

Figure 162 is an excellent example of what is believed to be an authentic artifact depicting the elephant. Here, etched in stone and having gone through an extensive study by BYU Archaeologist, the late Dr. Paul Cheesman, is what has been named the "Cuenca Elephant Stone" from the Crespi Collection in Ecuador. Unfortunately, this stone has been copied over and over and used as an exact copy by educators and other professionals. It is obvious that those who copied the stone were unfamiliar with the text. A simple mistake on one character will cause the piece to become recognized as a fake. The stone was discovered during an excavation of an airport in Cuenca. It was later copied incorrectly and used on the cover of *ESOP*, Vol., 3, Part 2. A corrected version was later published by Dr. Barry Fell.

Figures 163 and 164, are fakes but used and promoted as a reproduction of an authentic artifact

As Fred Rydholm wrote, "Ironically, the Illinois forger chose the wrong illustration to copy, and thus the newly 'excavated' tablet is the 1976 version, with a misshapen 'ya' symbol, and copyrighted by the Society. Thus the ludicrous situation arises that the 'antique' from Illinois has infringed the registered copyright of a drawing first published in 1976."

Megafauna bones have been discovered all over the western hemisphere. One source at Big Bone Lick, Kentucky, became one of the richest late Pleistocene deposits in eastern North America. Professor Paul Martin of the University of Arizona commented on this rich area, stating *"two samples of wood initially thought to be associated with bones of extinct species proved to be modern."* It may be true what Martin said, however, it also may prove that the elephant and other megafauna and man lived together later than most agree.

George Gaylord Simpson wrote an essay that is very interesting for investigators on this subject. He wrote:

In 1762 John Bartam, the Philadelphia Quaker who supplied Linnaeus and other European naturalists with descriptions and specimens of American plants and animals, heard that a large tooth and a fragment of a tusk had been brought to Fort Pitt by some Indians. He requested his friend James Wright to make inquiries among the Indians

264

concerning the place where these objects had been found. Through an interpreter, Wright secured an account of the site which came to be known as Big Bone Lick. According to Wright's informants, the lick contained five entire skeletons, the heads pointing toward a common center. The bones were of enormous size and were accompanied by tusks ten or twelve feet long. No such creatures as these had ever been seen alive by the Indians, but legend said that they had once been hunted through the forests by men of gigantic stature and that when the last of these men had died, God had destroyed their mighty prey in order to protect the present race of Indians.

Here is convincing evidence of elephants and other megafauna being upon our lands. It is also possible that elephants were brought here by ship when the North Africans set sail for the New World. Some evidence points to that possibility.

OGAM SCRIPT AND VARIATIONS ON A THEME

There are literally thousands of stones, rocks and tablets with script or animals inscribed on them. However, there is a form of writing that has been found throughout much of America that really raises the eyebrows of conventional archaeologists, scientists, epigraphers, etc.

Early on in the year 1712, Queen Anne of England ruled both at home and abroad in the Colonies of North America. During this time learned scholars under her direction were busy studying rock cairns, henges, strange writings and more and then reporting back to the Royal Society of London. A famous antiquary named Edward Lhyd reported to the Society that he had just discovered a previously unknown script engraved on a stone at Trabeg, near Dingle, in County Kerry. Lhyd had no idea what the inscriptions meant or the language in which it was written, but hoped someone in the Society might shed some light on his discovery. During the same time the Dighton Rock was discovered. (See Fig. 135.)

Barry Fell describes the way the British Society felt concerning the discoveries such as these, writing in *America B.C.* [1989, Chapter 3]:

No further advance in epigraphy was made for two generations, during which time span America became a separate nation, with her own learned societies publishing their own records of research and philosophical inquiry. One unfortunate result was that whereas Lhyd's inscription in Ireland continued to exercise the minds of savants in Britain, Cotton Mather's report from New England now ceased to have any direct interest for British investigators and (since it was recorded in a British journal) it was simply forgotten in America. This was the parting of the ways of British and American antiquaries, as well illustrated by the subsequent fate of the two reports that had been made in 1712. In contrast to the oblivion that now enveloped Cotton Mather's letter, the corresponding letter from Lhyd was to generate both a controversy and eventual enlightenment.

More than seventy years later, on June 24, 1784, a letter was received by the Society of Antiquaries in London from a certain Colonel Charles Vallancey, in Ireland, informing the Society that he had discovered an ancient Irish tombstone on Mount Callan, County Clare. He had been able to decipher the writing on it, so he reported, and found that it marked the grave of an ancient Irish chieftain named Conan Colgac. This startling information was accompanied by an explanation of how the decipherment had been carried out, and how he had recognized the writing as a script called "Ogam," identical with the unknown script that Lhyd had reported three generations earlier.

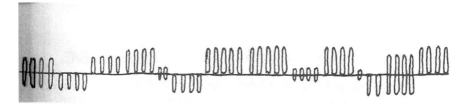

Fig. 165 Edward Lhyd's transcription of the Ogam inscribed at Dingle, County Kerry

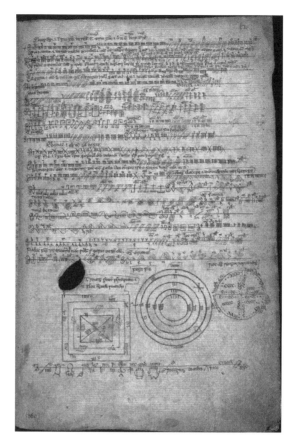

Fig. 166 The Ogam Tract in the Book of Ballymote shows a number of different alphabets known to the medieval author of the tract. The variety shown in the second line, called "Hinge Ogam" is one that occurs in North America, the vowels however being omitted from the American version.

Fig. 167 "Hinge Ogam"

267

Fig. 168   Michigan Tablet with Hinge Ogam Script.

American Ogam is not the only Ogam found in America. Several styles or varieties have surfaced over the years including the earlier style discovered by Lhyd. How or why these styles were used is the big question. Do they even read the same, are they forgeries, a prank, or are they authentic? Michigan tablets bearing American Ogam as well as hundreds of other tablets were long buried in mounds where huge trees grew and some were entangled in the aged old root system. They dated back to the Adena and Hopewell timelines, and that with the Hinge Ogam, and other ancient scripts should authenticate them as true artifacts of antiquity. Our west has its share of Ogam script. Some of the script is very strange but nevertheless it is still Ogam in one form or another. The following photographs will give the reader an idea of the diversity of Ogam script in the western part of our country. [See *America B.C..* Dr. Barry Fell, 1989, Chapter 3.]

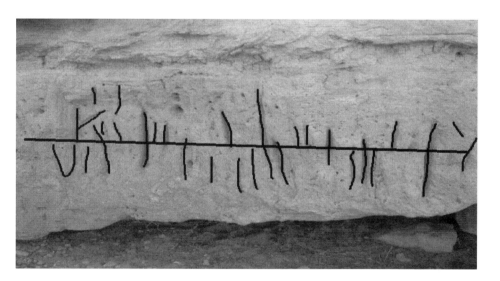

Fig. 169 Northwestern Arizona Ogam

 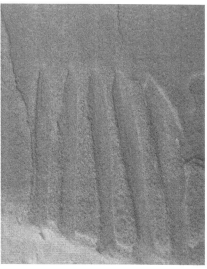

Fig. 170 Unidentified Ogam   Fig. 171 The equinox calendar

Both of these examples are from Utah's Navajo Reservation.

Fig. 172 Ogam from Nevada   Fig. 173 Ogam from Arizona

Fig. 174 Found near Cedar Mountain Utah   Fig. 175 Damaged Ogam

Fig. 176 Horse Creek panel

Figure 177 Virgin Birth Record in Stone

This panel has been deciphered to read: "She gave birth to a son in a cave; the name of the cave was the Cave of Bethlehem. His foster-father gave him the name Jesus, the Christ, Alpha and Omega. Festive season of prayer."

Ogam has been discovered in California as well. This style of Ogam is not the usual horizontal baseline or vertical baseline. The Celts wrote horizontal Ogam from left to right, but there is a Semitic form found on the Iberian Peninsula and in North Africa, written from right to left. There are several criteria used to determine whether a petroglyph is genuine Ogam or merely random scratches on rock. One is the presence of the baseline, which is sometimes only implied by the relative positions of other strokes. A second determinative is the number of strokes present and their particular grouping. A single Ogam letter may be from one to five strokes. If there are six or more it is most likely a number. Circle Ogam with holes in the center I refer to as "Solstice Zones." A stick inserted in the hole will cast a shadow, which will give the time of year. The site in California is a prime example how this works. Steve Bartholomew wrote an excellent article on the California Ogam Stones in *Ancient American Magazine* Issue # 61.

Ogam script in all its hundreds of styles is still being studied and analyzed. Finding this script in Northwestern Arizona was an exciting time for me. I couldn't believe what I saw! It was out of place, but knowing this made it all the more intriguing. Not only is it on the walls but on the ceiling and hidden behind large boulders. This site with its known history coupled with this new discovery is exciting.

CUP MARKS AND OGAM SCRIPT

In 2012, I was contacted by a man that claimed he had heard of a strange piece of pottery that came from a cave site in northwestern Arizona. He wanted to know if I would be interested in seeing the piece should he be able to acquire it. I assured him that I would very much like to see the piece and learn of its history. It was unfortunate that the cave had been pilfered years earlier by pot hunters. It was learned that besides pottery being taken there was a very fine pipe and arrows, shafts, feathers and points. It was much later that a young woman who had heard of the site was digging there when she unearthed a terracotta piece that appeared to be out of place for that environment.

Fig. 178a Author with cremation pits in Arizona

After a period of time my contact arranged a meeting between us so he could show me the piece that he had finally acquired from the young lady. Upon meeting with (I will call him Dave), I was surprised at what I saw. It was nothing like I supposed it to be and it was definitely part of the ever growing list of ooparts.

I learned that above the cave on top of the mesa there once stood an ancient Pueblo village. Pottery, arrow and spear points are still being discovered there, but not very many know of the hidden cave and over-hanging ledges just below the top of the mesa. Getting down to the area where the piece was discovered takes little effort, but without knowing where the trail is, one would not even know anything was there.

Once in the cave entrance I was shown where the piece was found. It was very apparent it was not part of the Pueblo group above and fur-thermore, I discovered three pits that contained human remains. Just above the center pit (see fig. 178a) is a small hole in the wall of the cave where the piece was extracted from.

Fig. 178 Terra-cotta effigy   Fig. 179 TLAZOLTEOTL

Figures 168, 171 and 172 are but a few of the examples of Ogam script found at the site where the effigy figure was discovered. This all seemed very strange because here we have three distinct cultures assembled at the same site and what appears to be around the same time line. Figures 178 and 179 represent the Goddess TLAZOLTEOTL, c 1300 – 1521, who was an earth, sex, childbirth and mother goddess. She was referred to as "Eater of Filth" because she visited people at the end of their lives to eat filth (sins) they confessed to on their deathbeds.

Most Tlazolteotl goddesses are made from Jade. Our goddess is terra-cotta. One of the legs was broken off from our goddess but was salvaged and sent to Professor James Feathers at the University of Washington Seattle for thermoluminescent testing.

Upon further inspection of the area it was determined that whoever inhabited these caverns worshiped the stars and planets. In a nearby hidden chamber we discovered what may very well be their rendition of our solar system. Or, perhaps these "cup markings" were used much like those found on prehistoric monuments in Briton. I observed at this site numerous circles, single and concentric, in groups or clusters which generally resembled the prehistoric markings of ancient Greco-

Phœnician and Syrio-Phœnicia contained analogous groups of circles associated with the same divinities as in the Briton coins, and that many of the whorls of terra-cotta dug up from the ruins of ancient Troy by Schliemann.

Fig. 180 Cup Marks indicating Planets or Numbers

However, I am not saying this site has anything to do with that period; I'm only showing the similarities. There are many strange designs using "Cup Marks" in this cave area. There are groupings of cups, lines of cups, either interacting with Ogam script or alone. They appear on the boulders, ceiling and the walls. Some take on the appearance of normal decay of the strata while others have the appearance of a superior hand in creating them.

Looking at Hitto-Sumerian Seals one can make out familiar patterns seen in the Cup Markers at this site with those used anciently.

Fig. 181 Ogam with "cup marks"

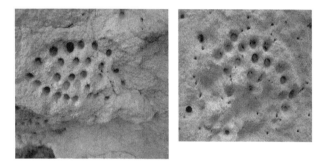

Figs.182 -183 Examples of the "Cup Marks" in groups.

We are puzzled by what we have seen here. Without needed artifacts to extract the history of the area, besides the Ancestral Pueblo who lived on top of the mesa, we have nothing to go on but what we can see and determine by our knowledge and experience. Once we have information back from Professor Feathers we might begin to see what happened here. We are now searching for any persons that have excavated the site legally or illegally so we can get to the bottom of this very exciting and mysterious story. The story of a long lost culture or a secret society is written here. In stone!

7

RUMORS: ANCIENT SOUTH AMERICA

"The topaz blazing like a lamp, Among the mines beneath."
—The Song of David A.D. 1760

"I have but one object: to bare the mysteries that the jungle fastnesses of South America have concealed for so many centuries. We are encouraged in our hope of finding the ruins of an ancient, white civilization [sic] and the degenerate offspring of a once cultivated race."

—This was the last message sent to London, England over the Overland Brazilian telegraph in Rondonia, by Col. P.H. Fawcett, April 20, 1925.

TAYOS CAVE

The story of Tayos Cave is not a new one. Much has been written on it since Fawcett's time. Explorers have searched long and hard but few have ever seen it or lived to tell about it. Ancient South America is as important to history as North America, and may even be of more importance.

Let's digress for the moment to give a little history of Ancient South America and what makes it worth discussing here. We begin with a report filed March 23, 1773, where by accident a Brazilian city was discovered that was deemed "Dead." *It was found in the wilds of the Rio Pequéry [spelled Pequeri in current listings].*

The report said that a fisherman, jumping ashore on a sandbank in the Rio Pequéry, in order to plunder a grove of wild limes and sweet oranges, found a curiously shaped stone of large diameter. He said it was like a mos de moinhos (grindstone of a mill-wheel). Nearby were the ruins of a house and an ancient stone wall. The commandant of the fort sent out from the garrison a canoe, manned by a sergeant and two ensigns, or soldiers, who penetrated the thick and unexplored forest and found vestiges of a city of unknown date. Said they:

> This ancient city is regularly laid out, and is of large size. It had a street that is half a league long. The city stood on the banks of two rivers and had a walled suburb. Moats stood between the city and the suburb; we unearthed two more of the strange mill-wheels, while we were making a stockade. All round are dense forests, the old men of the country side have traditions that a city stood on this spot which was called Guayra.

The unnamed fisherman from Medellin said that gold had been found and "*a lot of gold too!*" *He mentioned various tribes of "Indiós bravos (wild and unpacifiable Indians) whose territories they touched. Tribes such as the Uapes, Guaipunyos, Metas, the Cirecois, the Eperemenos, and the redoubtable Carib,*" whom not even the early conquistadores were able to subdue, and also from written histories that the territories are filled with pygmies and white Indians.

The man of Medellin continued his story of adventure into the heartland of Brazil and the headwaters of the mighty Amazon. "*There are dwarfish men, about four feet tall, with very red eyes. They have a thick bushy beard that reaches below the waist, and the arms were fat with muscles. Round the waist they usually wore a leather belt with gold buckles of some sort, other than that they are nude. These men are sickly white. Their women are beautiful with long hair, and either red or bluish eyes. They too are nude and their hair reaches down to their feet. They wear gold bracelets on their arms and gold necklets.*"

Whether or not anyone believes the story by the fisherman of Medellin, he claims it to be true. This same man told explorer Harold T. Wilkins a fantastic tale. He told him that he and others explored a great pyramid-temple whose interior fairly blazed with gold. It sheathed the pillars, the roofs and the walls. Strange letters were engraved on the gold plates. Some parts of the dead city were inaccessible. In fact, it would seem that only the suburbs of the dead city were entered by the roaming explorers. Wilkins' informant told him:

> In some of the pyramid-temples we entered, we saw deep, blue-veined marble alters, stained with ancient blood, or rust. Perhaps of ancient sac-

rifices, or, maybe, of some horrible cult of the decayed remnants of this very ancient civilization. But the gold, señor, not even the Incas had so much to hide when Don Francisco Pizarro killed the Emperor Atahualpha. High overhead, there were alcoves or galleries actually stuffed with splendid gold objects, vessels, chains, chalices, insignia, and shields and plates engraved with the strange hieroglificos. Some of these plates were three or four inches thick, all solid gold, tons, kilogrammes of it, señor. I took one of the gold knives in one of the temples. Eight or ten of them had been attached to one of the pillars. The hilts and the blades were marvelously chased and engraved, as by the finest goldsmiths ever known. Looking up, in another splendid ruined stone building, which cut into the side of the hill, I staggered with amazement to see eight glorious suns, of pure, shining, blazing gold from which rays were made to shine out like stars. Groups of handsome men, beautiful women, naked youths and maidens were carved on the walls of this mausoleum, and over their heads and shoulders, like the halo or nimbus round the head of the Virgin, and the Saints of God, shone stars or moons or pure shining gold. Chains hung down from the alcoves and pillars, and friezes were inscribed with strange signs in rows.

Did I tell you, señor, that each of the dwarfs in the outskirts of this dead city, living either in tunnels, or rooms in the rock, or the little stone houses we saw, carried a long curved knife of pure gold? It was not valued here. I could tell you a lot more especially about a queer sort of lock, like a stick with 9 rings, each ring forming one of the queer letters or hieroglificos, which we found on a gold chain in one of the queer pyramids. Apparently, you turned it to form a combination to open or lock the fetters.

The last message sent to London by Colonel Fawcett contained the warning that he might not be heard of for two or more years. According to Wilkins, Fawcett said that the dead city of the mountains was guarded by a strange race of troglodytes or small, squat Negros of ferocious disposition who were cannibals. Fawcett seems to have told no one where he located the dead city that was inhabited by these savage tribes.

If Colonel Fawcett became lost in the jungles of the Amazon, did he die in the jungle? Did he ever find what he was looking for? Now new blood explores the jungles in search for the caves of the ancients.

A very good friend of mine, Manuel Palacios Villavicencio has been searching for these caves and ancient sites for years. He has written extensively on the subject. Born and raised in Ecuador, Palacios has made it a lifelong quest to get into this *"Cave of Records" spoken of by certain natives.*

Fig. 184 Manuel Palacios (left) with unidentified friend holding two silver artifacts from the Crespi Collection

ARTIFACTS FROM THE CRESPI COLLECTION

Our story takes a turn here to re-introduce our readers to Father Carlos Crespi. He was born in Legnano, near Milan, Italy, on May 29, 1891. Despite statements of some sources, Crespi was not born into a family of dukes. At fifteen, he entered the novitiate in Foglizzo, and was subsequently ordained in Verona at twenty-six. Four years were spent studying at the University of Padua, with a thesis in anthropology, for which he earned a master's degree. Later he earned his doctorate in Natural Sciences.

Crespi came to Ecuador in 1923. It wasn't until he encountered an ancient potsherd during an excavation of the foundation for the Escuela Cornelio Merchan, a school for indigent Ecuadorian children, that he began to collect items from hungry Indians who would bring him amazing artifacts in exchange for money or food. He was a great humanitarian and was highly regarded within the ranks of the local citizens. Dr.

Warren L. Cook wrote an excellent paper on Crespi that can be read in *Ancient American Magazine Volume 11 No. 68.*

I bring the reader forward to the time I met the late Wendelle C. Stevens who visited Crespi and his little museum at Cuenca. There, Stevens was shown an array of artifacts that would change the way scholars view ancient South America.

Some of these ooparts were discovered in caves, embedded in foot-deep bat guano, or taken from ancient tunnels deep within the jungles of Ecuador. Moreover, it was reported tunnels ran for miles—filled with ancient artifacts of all types. Stevens brought with him the photos he took of some of the artifacts.

Over the years we became friends, and just before his death he gave me permission to publish the artifacts he was allowed to photograph at the little museum. Since the collection is vast, I have chosen those I felt would shed further light on those inhabited South America, or who had influenced the natives to create such wonderful pieces of art. [See the Shaffer Digital Library for full-color images of these photos and many other artifacts.]

Fig. 185 Crespi   Fig. 186 Solid Gold

Fig. 187 Several tablets of the Crespi Collection inscribed with indecipherable text

They have been identified by some scholars as "Neo-Libyan". However, Dr. Barry Fell opined they were more likely from an unknown form of early Cypriot.

Fig. 188   Fig. 189

Fig. 188 is a gold relief of what appears to be a High Priest or King. The snake staff at the left and the serpent-looking throne he is sitting on suggests that he ruled by using witchcraft. Although the term "witchcraft" is a rather emotionally charged term, and ancient societies and cultures used images such as serpents in their artifacts or writings, it does not pre-suppose an evil intent or origin—even when it differs from Judeo/Christian thought.

Fig. 189 seems to be the artifact most studied by linguists and epigraphers. Dr. Warren L. Cook was something of a genius, with both written and spoken fluency in German, French, Portuguese and Spanish. He attended the Universidad Nacional Mayor de San Marcos, the oldest university in the Western Hemisphere, located in Lima, Peru. There, he earned his first Doctorate of Letters. He continued his education at Yale University where he obtained an M.A. and Ph.D. His award winning doctoral dissertation was published by Yale University Press and nominated for the Pulitzer Prize in 1973. Subsequent research of pre-Conquest cultures in the Peruvian Andes gained him international acclaim and distinction among his academic peers. Said he of this tablet:

Not only the fine execution of this metal tablet, but its consistent and intricate historical detail are far beyond the capabilities of desperately impoverished, uneducated Ecuadoran Indians. The relief image appears to portray a Syrian or Phoenician astrologer-priest (note the stars depicted beneath the cosmic serpent), and may have originally decorated a shrine or temple as early as circa 1100 B.C., when Phoenician mariners began long-distance voyaging, to the mid-1st century A.D, which witnessed the last manifestation of Phoenician culture in North Africa kingdom of Mauretania.

The artifacts in Crespi's collection spanned many hundreds of years and cultures. Gold, silver, bronze, copper and iron was housed in his little museum. Some artifacts had been dubbed "fakes" for different reasons. Like so many other collections, if one or two artifacts from a given collection have been proven to be fakes or of dubious authenticity, then it casts a dark shadow of impropriety on the whole collection. Some of the most elaborate items were cast bronze plaques, using a lost wax process. Others are castings reflective of the same motifs encompassing several distinct cultures that many believed to have originated in Ecuador, and by a local artisan. We may never know the truth.

Fig. 190. In Assyrian myth, a winged genie dispensed blessings with an acorn dipped in holy water. Although the acorn in its right hand has been effaced, a portion of the container is still partially visible above the knee. The eagle's head personified spiritual power. Receiving the genie's blessing, the central figure is a priest holding another emblem of regeneration, the lotus flower. Significance of the coiffured head (far right) is unknown. The rendering of such obscure, even arcane symbolism, and in so competent a style, defines this Crespi Collection object as physical proof of ancient Near Eastern influence in Ecuador.[22]

SPECIAL ARTIFACTS

Wendelle Stevens told me of three fantastic artifacts that Father Crespi valued more than all the rest. The "Zodiac Plate," measuring 51 inches X 13 Inches with fifty-six symbols embossed on copper alloy, a rectangular "Pyramid Plaque," embossed on the same type of alloy, and a large brownish ceramic jar bearing symbols that may be either Cypriot or Quechuan. Stevens stated that not all of the artifacts were accessible, nor even permitted to be photographed. However, after some discussion he was allowed to see a few of them.

Fig. 191   Chieftain   Fig. 192   "Zodiac Tablet"

Fig. 193

These three metal artifacts may depict astronomer priests, given the prominence of stars in each one. Each piece seems to refer to the mastery of their office. Note the bearded figure at the far left, the Phoenician at the center and the oriental at far right.

Fig. 194 Bonnie Stevens, Father Crespi and Wendelle Stevens

Fig. 195 Some of the more valuable artifacts of the Collection

Fig. 196 High Priest.   Fig. 197   King or Wizard

Fig. 19 8 Note the little heads at the   Fig. 199 A dwarf imp
bottom and on his person

Note: Readers are invited to subscribe to the SDL (Shaffer Digital Library) to learn the "rest of the story" on these and many other mysteries as well as to stay current with breaking news, new discoveries and more insights about Ancient America. For more information about later news regarding the disposition of Crespi's artifacts following his death, follow this link: http://www.ancient-origins.net/news-general/truth-about-father-crespi-and-his-missing-artifacts-finally-revealed-005498

Fig. 200 A silver skeleton   Fig. 201   Fine gold

Fig. 202 Crespi with a large copper sheet with inscriptions on it

Fig. 203 A skeleton in a casket of pure gold and an Assyrian High Priest, or wizard

Fig. 204   Two items thought to be fakes.

Fig 205 Tablet with Inscriptions

I am showing this tablet (see also Fig. 187) for the purpose of bringing to the attention of the reader that no circular letters are seen in this primitive alphabet. Claims to this being an early form of Cypriot may be a bit premature. Some of these figures and a few modified later on suggest these letters were brought out of Egypt into Greece and that they may be an early form of the Eastern Greek alphabet.

Unfortunately, this great collection has been dis-assembled and, in part, taken out of South America to Europe—stolen, destroyed, lost and some artifacts returned to the caves from which they came. Many objects have been authenticated while others have been dubbed "fakes." *As with all artifacts, there are the nay-sayers and the proponents. Although many of these artifacts fall into the "ooparts" category, many do not. If that great cave of records is ever found and archaeologists are allowed to enter and investigate what may be there, we will have re-discovered one of the greatest literary libraries of all time. [See Tayos Gold: The Archives of Atlantis*, Stan Hall, 2006 for more background on this discovery.]

Note: This link may provide updated information regarding the Crespi Collection

http://www.ancient-origins.net/news-general/truth-about-father-crespi-and-his-missing-artifacts-finally-revealed-005498

8

FICTIONS & MYTHS: STRANGE STORIES

"Unorthodoxy breeds contempt, but facts breed reality."
—Author unknown

Perhaps one of the strangest stories of the early 20th century was that of G.A. Kincaid. The story has been published numerous times; however, for those who haven't read it or know much about it, we repeat the story here *and include* further information for your reading and studying.

It was late in 1881 that the Smithsonian Institute committed itself to the idea of Isolationism, thereby deciding (on their own initiative) that there never was or had been very little contact between ancient civilizations of the east to the America shores. When new evidence contrary to their view began to surface, there commenced an active suppression of any knowledge or proof relating to these discoveries. As Professor Gunnar Thompson so bluntly but accurately put it:

> In order to protect vested interests, the custodians of orthodoxy invented a bastardized form of "science" that really wasn't scientific at all. Enlightened thinkers who came close to the truth were branded as heretics and expelled from the academic community. Those who found artifacts that challenged established beliefs were called "hoaxers." Those who tested the ability of ancient mariners to sail across the oceans were described as "non-scientific adventures.

EXTRAORDINARY DISCOVERY

G.A. Kincaid Photos

On April 5, 1909, a lengthy front page story in the *Phoenix Gazette* gave a highly detailed report of the discovery and excavation of a rock-cut vault in the Grand Canyon. The expedition, led by a Professor S.A. Jordan of the Smithsonian Institution and a man named G.A. Kincaid, an explorer working with Jordan, supposedly discovered a network of caverns, artificially hewn into the side of the canyon wall. The explorers described hundreds of rooms radiating from a central point like spokes in a wheel. Everywhere they looked, hieroglyphics were to be seen, as well as Egyptian artifacts.

Kincaid was the first white child born in Idaho. He had been an explorer and hunter all his life, serving 30 years with the Smithsonian. In his brief to the Smithsonian he wrote:

> *I was journeying down the Colorado river in a boat alone, looking for mineral. Some 42 miles up the river from El Tovar Crystal Canyon, I saw on the east wall, stains in the sedimentary formation about 2,000 feet above the river bed. There was no trail to this point, but I finally reached it with great difficulty. Above a shelf which hid it from view of the river, was the mouth of a cave. There are steps leading from the entrance some 30 yards to what was, at the time the cavern was inhabited, the level of the river. When I saw the chisel marks on the wall inside the entrance, I*

became interested [and] securing my gun went in. During that trip I went back several hundred feet along the main passage until I came to the crypt in which I discovered the mummies. One of these I stood up and photographed by flashlight. I gathered a number of relics, which I carried down the Colorado to Yuma from whence I shipped them to Washington with details of the discovery. Following this, the explorations were undertaken.

Kincaid's report continued:

The main passageway is about 12 feet wide, narrowing to 9 feet toward the farther end. About 57 feet from the entrance, the first side-passages branch off to the right and left, along which, on both sides, are a number of rooms about the size of ordinary living rooms to today, though some are 30 by 40 feet square. These are entered by oval-shaped doors and are ventilated by round air spaces through the walls into the passages. The walls are about 3 feet six inches in thickness. The passages are chiseled or hewn as straight as could be laid out by an engineer. The ceilings of many of the rooms converge to a center. The side-passages near the entrance run at a sharp angle from the main hall, but toward the rear they gradually reach a right angle in direction.

The fantastical tale continues with even more amazing disclosures:

Over a hundred feet from the entrance is the cross-hall, several hundred feet long, in which are [is] found the idol, or image, of the people's god, sitting cross-legged, with a lotus flower or lily in each hand. There are two large cactus with protruding arms, one on each side of the Dias on which the god squats. All this is carved out of hard rock resembling marble. In the opposite corner of this cross-hall were found tools of all descriptions, made of copper. These people undoubtedly know the lost art of hardening this metal, which has been sought by chemists for centuries without result.

As if that weren't enough, the author describes still more amazing discoveries:

Among the other finds are vases or urns and cups of copper and gold, made very artistic in design. The pottery work includes enameled ware and glazed vessels. A grey metal is also found in this cavern, which puzzles the scientists, for its identity has not been established. It resembles platinum. One room, about 40 by 700 feet, was probably the main dining hall, for cooking utensils are found here. Upwards of 50,000 people could have lived in the caverns comfortably.

One thing I have not spoken of may be of interest. There is one chamber, the passageway to which is not ventilated, and when we approached it a deadly, snaky smell struck us. Our light would not penetrate the gloom, and until stronger ones are available we will not know what the chamber contains. No sounds are heard, but it smells snaky just the same. The whole underground installation gives one of shaky nerves the creeps. The gloom is like a weight on one's shoulders, and our flashlights and candles only make the darkness blacker. Imagination can revel in conjectures and ungodly daydreams back through the ages that have elapsed till the mind reels dizzily in space.

On all the urns, or walls over doorways, are tablets of stone which were found by the image are the mysterious hieroglyphics, the key to which the Smithsonian Institute hopes yet to discover. The engraving on the tables probably has something to do with the religion of the people. Similar hieroglyphics have been found in southern Arizona. Among the pictorial writings, only two animals are found. One is of prehistoric type.

The saga continues unabated in its descriptions of yet additional finds:

The tomb or crypt is which the mummies were found is one of the largest of the chambers, the walls slanting back at an angle of 35 degrees. On these are tiers of mummies, each one occupying a separate hewn shelf. At the head of each is a small bench, on which is found copper cups and pieces of broken swords. Some of the mummies are covered with clay, and all are wrapped in a bark fabric.

The urns or cups on the lower tiers are crude, while as the higher shelves are reached, the urns are finer in design, showing a later stage of civilization. It is worthy of note that all the mummies examined so far have proved to be male, no children or females being buried here. This leads to the belief that this exterior section was the warriors' barracks.

Among the discoveries no bones of animals have been found, no skins, no clothing, no bedding. Many of the rooms are bare but for water vessels. What these people lived on is a problem, though it is presumed that they came south in the winter and farmed in the valleys, going back in the summer.

. . . One theory is that the present Indian tribes found in Arizona are descendants of the serfs or slaves of the people which inhabited the cave.

Undoubtedly a good many thousands of years before the Christian era, a people lived here which reached a high stage of civilization. The chronology of human history is full of gaps. Professor Jordan is much enthused over the discoveries and believes that the find will prove to find calculable value in archeological work.

There are a few theories of the origin of the Egyptian people according to some. One theory is that they came from Asia; another theory holds forth that the racial cradle was in the upper Nile region, and believes the Indian origin of the Egyptians—namely—that the Burrows Cave Egyptian discoveries have a direct connection with the Grand Canyon discovery—that they might be one and the same people. However, since we have *no* evidence, no artifacts—nothing at all—what can be proven?

THE KINCAID EGG

Supposedly, the only artifact that came out of the Grand Canyon was sneaked out by Kincaid himself; he personally took it back to Idaho.

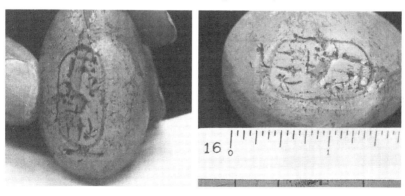

Fig. 206 The Kincaid Egg   Fig. 207 Another view of the Kincaid Egg

In the photos above is what is referred to as the "Kincaid Egg." It was given to a woman by the name of Kathy Kincaid. According to the recipient of this stone, she acquired it from her great-grandmother:

This very interesting 'artifact' was found by my great-grandmother Laura B. Sloan at the turn of the century in the state of Idaho. The egg was given to me approximately three years prior to her death. Discovery that the carvings on the egg was Egyptian was brought to light by the November 1976 publication of a Smithsonian (article on

King Tut's Treasure). Heretofore it was thought that the carvings were Indian petroglyphs. Known facts about the egg:

- Family possession of 77 years. (No tests have been taken at this time to determine age of material)
- Carved from quartz-like stone
- Microscopic examination verifies that the shape and carvings are hand-hewn
- Weight is .253 lbs
- Girth dimensions are 1.495 x 1.495 inches diameter
- Height dimension is 2. 085 inches

Point of interest: The incredible exactness of the hand-carved shape of the egg. Calculations of the known dimensions of the pyramids of Egypt disclose the hypotenuse or pitch angle inch to be 1.0510 inches. The height of the egg divided by two is 1.0425 inches, within .009 inches of the calculation.

When Kathy Kincaid decided to go public with the stone, she contacted local reporter Ted Krec of the Garden Grove newspaper to tell her story. Krec wrote:

Wide-eyed Kathy Kincaid of Garden Grove is a little awed by it all, for she may have uncovered one of the archaeological mysteries of the ages.

The center of the mystery is an egg-shaped, quartz-like piece of stone weighing about a quarter of pound, about one and one half inches in diameter and a little more than two inches long. The stone has been in her family about 77 years, ever since her great-grandmother found it when she was a girl in Idaho back at the turn of the century.

Great-grandmother Laura B. Sloan later gave it to Kathy and told her it was an Indian artifact; it has carvings on opposite sides of the surface.

Curious about the stone, Kathy had some photos taken of the carvings and sent them to Frank A. Norick, principal museum curator at University of California, Berkeley.

She was stunned by Norick's reply. He said it could be an unfinished mace head or an early darning egg of some sort, but the carving isn't Indian, it's Egyptian. Furthermore it's the personal seal of King Tutankhamen, who ruled in Egypt about 1352 B.C.!

Here's the mystery—the stone was found in Idaho at the turn of the century and King Tutankhamen's tomb was not discovered until 1922!

She still doesn't know for sure what the stone is, but she knows it must be super-valuable. She's looking for more information. Meanwhile, to be safe, the creamy-colored egg is locked up in a safe deposit box.

Kathy is anxious to interest a museum in taking it on a loan basis, as soon as she finds out exactly what it is, so that the public can share in the mystery of how an Egyptian King Tut relic could be found in Idaho 22 years before the tomb of King Tutankhamen was discovered by Howard Carver and Lord Carnarvon in 1922!

A couple of more bizarre facts, Kathy's dad computed the egg's measurements and came up with the shocker that it is scaled in the so-called "Pyramid Inch"—the measurement used by the ancients in the construction of the Egyptian pyramids. [Interestingly, Ra—the Egyptian sun-god, supposedly came out of an egg.]

Kathy Kincaid got busy by sending out numerous letters around the country looking for answers. As the word got out, more people became interested. In a letter written 23 May 1977, to Dr. Paul Cheesman we find the following:

Dear Bro. Cheesman:

I was quite surprised this week to discover that right next door, as it were, there is a woman who may have something that may be of interest to the Church.

I am sending you the enclosed article for your evaluation. I know nothing more about it than is in the article.

I have some theories of my own that probably only Latter-day Saints would understand. If this item seems to be of any real significance I would appreciate hearing your conclusions.

The letter was signed by M. Kay Johnson, Ed D, Director of the Santa Ana Institute.

Johnson and Cheesman corresponded back and forth; then on April 20, 1978, Cheesman penned the following response to Johnson:

Enclosed please find the original pictures belonging to the Kincaids. I have copied them and have forwarded them to Boston to get the best opinion. As soon as I hear from him I will let you know.

The final correspondence between the two men as far as we can determine was on March 31, 1978, where Kay Johnson wrote on Huntington Beach Institute of Religion letterhead:

In mid-march I met with Mrs. Kincaid who is the owner of the egg-shaped stone. I got the impression that her main interest is in the monetary value of the stone; but be that as it may, perhaps her stone can help us further verify links between Egypt and the ancient Americans.

As I indicated on the phone, she is only loaning the pictures and wants to have them returned. She is loaning them with the intent that you will provide her the best expert opinion you can get, both your own as well as other sources you may have. She seemed to be quite anxious and I promised her that as soon as anything worthwhile is known that she would be informed.

While I would appreciate being kept abreast of any meaningful information that may develop, you may have reason to contact her directly. I cannot be sure of her address as she was reluctant to give it. It may be the same as on the Xeroxed attachments; at any rate her phone number is in Garden Grove, Calif. Her father, however, that you will read about in some of the attachments, is now in Parowan, Utah and is anxious to talk to anyone "official" such as yourself, and I believe she has mentioned you to him. I suspect he knows more about the stone than she does. His address is:

Herbert C. Kincaid

P.O. 819

Parowan, Utah

She will allow the stone to be examined only in her presence. She has not submitted it for scientific dating for fear of any damage that might occur. The attachments are pretty much self-explanatory. The magazine page is from the article in the Smithsonian, referred to in her story. She saw it in a doctor's office and recognized the carvings as the same as those on her egg. She said the stone is the same color and looks like the same material as in the colored pictures.

With this letter and the attachments, you will know as much about it as I do. I realize you are busy in both your professional and ecclesiastical pursuits, but would appreciate knowing whenever anything turns up that is worth knowing.

Sincerely,

M. Kay Johnson, Ed D

Instructor, Huntington Beach Institute of Religion

Strange that we have the Kincaid name associated with Egyptian artifacts and the state of Idaho. Was this the egg that old man Kincaid slipped out of the Grand Canyon like it is believed? Was Herbert Kincaid a relative of G. A. Kincaid? How did a replica of King Tut's egg make it to Idaho if G. A. Kincaid did not take it there? More importantly—*why* was it there? Were the Egyptians more deeply entrenched in American pre-history than we know?

CAVE IN SOAPSTONE BASIN

In 2004, an elderly woman came to visit me (whom I'll call Alice) with a story to tell. Her father used to help out one of the museums around Utah Valley, Utah, when he had time and often was brought in to help remove or to hide valuable discoveries. The discoveries that were hidden up were done because of the perceived narrow-mindedness of local universities and government officials. She told of several items of discovery that were left in place that I would have given anything to see and to hold!

Alice began her story by telling us that her father and his friend would often sit at the family kitchen table and talk about where they would go next and who would be helping them. Usually it was a Ute or Paiute Indian that took them to the different sites around the valley. Everybody knew her father and his friend and what they were doing. Their primary motive was to preserve history so everyone could enjoy Utah's past.

One particular evening while helping with dinner, her father and his friend came in the door excited about a site they had been led to on the west side of Utah Lake. While discussing this site a knock came at the door. Alice went to the door and opened it. There stood two young men who asked to see her father's friend. She let them in and they immediately went directly to the table where the two men were sitting. Alice told us that they had on WWII flight jackets and she noticed that they were bulging! The two young men opened their jackets and let the contents fall upon the table. Her father and his friend actually stood up and backed away from the table. "*Where did you get this stuff?*" they demanded emphatically. The two men then told their story.

They claimed they went deer hunting up on Soapstone Basin, 40 miles east of Salt Lake City and some 15 miles from Kamas. Their hunting took them along a long white ridge where it looked like a natural place for a big mule deer buck to hide out. Upon finding a nice spot to sit, they hunkered down to wait for that special buck to appear. Soon what they had hoped for happened, for out of the rocks trotted a very large 4 x 4 muley. Both shot at the same time but did not kill the buck outright—meaning they had to go hunt for him to finish the job. When they found the buck they found something else that would cause them to forget all about hunting for quite some time.

They found their buck lying dead at the base of the white cliffs with his antlers tangled up in a bush. Excited about their kill they laid their rifles down, and each grabbing a hind leg began pulling the buck out of the bush when something caught their attention. A hole appeared behind the bush, and could only be seen when the bush was being pulled away from it.

After dressing their deer they decided to explore the now exposed hole thinking perhaps it was a lost Spanish Gold mine. The entrance was small, but large enough for a man to crawl in with a little effort. Once inside it opened up where one could stand but not fully erect. As soon as both men were inside they could see they were standing in a tunnel that went back into the cliff a few yards before turning to the right. They followed the tunnel; turning right and into a room. What their eyes beheld was unbelievable! There in that room were dozens of ancient looking artifacts of all kinds, shapes and sizes! They knew right away that what they found was something out of this world!

The two men spent some time trying to decide what to do about this remarkable discovery. They decided the best move to make at that time was to gather up some of the artifacts and take them to a man they had heard of that collected such things for a museum in Lehi. After they had secured a few of the objects they left the cave, but before leaving the mountains they covered the hole with loose rock, marking the spot with a certain object only they knew about.

The items they dropped on the table at the home of Alice and her father were remarkable. Alice did not have photographs to show me but she drew on paper what she had seen to the best of her ability. She stated that she couldn't remember everything but a few things still stuck in her mind. Some of the items she said she seen were rings and necklaces with strange inscriptions on them but couldn't remember exactly what they looked like.

Fig. 208 The Knife   Fig. 209 The Goblet

Alice drew the above items on a piece of paper saying these two items impressed her the most. The knife was about ten inches long with a double blade. It was very old looking because *"the blade looked dark like something had tarnished it, but the handle was exquisite! My father said it was gold and it had wire gold wrapped around the hilt with a pure gold button on its end piece."* The next item she drew for us was the goblet. *"It was amazingly beautiful and it was gold with strange characters on it. I think I remember a few of them."* She drew the characters out as she remembered them and placed question marks where she saw characters but couldn't recall what they were. She said the goblet was very heavy. [The drawings are in possession of the author.]

When the two young men finished their story, our museum friend told them, no, demanded that they return the items back to the cave—and never go back again—and to forget all about it, because bringing this out now would be a curse!

We may never know whether or not our two young friends ever took the cache back to the cave nestled beneath the white cliffs in Soapstone Basin or not. The subject was never brought up again according to Alice. It makes one wonder why this discovery was kept so secret. What a great discovery this could have been if brought forth properly. Like so many others, it is hidden away until that time when it is expedient for it to come forth for mankind to see and to ponder.

More strange stories have come forth over the years that have raised the eyebrow on many a scientist. Anomalies and ooparts come in faster than they can be studied; therefore, even before these discoveries *can* be studied, many are summarily dismissed as fakes or fairy tales. No matter how dubious it may sound—the account of these two men who allegedly found this magnificent cave is most likely a true story. [25]

CAVE DWELLERS

From *The Deseret Weekly*, 1881 we find the following equally incredible story:

The caves of Crawford county, Indiana, have long excited the wonder of pleasure-seekers who enjoy subterranean curiosities of nature and the further these caves have been explored the greater marvels have been disclosed. But the last discovery is the climax. Some boys went into the cave a week ago Sunday with the intention of spending the day, but they lost their path and were three days finding their way out. When they returned to the outer world they reported having found new and vast extensions of the cave, parts of which they insist, are inhabited by a race of diminutive men, almost Lilliputian in stature.

The young explorers were laughed at, but their earnestness begot confidence in a few, and they returned to search out the cave dwellers. After an absence of nearly four days, they came back again yesterday, and on hearing their second report hundreds of people flocked to the spot to learn the facts and prepare for thorough exploration. Excitement is [at] a fever heat.

The cave dwellers appear, according to descriptions by the boys, to be the lowest type of humanity, averaging less than three [feet] in height and about forty pounds in weight. They run upon all fours when they tire of the erect position. They exhibited extreme fear of the intruders, and clambered with great agility over large heaps of stones in their frantic flight. Not a vestige of clothing covered them and the boys say they noticed no signs of hirsuteness [furriness] or other physical marks of the lower orders of the animal kingdom.

The form is not well developed, and the males are little, if any, superior to the females. The heads are all well supplied with long hair, so densely tangled and matted that the true color could not be discerned. Their food can be nothing except fish from the streams which abound in the caves, for long before their place of abode is reached every vestige disappears of animals which haunt caves or seek refuge therein.

The singular beings have some form of language, for when the youthful explorers were [there] a baby-like chatter arose. Which, awakening the echoes of the cave, was almost deafening. Efforts will be made to capture some of these remarkable people. —*Detroit News*. (author's brackets)

It sounds like a chapter out of a Harry Potter Story, but—can it be true? Or were the boys just looking for attention? Can we be positive that it never happened? We always need to keep an open mind, regardless of circumstance or opinion until a thing is proven one way or the other.

I've always been intrigued by stories of the west. I love a good Indian story—especially when it revolves around something out of the ordinary or not in line with today's modern thinkers. I thought I would share this little story as the last in this chapter. I have left spelling and grammar is it was written.

THE GREAT CAVE

From a little booklet *Pioneering the West* by Howard R. Egan (1840-1916) republished by Andesite Press. In it I came across the story titled "The Indian Story of a Great Cave," author unknown. Here's the account:

I first got this from a young buck and just enough to cause me to want to hear all there was to it, and I told the young man so. He said there were some old men that knew all about it, and he would tell me who they were as soon as he could. Some time later I was at the Indian camp that was near the station taking lessons in their dialect. When the young man came in and said there was an old man over there in another wigwam, that could tell me about the big cave. I was soon over there and after a friendly smoke; this is what he said as near as I can remember:

There was camped at the very south end of the Schell Creek range of mountains [east of present-day Ely, Nevada] a large band of Indians, and a little ways from the camp was a large knoll. In the side of it was a cave that no one had ever been to the end of, and in fact none would try to explore it, on account of it being said that the bad spirit lived there, and killed all who entered very far inside.

The chief of this band of Indians had two squaws, one was quite old and cross, the other was very young and gentle and good looking, but the two squaws were most always quarreling, and the chief had frequently given the old one a good thrashing, thinking she was to be blamed for being so cross but the time came when he thought he would try whipping the young one, but first asked her why she could not get along without quarreling with the old lady. She said the other woman was always scolding her for not working harder and thereby making it lighter work for her and if he didn't make her stop her growling, she would run away as she was tired of living this way.

That kind of talk made the chief very mad so he gave the young squaw a very hard whipping, using his horse whip and holding her by the hair of her head while he laid the whip on till the blood had started out most all over her, then throwing her to one side said let us have peace or there will be something worse coming.

That night the sore little squaw took some dried meat and a few pine nuts and went to the cave determined to go as far in as the bad spirit would allow her to go, and, if she did not see him, to go as far as she had strength to crawl as she never wanted to go back or have the Indians find her body if they tried to do so.

For some distance the floor of the cave was covered with sand that laid in small wave like ridges and on the whole nearly level, but further on took a steep grade down for a long way, then a nearly level stretch, then again down grade, this kept on she did not know how long, for when she got tired she would lie down and sleep, and when she woke up would continue feeling her way down.

She had no idea how far she was from the mouth of the cave when she stepped into a pool of water that came nearly up to her knees and was cold as ice. She felt around and found there was quite a stream that was running out of the spring on the opposite side and she could hear a small waterfall a little further down. She soon made her way to this fall and over it and down the creek.

This went on for a long time, her food had all been eaten and she expected to soon have to give up and die, but what was this under her feet so soft? It was grass. She tried to eat some of it but it did not taste good, so went on and when tired out laid down beside the creek to sleep and lying on her back opened her eyes and saw that there was stars above her and in watching these discovered there were clouds up there too, and this kept her awake for a long time, but she did sleep again and then was awakened by something running by her.

She found it was day light and the sun was coming up over the hills and she could now hear birds singing, and she saw numerous wild animals the like of which she had never seen before. Everywhere she looked the ground was covered all over with grass, bushes, and trees. Anywhere else in her life, she had not seen such a beautiful country not even in small patches, having lived in a desert country.

Hunger caused her to look around to see if she could find any berries or roots that she could eat. Going on down the creek she found there was plenty of berries and many kinds that she had never seen before, some very large, and others very small. She ate of them such as tasted good until satisfied. She then went on still following the winding brook.

She had not traveled over a half a sun when she saw a large herd of very white animals feeding on a large open space where there was nothing but fine grass. She had never seen any animals like these. They were not as tall as an antelope, nor as little as a coyote. They were covered all over with long curly hair, and as she drew near to them they raised their heads and looked at her, then went on with their feeding, and seemed to know that she was not dangerous. While watching these animals, she saw something else that gave her quite a scare. It was a man and , as he had seen her and was coming towards her [but] there was no use in running away, so she stood still but watching to see if he was friendly or not. He came up pretty close and stopped then spoke to her in a language she had never heard and could not understand.

After some time he seemed to know that she was of some other people, and was lost, and was probably hungry, so putting one hand on his stomach and the other pointing to his mouth then pointing down the brook motioned for her to follow him, which she did as he seemed very friendly.

After going some distance they came to where a broad trail led to the door of a big house that had four or five other houses inside of it, and in the sides of all of them were big holes that had something over them that kept the wind and rain out, but you could see outside through them. In this very house the ground was covered with wood and the whole houses seemed to be made of wood with different kinds and colors of paint. There were places to sit on, places to eat on, and places to sleep on, all very beautiful to look at.

The man went to one of the walls and opened a door that did not open clear through the wall and brought out some meat that looked cooked and some very white bread and some yellow grease, and a pan of berries, a cup of sugar and put these on the place to eat on, then got some water in a cup you could see through. Then motioned for her to sit there, and he sat opposite, all the time talking in a kind voice.

He would point to something and say one word, and keep saying it till she would repeat it, then he would laugh and seemed much pleased. She knew that he was trying to teach her to talk his language and she was anxious to learn, and it was not long before she was able to ask questions and understand the answers. She slept in one of the inside houses and the man in another. The man done all the cooking for a long time, or until she had learned to talk well, and also how the cooking was done. Then she took hold of that part, which left the man more time to attend to his flocks and herds of which he had a good many. Some days he would take her out with him to get the fresh air and view the country, and at such times she could see scattered around at quite a distance numerous houses like the one where she lived and could also see many herds of different kinds of animals. When she asked the man if friendly people lived there he said yes. It is a very big country and all over it just like it is as far as you can see.

One day the man dressed himself in finer clothes and told the girl he was going away, but would come back by sundown. He was back by the time, called the girl to come and see what he had brought for her. It proved to be a dress that would reach from neck to ankles, and cover the arms too. It was covered most all over with different colored beads which were put on so as to show trees, birds, etc., and was very beautiful to look at. There were some leggings and shoes all finished off with beads like the dress. She was much pleased with the present as her own clothes were badly worn. The man told her to put them on and wear them every day, and after a while would get her another, and better outfit.

One day he called her to set down, and as she could talk good enough to make him understand, to tell him her story of where she came from and how and all about her people, as he was satisfied she was not of his country. So she commenced her story from the time she could first remember, up to the time her husband had whipped her, which seemed to make the man very mad.

He frequently asked her questions as she was telling her story. Then when she was telling of her running away and entering the cave to die he was all excited as there was an old story in his country that the cave had another opening far in the mountains that led to a bad country.

Well, she ended her story, after telling all that happened to her up to the time she met him. He knew the rest. One day he took her out to the side of the great trees, where he sat down and said three years ago I had a wife, she died and is laying there pointing to a small mound near him and two years more must pass before I can marry again, as that is our custom here. Then maybe I will talk to you about it.

One day some time later he found the girl sitting out in the shade she was crying and sobbing like her heart would break. After a good deal of coaxing she told him she was thinking about her husband and her boy, and wanted to see them again, at least her boy that was one year old when she left them. The man seemed very much depressed but said, "your husband is no good I wouldn't cry for him, but I do not blame you for wanting to see your boy, and if there was any way to help you get him I would, *but there is no way, so try and forget them." And soon she was crying most of the time, till at last she told the man if he would let her go she would try and go back the way she had come, and get her boy.*

The man tried to make her understand that it would be impossible for her to find her way back. But she was determined to make the attempt. So seeing that he could not persuade her to his views, he told her that if she was bound to take the chance of getting back through that awful hole he would help her all he could but would not go one step inside of the cave to save his own life or her's either. So as she wanted to start at once they both began getting together such articles as they thought would help her to make the journey through the cave.

The man got a small bundle of grass torches any one of which would burn a whole day, and advised the girl to use as few as possible while she had the creek to follow, and after leaving the spring at the head of the creek might be able to trace her steps back if she had light enough. Well, one day when they could think of nothing [else] that would help her, the man went with her to where the creek came out of the mountains; tried again to have her give up such an awful undertaking, but as she would go, made her promise that if she could not find her way out at the other end, or did get through and found her boy she would come back to him and he would wait two years for her.

So they parted, the man to his peaceful home, the girl to the dismal cave, where, after a very long time, and her provisions were about all used up, and the torches all burned out, she came to the light of day, about noon. She climbed a small hill where she could view the country around her at least some distance away discovered a smoke that showed her where there was a camp of Indians.

She went to it and found it to be her husband's band who was all very much surprised to see her again and alive, and dressed so fine and looking as pretty as ever, only tired out, and whiter than when she left them. The old woman had died while she was gone. Her husband said he would never whip here again and she must come and live with him and the boy, which she did.

There is another Indian story about that same cave, of how a small band of Indians lived near it, and was attacked by a large band of strange and hostile Indians, that was determined to kill all of the men and children and keep the squaws for servants. They had a running fight and all that were not killed took refuge in this cave. Their enemy placed a guard near the entrance to prevent any from escaping and they were determined to kill or capture the whole band. But after keeping their guards there for a whole moon, and not seeing or hearing of anyone that had went in they came to the conclusion that all had starved to death. So they went in to investigate, and could plainly see the tracks of the fleeing party all pointing further in, not one had turned back. This was enough, all had gone to their heaven or their hell.

Now a white man story about this same cave. It goes as follows:

We had a number of men hired for haying season, and among them were some that had lived in the settlements south of Utah Lake. I had been telling a bunch of them some of what the Indians had told me about this cave, when one of the men said there must be something in it, for I heared a man down south say he was acquainted with some of the party that had done some exploring there.

The parties were returning from California and making a cut off across the desert, when they camped near and discovered the cave. Some of the party went in quite a long ways, but had to retreat as their light gave out. Then they made a number of torches and with what lighting material they had, attempted to again reach the far end of the cave. There were many leads off to the sides but only one led down, kept one general direction. By following this, and just as they were about to back out going any further, they came to a spring of nice clear and pure water. The stream from which ran on down into the cave. There seemed to be plenty of room to follow it but they could not at that time.

All said they would go to the settlements and provide themselves with the means of finding the end of that cave if it took them six months to do it. I know that a good many men have been willing at any time to go and explore it. But there was always lacking a leader that would go ahead and organize a party for that purpose.

Yet another "Indian tale" you think? Well, maybe so but can you be so certain?

THE MUMMY OF PELICAN POINT

Many years ago a man by the name Robert Leonard, who was a Forest Service archaeologist, contacted me with a strange story. He handed me a paper to read. The following is a copy of that document, with the addition of my own headers and clarifying information in square brackets.

ROBERT LEONARD BACKGROUND

In 1989-91 I and my father were researching an old pioneer site on the west side of Utah Lake near what was once called Pelican City. I worked closely with John Hutchings from the Hutchings Museum in Lehi [Utah] to learn where the old pioneer homesteads were located and donated artifacts [to the museum] I found from various sites. Near the long peninsula known as Pelican Point, and then owned by Arnold Cedarstrom, we located a unique site. This site, we learned through records and the efforts of John Hutchings, was the homestead of one Holstrom family who had only lived there for two years before leaving because of poor well water. The site was made of local stones found in the Lake Mountains to the [west] east and was sectioned into several rooms, the wall long since collapsed. Sage brush grew high over it and except that you stumble into as we did you would never see it, not even from 30 feet away on the dirt trails used by fisherman at Utah Lake.

LENGTHY PROJECT

Over the next five years we gradually cleared out the sage engulfing the site, took measurements and excavated the rooms to rock floor. As we did I noticed that the shape of the structure was closer to the design used by Fremont Indians than pioneers. John Hutchings learned through connections that the granddaughter of the homesteaders was still alive and living near Lehi, [Utah] a short distance away. She had in her possession the diaries of her family as well as drawings and sketches made by the settlers while living there. An interesting note in one of the diaries stated that they had built from materials on an older structure and *used all the same stones*. They only had to quarry a small amount from Lake Mountain to make it a livable home (emphasis added).

SURPRISING DISCOVERY

Taking this into consideration and sharing my thoughts with John Hutchings, [we] returned to the site believing that beneath the stone floor would be found the original floor and perhaps artifacts to help date it. What we found was more odd than we expected. There were not two layers of habitation but three!

The latest was the Holstrom family who were the last to live there. In the layer just inches immediately below the stone floor they built was found gun parts belonging to Spanish matchlock pistols from the period of the early 1800s [actually this firing mechanism was invented sometime before 1475 and obsolete by at least 1720 when the flintlock mechanism replaced it]. Digging deeper still we came to yet another layer of pottery shard and strange hammered lead and copper plates, three actually.

The lead plate was about the size of a 50-cent piece and had odd writing in tiny symbols around the outer edge of one side. Nothing else was on the plate and the lead was extremely soft. The two copper plates were only a bit larger, about 2 1/2 inches in rough diameter and all signed [signs] of being crudely hammered. John Hutchings could not identify these nor the shards I left with him but he said the writing on the lead plate appeared to [be] very old 16th century letters.

AMAZING FIND

In 1992 a fisherman and his son were walking along the shoreline where the lake had eroded the bank. Sticking partly out of the rock and soil was the remains of a human body. Believing it may be a pioneer grave of [or] a murder scene, the fishermen contacted the local sheriff's department who came to investigate. It was soon revealed that the body was [that of an] extremely old mummy and had been buried with arms folded and embracing a long broadsword.

There was a small mention in the *Salt Lake Tribune* about the event then it quietly disappeared. John Hutchings had a son who worked for the BYU (Brigham Young University) archaeology department (who had taken charge of the body). John spoke with his son to see if John and I could get permission to view the mummy. John's son informed him that the body was under tight security and they were not letting anyone see it, not even John's son. This was swept under the rug from the public and try as we might John Hutchings nor myself could find anyone who was willing to discuss the mummy; other than it was a large male, about eight feet call, and very ancient. About two weeks later I returned to the Utah Lake site I had been working to pass some time metal detecting in the region. I was amazed to [see] a group of very official looking people in expensive Chevy Suburbans and one green Jeep poking around in the brush and along the bank of the lake. As I drove down the rough dirt trail towards my site and the group, a man jumped into the green Jeep and promptly headed toward me, stopping abruptly in front of me and got out. The guy ordered me to leave the region and gave no reason why except that the area was under BYU authority. I immediately knew why they were there—because of the mummy find and were searching for further artifacts.

Being on public land and armed with the knowledge I had of my site and authority of John Hutchings to vouch for the odd discoveries, I told the man I had knowledge of an old site that appeared to be several hundred years old and may be related to the mummy. The guy became angered and ordered me again out of the area (public land) on the threat of being arrested and wouldn't listen to what I had to say. From that day on, the belligerent and unnecessary treatment I received and coupled with the secrecy and cover-up [of] the ancient mummy, I lost all respect for academia and never again disclosed what unusual discoveries I would find in life. Typically, it's the "amateurs" or causal hiker who makes the most important discoveries only to be forgotten, threatened or belittled by academia in order to maintain control and authority. That wouldn't be the last time I butted heads with the so called *scholars*!

A very short time after this incident the land was sold to become a gravel quarry to provide construction materials for the upcoming Salt Lake Winter Olympics. The site I had worked was bulldozed and is today just a raw scar on the land. I know the BYU "professionals" never found the site I worked because John Hutchings had quite a few connections. He himself had little respect for BYU academia and often griped about their policies. But this region on the west side of

FICTIONS & MYTHS: STRANGE STORIES

Utah Lake may have once held the remains of an [a] pre-Columbian European settlement.

There are many rock writings in the region to attest to pre-Columbian European visitors also, but because of their [BYU] arrogance we will never truly know what secrets Lake Site Ruins No. 1 would have revealed. One day I may talk about Lake Site ruins No. 2, but it's doubtful [brackets mine].

And thus we see . . . that failure to approach new/old discoveries with an inquisitive and unbiased view of possibilities, not only destroys credibility, but potentially discredits otherwise legitimate artifacts, sites and settings.

9

ARCHAEOLOGICAL/ HISTORICAL COVER-UPS

Any time you allege a conspiracy is afoot, especially in the field of science, you are treading on thin ice. We tend to be very skeptical about conspiracies. However, the evidence is overwhelming; what is ironic is that much of it is in plain view—especially to those of discerning minds. The good news is that the players who may be considered to be power-brokers are obvious. Their game plans, and even their play-by-play tactics are transparent, once you learn to spot them.

It is not so easy to penetrate through the smoke screen of propaganda and disinformation to get to their underlying motives and goals. It would be convenient if we could point to a covert Watergate team of purported plumbers aligned with a bold-faced liar such as Richard Nixon, but this is a far more subtle operation.

The bad news—the conspiracy is global and there are many vested interest groups. A cursory investigation yields the usual suspects: scientists with a theoretical axe to grind, careers to further and the status quo to maintain. Their modus operandi is "The Big Lie" and the bigger and more widely publicized, so much the better. They rely on invoking their academic credentials to support their arguments, and the presumption is that no one has the right to question their authoritarian pronouncements. Some of these lies are listed below, though by no means are these all-inclusive:

- There is no mystery about who built the Great Pyramid or what the methods of construction were, and the Sphinx shows no signs of water damage
- There were no humans in the Americas before 20,000 B.C.
- The first civilization dates back no further than 3000 B.C.
- There are no documented anomalous, unexplained or enigmatic data to take into account
- There are no lost or unaccounted for civilizations

Let the *documented* evidence to the contrary be damned!

A HOUSE OF CARDS

In 1993, NBC Television aired "The Mysteries of the Sphinx," which presented geological evidence showing that the Sphinx was at least twice as old (9,000 years) as establishment Egyptologists claimed. This difference of opinion has become well known as the "water erosion controversy." An examination of the campaigning that mainstream Egyptologists deployed to combat this undermining of their turf is instructive. Self-taught Egyptologist John Anthony West, brought the water erosion issue to the attention of geologist Dr. Robert Schoch. They went to Egypt and launched an intensive on-site investigation. After thoroughly studying the Sphinx first hand, the geologist came to share West's preliminary conclusion and they announced their findings.

Dr. Zahi Hawass, the Giza Monuments chief, wasted no time in firing a barrage of public criticism at the pair. Renowned Egyptologist Dr. Mark Lehner, who is regarded as the world's foremost expert on the Sphinx, joined in the attack. He charged West and Schoch with being "ignorant and insensitive." This attack was a curious accusation which took the matter from the professional level and put the whole affair on the personal plane. It did not address the facts or issues at all, and was highly unscientific in its approach to evidence.

We must note the standard tactic of discrediting anyone who dares to call the accepted theories into question. Shifting the focus away from the issues and "personalizing" the debate is a highly effective strategy—a tactic favored by politicians who feel insecure about their positions.

Accordingly, Hawass and Lehner invoked their untouchable status and presumed authority. (One would think that a geologist's assessment would hold more weight on this particular point.)

A short time later, Schoch, Hawass and Lehner were invited to debate the issue at the American Association for the Advancement of Science. West was not allowed to participate because he lacked the required credentials. This barring points to a questionable assumption that is part of the establishment's arsenal: only scientists with academic degrees can practice science. Two filters keep the independent researcher out of the loop: 1) credentials, and 2) peer review. You do not get to number two unless you possess number one.

Science is a method that anyone can learn and apply. It does not require a degree to observe and record facts and think critically about them, especially in the non-technical social sciences. In a free society, science has to be an open process. Be that as it may, West was barred. The elements of the debate have been batted back and forth since then without resolution. It is similar to the controversy over who built the Giza pyramids and how.

This brings up the issue of "The Big Lie" and how it has been promoted for generations in front of God and everyone. The controversy over how the Great Pyramid was constructed is one example. It could be easily settled if Egyptologists wanted to resolve the dispute. A simple test could be designed and arranged by impartial engineers that would either prove or disprove their longstanding disputed theory—that it was built using the primitive tools and methods of the day, circa 2500 B.C. Why hasn't this been done?

The answer is so obvious, it seems impossible: the power-brokers within the academic community know that the theory is bogus. Could a trained, highly educated scientist really believe that 2.3 million tons of stone, some blocks weighing 70 tons, had been transported and lifted by primitive methods? That seems improbable, though they have no compunction against lying to the public, writing textbooks and defending this theory against alternative theories. However, we must note that they will not subject themselves to the bottom-line test. [Editor – what is this acid test? It would be instructive to the readership to give them a possible scenario of testing procedures to ensure that the scientific community plays by the same rules they impose upon others. If you read some of Hugh Nibley's stuff, he actually calls a spade a spade, i.e., many of the scientists are in actuality, the high priests of the religion of their particular science—no less dogmatic than the Holy Inquisition of Torquemada's era.]

We think it is incumbent upon any scientist to bear the burden of proof of his/her thesis; however the social scientists who make these claims have never stood up to that kind of scrutiny. [by social scientists, what discipline[s] do you speak of?] That is why we must suspect a conspiracy. No other scientific discipline would get away with bending the rules of science. All that Egyptologists have ever done is put down alternative theories using underhanded tactics. It is time to insist that they prove their own proposals.

Why would scientists try to hide the truth and avoid any tests of their hypotheses? Their motivations are equally transparent. If it can be proved that the Egyptians did *not* build the Great Pyramid in 2500 BC using primitive methods, or if the Sphinx can be dated to 9000 BC, the whole house of cards comes tumbling down. Orthodox views of cultural evolution are based upon a chronology of civilization having started in Sumer no earlier than 4,000 BC. The theory does not permit an advanced civilization to have existed prior to that time. Thus—one must reasonably conclude that it is the end of the discussion. *Archaeology and history lose their meaning without a fixed timeline as a point of reference.*

Since the theory of "cultural evolution" has been tied to Darwin's general theory of biological evolution, even more is at stake. Does this explain why facts, anomalies and enigmas are denied, suppressed and /or ignored? Yes—it does. The biological sciences today are based on Darwinism.

CASE STUDY: NBC BROADCAST

The case of author Michael Cremo is well documented, and it also demonstrates how the scientific establishment openly uses pressure tactics on the media and government. His book, *Forbidden Archeology, The Hidden History of the Human Race*, examines many previously ignored examples of artifacts that prove modern man's antiquity far exceeds the age given in accepted chronologies. The examples which he and his co-author present are controversial; however, the book itself became far more controversial than its contents when it was used in a documentary.

In 1996, NBC broadcast a special called "The Mysterious Origins of Man," which featured material from Cremo's book. The reaction from the scientific community went off the Richter scale. NBC was deluged with letters from irate scientists who called the producer "a fraud" and the whole program "a hoax."

But the scientists within this faction went further than this—a lot further. In an unconscionable sequence of bizarre moves, they tried to force NBC not to re-broadcast the popular program, but that effort failed. Then they took the most radical step of all—they presented their case to the federal government, requesting the Federal Communications Commission to step in and bar NBC from airing the program again.

This was not only an apparent infringement of free speech and a blatant attempt to thwart commerce, it was also an unprecedented effort to censor intellectual discourse. If the public or any government agency made an attempt to handcuff the scientific establishment, the public would never hear the end of it. A letter to the FCC written by Dr. Allison Palmer, President of the Institute for Cambrian Studies, is most revealing.

> At the very least, NBC should be required to make substantial prime-time apologies to their viewing audience for a sufficient period of time so that the audience clearly gets the message that they were duped. In addition, NBC should perhaps be fined sufficiently so that a major fund for public science education can be established. I think we have some good leads on who "the Brain Police" are.

I really do not think "conspiracy" is too strong a word, because for every case of this kind of attempted suppression that is exposed, ten others are going on successfully. We have no idea how many enigmatic artifacts or dates have been labeled "error" or "fraud" or "scam" and tucked away in storage warehouses or circular files, never to see the light of day.

CASE STUDY: STEEN-MCINTYRE

Then there is the high-profile case of Dr. Virginia Steen-McIntyre, a geologist working for the US Geological Survey (USGS), who was dispatched in the 1970s to an archaeological site in Mexico to date a group of artifacts. This travesty also illustrates how far many established scientists will go to guard orthodox tenets.

Steen-McIntyre used state of the art equipment and backed up her results by using four different methods, but her results were off the chart. While the lead archaeologist expected a date of 25,000 years or less, her finding was 250,000 years or more. The figure of 25,000 years or less was critical to the Bering Strait "crossing" theory, and it was the motivation behind the head archaeologist's tossing Steen-McIntyre's results in the circular file and asking for a new series of dating tests. This sort of reaction does not occur when dates match the expected chronological model that supports accepted theories.

Steen-McIntyre was given a chance to retract her conclusions, but she refused. From that point onward, she found it difficult to get her papers published, and she lost a teaching job at an American university.

In New Zealand, the government actually stepped in and enacted a law forbidding the public from entering a controversial archaeological zone. This story appeared in *Ancient Celtic New Zealand*, a book by Mark Doutré. However, as we will find, this is a complicated conspiracy. Scientists trying to protect their "hallowed" theories while furthering their careers are not the only ones who want artifacts and data suppressed. There are others—and they have their own agendas. This is where the situation gets sticky.

CASE STUDY: WAIPOUA FOREST

The Waipoua Forest became a controversial site in New Zealand, because an archaeological dig apparently showed evidence of a non-Polynesian culture that preceded the Maori—a fact that the tribe was not happy with. They learned of the results of the excavations before the general public did and complained to the government. According to Doutré, the outcome was "an official archival document, which clearly showed an intention by New Zealand government departments to withhold archaeological information from public scrutiny for 75 years." The public got wind of this fiasco but the government denied the claim.

However, official documents show that an embargo had been placed on the site. Doutré is a student of New Zealand history and archaeology. He is concerned because he says that artifacts proving that there was an earlier culture which preceded the Maori are missing from the museums. He asks what happened to several anomalous remains. "Where are the ancient Indo-European hair samples (wavy red brown hair), originally obtained from a rock shelter near Watakere, that were on display at the Aukland War Memorial Museum for many years? Where is the giant skeleton found near Mitimati?"

Unfortunately, this is not the only such incident. Ethnocentrism has become a factor in the conspiracy to hide mankind's true history. Author Graham Hancock has been attacked by various ethnic groups for reporting similar enigmatic findings. The problem for researchers concerned with establishing humanity's true history is that the goals of nationalists or ethnic groups who want to lay claim to having been in a particular place first, often dovetail with the goals of cultural evolutionists.

Archaeologists are quick to go along with suppressing these kinds of anomalous finds. One reason Egyptologists so jealously guard the Great Pyramid's construction date has to do with the issue of national pride.

CASE STUDY: TAKLA MAKAN DESERT MUMMIES

The case of the Takla Makan Desert mummies in western China is another example of this phenomenon. In the 1970s and 1980s, an unaccounted for Caucasian culture was suddenly unearthed in China. The arid environment preserved the remains of a blond-haired, blue-eyed people who lived in pre-dynastic China. They wore colorful robes, boots, stockings and hats. The Chinese were not happy about this revelation and they have downplayed the enigmatic find, even though Asians were found buried alongside the Caucasian mummies.

National Geographic writer, Thomas B. Allen, mused in a 1996 article about his finding a potsherd bearing a fingerprint of the potter. When he inquired if he could take the fragment to a forensic anthropologist, the Chinese scientist asked whether he "would be able to tell if the potter was a white man." Allen said he was not sure, and the official pocketed the fragment and quietly walked away. It appears that many things get in the way of scientific discovery and disclosure.

CASE STUDY: OLMEC CULTURE

The existence of the Olmec culture in Old Mexico has always posed a problem. Where did the Negroid people depicted on the colossal heads come from? Why are they there?

Caucasians are carved on the stelae in what is considered to be from Mexico's seed civilization. However, why aren't the indigenous Mexican people found on the Olmec artifacts?

Recently, a Mexican archaeologist solved the problem by making a fantastic claim: the Olmec heads, which generations of people of all ethnic groups have agreed bear a striking resemblance to Africans, were really representations of the local tribe.

The public does not seem at all aware of the fact that the scientific establishment has a double standard when it comes to the free flow of information. In essence, it goes like this—scientists are highly educated, well trained and intellectually capable of processing all types of information, and they can make the correct critical distinctions between fact and fiction, reality and fantasy. The unwashed public, on the other hand, is simply incapable of functioning on this high mental plane.

The noble ideal of the scientist as a highly trained, impartial, apolitical observer and assembler of established facts into a useful body of knowledge seems to have been shredded under the pressures and demands of the real world. Science has produced many positive benefits for society; but we should know by now that science has a dark, negative side. Didn't those meek fellows in the clean lab coats give us nuclear bombs and biological weapons? The age of innocence ended in World War II.

The scientific community has an attitude of intellectual superiority that is thinly veiled under a carefully orchestrated public relations guise. We always see Science and Progress walking hand in hand. Science as an institution in a free society has to function in the same way as the society at large—it should be open to debate, argument and counter-argument. There is no place for unquestioned authoritarianism. Is modern science meeting these standards? The evidence seems to argue against that premise.

CONVENTIONAL WISDOM

In the Fall of 2001, PBS aired a seven-part series, titled "Evolution Taken at Face Value," that seems harmless enough. However, while the program was presented as pure, objective, investigative science journalism, it completely failed to meet even minimum standards of impartial reporting. The series was heavily weighted towards the view that the theory of evolution is "a science fact" that is accepted by "virtually all reputable scientists in the world" and not a theory that has weaknesses and strong science-educated critics.

The series did not even bother to interview scientists who have criticisms of Darwinism: not "creationists," but bona fide scientists. But the issue has overtones of bias because how can we write something that emphasizes the fact that the objecting scientists truly had the "proper" credentials to be taken seriously without aligning them with the typical stereotypic connotation of what might be termed a creationist? To the minds of many, a creationist is an uneducated individual that ascribes magical thinking to God, and all reason goes out the window.

To correct this deficiency, a group of 100 dissenting scientists felt compelled to issue a press release. "A Scientific Dissent on Darwinism," on the day the first program was scheduled to go to air. Nobel Prize nominee Henry "Fritz" Shaefer was among them. He encouraged open public debate of Darwin's theory. Said he, "Some defenders of Darwinism embrace standards of evidence for evolution that as scientists they would never accept in other circumstances."

We have seen this same "unscientific" approach applied to archaeology and anthropology, where "scientists" simply refuse to prove their theories yet appoint themselves as the final arbiters of "the facts." It would be naïve to think that the scientists who cooperated in the production of the series were unaware that there would be no counter-balancing presentation by critics of Darwin's theory.

Richard Milton is a science journalist. He had been an ardent true believer in Darwinian doctrine until his investigative instincts kicked in one day. After twenty years of studying and writing about evolution, he suddenly realized that there were many disconcerting holes in the theory. He decided to try to allay his doubts and prove the theory to himself by using the standard methods of investigative journalism. Milton became a regular visitor to London's famed Natural History Museum. He painstakingly put every main tenet and classic proof of Darwinism to the test. The results shocked him. He found that the theory could not even stand up to the rigors of *routine* investigative journalism.

The veteran science writer took a bold step and published a book titled *The Facts of Life: Shattering the Myths of Darwinism.* It is clear that the Darwinian myth had been shattered for him, but many more myths about science would also be crushed after his book came out. Milton says: "I experienced the witch-hunting activity of the Darwinist police at first hand. It was deeply disappointing to find myself being described by a prominent Oxford zoologist (Richard Dawkins) as 'loony', 'stupid' and 'in need of psychiatric help' in response to purely scientific reporting." (Does this sound like stories that came out of the Soviet Union twenty years ago when dissident scientists there started speaking out?) Indeed, many dissenters were forcibly detained within mental institutions within the former USSR.

Dawkins launched a letter-writing campaign to newspaper editors, implying that Milton was a "mole" creationist whose work should be dismissed. Anyone at all familiar with politics will recognize this as a standard Machiavellian by-the-book "character assassination" tactic. Dawkins is a highly respected scientist, whose reputation and standing in the scientific community carry a great deal of weight.

According to Milton, the process came to a head when the *London Times* Higher Education Supplement commissioned him to write a critique of Darwinism. The publication foreshadowed his coming piece: "Next Week: Darwinism, Richard Milton goes on the attack," Dawkins caught wind of this and wasted no time in nipping this heresy in the bud. He contacted the editor, Auriol Stevens, and accused Milton of being a "creationist," and prevailed upon Stevens to pull the plug on the article. Milton learned of this behind-the-scenes backstabbing and wrote a letter of appeal to Stevens. In the end, however, she caved in to Dawkins and scratched the piece

Imagine what would happen if a politician or bureaucrat used such pressure tactics to kill a story in the mass media—it would ignite a huge scandal. Not so with scientists, who seem to be regarded as "sacred cows" and beyond reproach. There are many disturbing facts related to these cases. Darwin's theory of evolution is the only scientific theory routinely taught in our public school system that has never been subjected to rigorous scrutiny; moreover, none of any writings critical of Darwinian Theory have been allowed into the curriculum. This is an interesting fact, because a recent poll showed that the American public wants the theory of evolution taught to their children; however, "*71 per cent of the respondents say biology teachers should teach both Darwinism and scientific evidence against Darwinian Theory.*" Nevertheless, there are no plans to implement this balanced approach.

It is ironic that Dawkins has been appointed to the position of Professor of the Public Understanding of Science at Oxford University. His is a classic "Brain Police" office, patrolling the neurological front lines. The Western scientific establishment and mass media pride themselves on being open public forums devoid of prejudice or censorship. However, no television program examining the flaws and weaknesses of Darwinism has ever been aired in Darwin's home country or in America.

REPERCUSSIONS

A scientist who opposes the theory cannot get a paper published. The Mysterious Origins of Man, a 1996 television documentary movie, was not frontal attack on Darwinism; it merely presented evidence that is considered anomalous by the precepts of his theory of evolution.

Returning to our bastions of intellectual integrity, Forest Mims was a solid and skilled science journalist. He had never been the center of any controversy and so he was invited to write articles for the most-read column in the prestigious *Scientific American*, "The Amateur Scientist," a task he gladly accepted. According to Mims, the magazine's editor, Jonathan Piel, then learned that he also wrote articles for a number of Christian magazines. The editor called Mims into his office and confronted him.

"Do you believe in the theory of evolution?" Piel asked.

Mims replied, "No, and neither does Stephen Jay Gould."

His response did not affect Piel's decision to bump Mims off the popular column after just three articles. This has the unpleasant odor of a witch-hunt. The writer never publicly broadcast his private views or beliefs, so it would appear that Establishment academics now believe they have orders to make sure "unapproved thoughts" are never publicly disclosed.

So, the monitors of "good thinking" are not just the elite of the scientific community, as we have seen in several cases; they are television producers and magazine editors, as well. It seems clear that they are all driven by the singular imperative of furthering "public science education," as the president of the Cambrian Institute so aptly phrased it.

However, there is a second item on the agenda, and that is to protect the public from "unscientific" thoughts and ideas that might infect the mass mind. We outlined some of those taboo subjects at the beginning of the article; now we should add that it is also "unwholesome" and "unacceptable" to engage in any of the following research pursuits: Paranormal phenomena, UFOs, cold fusion, free energy and all the rest of the "pseudo-sciences." Does this have a familiar right to it? Are we hearing the faint echoes of religious zealotry?

Who gave science the mission of engineering and directing the inquisitive pursuits of the citizenry of the free world? It is all but impossible for any scientific paper that has anti-Darwinian ramifications to be published in a main-stream scientific journal. It is also just as impossible to get the "taboo" subjects even to the review table, and you can forget about finding your name under the title of any article in *Nature*, unless you are a credentialed scientist, even if you are the next Isaac Newton.

To re-state how this conspiracy begins, it is with two filters: credentials and peer review. Modern science is now a maze of such filters set up to promote certain orthodox theories, and at the same time to filter out that data already prejudged to be unacceptable. Evidence and merit are not the guiding principles because conformity and position within the Establishment community have replaced objectivity, access and openness.

Many scientists do not hesitate to launch the most outrageous personal attacks against those whom they perceive to be the enemy. Eminent paleontologist, Louis Leakey, penned this acid one-liner about *Forbidden Archeology*: "Your book is pure humbug and does not deserve to be taken seriously by anyone but a fool." Once again, we see the thrust of a personal attack; the merits of the evidence presented in the book are not examined or debated; and it is a blunt, authoritarian pronouncement.

Modern day archaeology and anthropology have nearly sealed the door on our imaginations, broadly interpreting the North American past as devoid of anything unusual in the way of great cultures characterized by a people of an unusual demeanor. The great interloper of ancient burial grounds, the nineteenth century Smithsonian Institution, created a one-way portal, through which uncounted bones have been spirited. This door and the contents of its vault are virtually sealed off to anyone but government officials concerning the deep past. (Ross Hamilton from *The Holocaust of Giants: The Great Smithsonian Cover-up*)

Fig. 210 John Wesley Powell

While the idea of the prestigious Smithsonian covering up a valuable archaeological find is difficult for some to accept, there is, sadly, a great deal of evidence to suggest that this institution has knowingly covered up and "lost" important archaeological relics throughout their history. Powell, as argued above, has done irretrievable damage by damning any and all artifacts or theories outside the parameters of his own thinking. This biased attitude has prevailed to the point where it became "law" amongst the scientists of the day. This attitude continues to this day—largely unabated.

This book has attempted to furnish the reader with what the author has been able to learn and study through his own investigations and those of others, many *uncredentialed* in the classical sense. It is hoped that though sketched hurriedly and sometimes vaguely, this effort will suffice to convey some ideas of the human interest and the great importance of histories past.

Not the End!

AFTERWORD

ALTHOUGH WE MAY BE TITILLATED by fantastical stories of monsters, creatures and visitors from outer space, there are real life mysteries that demand answers and resolution. In addition to the recorded history of our planet, there are other evidences of man's existence that are just as intriguing and the fascinating insights just as demanding of careful and unbiased research.

As I examined the stories, histories, myths, legends as well as the discoveries and evidences of ancient peoples of North, Central and South America, the challenge grew into almost an obsession to find the truth of their origins. The *so-called* frauds and fakes—of which there are admittedly obvious counterfeits—are so extensive in volume and so widespread in the world, that forgeries and fabrications can account for only a small portion of the many artifacts that have been documented and continue to be found, many with full provenance. Further, the oral traditions of the aboriginal inhabitants of the Americas invite additional study and field work.

Thanks to the monumental efforts of many researchers and chroniclers throughout the ages, we are the recipients of a variety of publications, collections, discoveries and works that are capable of expanding our minds and enriching our understanding of those who preceded us on this planet. In particular, my commendation to those explorers, biographers, writers, researchers and students of the sciences who were and are willing to stake their career and reputation on findings that do not fit the popular or conventional interpretation, in many cases disputing the scholarly explanations and theories of academia.

The accounts, images, records and stories in the pages of this manuscript raise more questions than they answer and yet provide a model for further pursuit of truth, wherever it may lie—especially if it contradicts credentialed and theoretical explanations. They say that history is written by the victorious, but even long-held and "canonized" theories can be destroyed or modified by simple, solid, honest and true facts.

When actually handling artifacts from Crespi, Brewer, Burrows and others, exploring rock art, pictographs and other script "written in stone," and actually discovering hidden meanings in the oral traditions of the ancients, my thinking underwent a *metamorphosis*—a transformation.

A refusal to believe the oral accounts of great Indian leaders of our nations, for example, whose testimony is that the Savior actually conversed with them, giving them instructions and teaching them life truths, is tantamount to dismissing the witness of hundreds if not thousands who were participants in these remarkable and life-changing experiences.

My intent here—and in subsequent publications and resources—is to present new ideas and discoveries in such a way that readers will be enticed to learn more, to study with an open mind and to enjoy the enlightenment that can boost morale, strengthen resolve and inspire hearts. What greater joy and satisfaction can come to one's mind than the resolution of what has been a mystery, a myth, or a rumor through the linking of *true* facts, *real* artifacts and *actual* evidences.

—The Author

Cruelties of the Spanish in the Americas

[https://www.encyclopediavirginia.org/The_Black_Legend_an_excerpt_ from_A_Brief_Account_of_the_Destruction_of_the_Indies_by_Barto- lome_de_las_Casas_1552]

The following excerpt comes from an English edition of A Brief Account of the Destruction of the Indies *by Bartolomé de las Casas published in London in 1689. A Dominican friar who had performed missionary work in the New World, Las Casas published the original in 1552 in Seville, Spain. The book criticized the Spaniards' conquest of Central and South America and, in particular, their treatment of American Indians. It became the foundation for the so-called Black Legend, which portrayed Spanish in- fluence in the New World as unrelentingly negative.*

Note: the quoted sections are shown in the original spelling, punctuation and format of the English translation of the friar's document. Sections have been summarized to avoid repetition from one group of natives to another on a different island or continent. This is primarily the firsthand account of Fray Bartolomé de las Casas.

The preface outlines the purpose and briefly give the reasons for pub- lishing this account in order to dissuade further harms on the natives of the Americas.

The Argument of this Narrative by way of Preface to the Reader

. . . I earnestly beg and desire all men to be persuaded, that this summary was not published upon any private design, sinister ends or affection in favor or prejudice of any particular Nation; but for the pub- lich Emolument and Advantage of all true Christians and moral men throughout the whole world.

THE CRUELTY OF THE SPANIARDS COMMITTED IN AMERICA

America was discovered and found out Ann. Dom. 1492, and the Year insuing inhabited by the Spaniards, and afterward a multitude of them travelled thither from Spain for the space of nine and forty years. Their first attempt was on the Spanish Island which indeed is a most fertile soil, and at present in great reputation for its spaciousness and length, containing in circumference six hundred miles: Nay it is on all sides surrounded with an almost innumerable number of Islands, which we found so well peopled with Natives and forreigners, that there is scarce any region in the Universe fortified with so many inhabitants: But the main land or continent, distant from this island two hundred and fifty miles and upwards, extends itself about ten thousand miles in length near the sea-shore, which lands are some of them already discover'd, and more may be found out in process of time: And such a multitude of people inhabits these countries, that it seems as if the Omnipotent God has assembled and Convocated the major part of mankind in this part of the world.

Now this infinite multitude of men are by the creation of God innocently simple, altogether void of and averse to all manner of craft, subtlety and malice, and most obedient and loyal subjects to their native sovereigns; and behave themselves very patiently, sumissively and quietly towards the Spaniards, to whom they are subservient and subject; so that finally they live without the least thirst after revenge, laying aside all litigiousness, commotion and hatred.

This is a most tender and effeminate people, and so imbecile and unequal-balanced temper, that they are altogether incapable of hard labour, and in few years, by one distemper or other soon expire, so that the very issue of Lords and Princes, who among us live with great affluence, and fard deliciously, are not more effeminate and tender than the children of their husbandmen or labourers: This nation is very necessitous and indigent, masters of very slender possessions, and consequently, neither haughty, nor ambitious. They are parsimonious in their diet, as the Holy Fathers were in their frugal life in the Desert, known by the name of Eremites. They go naked, having no other covering but what conceals their pudends from publick sight. An hairy Plad, or loose coat, about an ell, or a coarse woven cloth at most two ells long serves them for the warmest winter garment. Ley lye on a course rug or matt, and those that have the most plentiful Estate or fortunes, the better sort, use net-work, knotted at the four corners in lieu of beds, which the inhabitants of the island of Hispaniola, in their own proper Idiom, term Hammacks.

Fig.1 Spaniards burning men and women to death

The men are pregnant and docible. The natives tractable, and capable of morality or goodness, very apt to receive the instill'd principles of Catholick religion; nor are they averse to civility and good manners, being not so much discompos'd by variety of obstructions, as the rest of mankind; insomuch, that having suckt in (if I may so express myself) the very first rudiments of the Christian faith, they are so transported with zeal and furvor in the exercise of Ecclesiastical sacraments, and Divine service, that the very religioso's themselves, stand in need of the greatest and most signal patience to undergo such extreme transports. And to conclude, I myself have heard the Spaniards themselves (who dare not assume the confidence to deny the good nature praedominant in them) declare, that there was nothing wanting in them for the acquisition of Eternal Beatitude, but the sole knowledge and understanding of the Deity.

The Spaniards first assaulted the innocent sheep, so qualified by the Almighty, as is premention'd, like most cruel Tygers, Wolves and Lions hunger-starv'd, studying nothing, for the space of Forty years, after their first landing, but the massacre of these wretches, whom they have so inhumanely and barbarously butcher'd and harass'd with several kinds of torments, never before known or heard (of which you shall have some account in the following discourse) that the three millions of persons, which lived in Hispaniola itself, there is at present but the inconsiderable remnant of scarce three hundred. Nay the Isle of Cuba, which extends as far, as Valledolid in Spain is distant from Rome, lies now uncultivated, like a desert, and intomb'd in its own ruins. You may also find the Isles of St. John, and Jamaica, both large and fruitful places, unpeopled and desolate. The Lucayan Islands on the north side, adjacent to Hispaniola and Cuba, which are sixty in number, or thereabout, together with those, vulgarly known by the name of the Gigantic Isles, and others, the most infertile whereof, exceeds the Royal Garden of Sevil in fruitfulness, a most healthful and pleasant climate, is now laid waste and uninhabited; and whereas, when the Spaniards first arriv'd here, about five hundred thousand men dwelt in it, they are now cut off, some by slaughter, and others ravished away by force and violence, to work in the mines of Hispaniola, which was destitute of native inhabitants; for a certain vessel, sailing to this Isle, to the end, that the harvest being over (some good Christian, moved with piety and pity, undertook this dangerous voyage, to convert souls to Christianity) the remaining gleanings might be gather up, there were only found eleven persons, which I saw with my own eyes. There are other Islands Thirty in number, and upward bordering upon the Isle of St. John, totally unpeopled; all which are above two thousand miles in length, and yet remain without inhabitants, native, or people.

As to the firm land, we are certainly satisfied, and assur'd, that the Spaniards by their barbarous and execrable actions have absolutely depopulated ten Kingdoms, of greater extent than all Spain, together with the kindoms of Arragon and Portugal, that is to say, above one thousand miles, which now lye waste and desolate, and are absolutely ruined, when as formerly no other country whatsoever was more populous. Nay we dare boldly affirm, that during the forty years space, wherein they exercised their sanguinary and detestable tyranny in these regions, about twelve millions (computing men, women and children) have undeserv-

336

edly perished; nor do I conceive that I should deviate from the truth by saying that above fifty millions in all paid their last debt to nature.

Those that arriv'd at these Islands from the remotest parts of Spain, and who pride themselves in the name of Christians, steer'd two courses principally, in order to the extirpation, and exterminating of this people from the face of the earth. The first whereof was raising an unjust, sanguinolent, cruel war. The other, by putting them to death, who hitherto, thirsted after their liberty, or design'd (which the most potent, strenuous and magnanimous spirits intended) to recover their pristine freedom, and shake off the shackles of so injurious a captivity. For they being taken off in war, none but women and children were permitted to enjoy the benefit of that country-air, in whom they did in succeeding times lay such a heavy yoke, that they very brutes were more happy than they; to which two species of tyranny as sub-alternate things to the genus, the other innumerable courses they took to extirpate and make this a desolate people, may be reduced and referr'd.

Now the ultimate end and scope that incited the Spaniards to endeavor the extirpation and desolation of this people, was GOLD only; that thereby growing opulent in a short time, they might arrive at once at such degrees and dignities, as were no ways consistent with their persons. Finally, in one word, their ambition and avarice, than which the heart of man never entertained greater, and the vast wealth of those regions; the humility and patience of the inhabitants (which made their approach to these lands more facil and easie) did much promote the business; whom they so despicable contemned, that they treated them (I speak of things which I was an eye witness of, without the least fallacy) not as beasts, which I cordially wished they would, but as the most abject dung and filth of the earth; and so solicitous they were of their life and soul, that the above mentioned number of people died without understanding the true faith or sacraments. And this also is as really true as the precedent narration (which the very tyrants and cruel murderers cannot deny without the stigma of a lye) that the Spaniards never received any injury from the Indians, but that they rather reverenced them as persons descended from Heaven, until that they were compelled to take up arms, provoked thereunto by repeated injuries, violent torments, and in just butcheries.

Editor Note: The depredations on the populations of the various islands continued, including the islands of Hispaniola, St John, Jamaica, and

Cuba, including smaller isles where the natives fled to escape death, but to no avail. Entire islands were left void of people, de las Casas having witnessed the hanging of 200 indians "of their own accord" to escape the torture of the invaders and another 3,000 men, women and children slaughtered without provocation.

Once it so happened that the citizens of a famous city, distant ten miles from the place where we then resided, came to meet us with a splendid retinue, to render their visit more honorable, bringing with them delicious viands, and such kind of dainties, with as great a quantity of fish as they could possible procure, and distributing them among us; but behold on a sudden, some wicked devil possessing the minds of the Spaniards, agitated them with great fury, that I being present, and without the least pretence or occasion offered, they cut off in cold blood above three thousand men, women and children promiscuously, such inhumanities and barbarisms were committed in my sight, as no age can parallel.

Fig. 2. Vicious dog ripping the heart out of an Indian

OF THE CONTINENT

In the Year 1514, a certain unhappy Governour landed on the firm land or Continent, a most bloody Tyrant, destitute of all mercy and prudence, the instrument of God's wrath, with a resolution to people these parts with Spaniards; and although some tyrants had touched here before him, and cruelty hurried them into the other world by several wayes of slaughter, yet they came no farther than to the sea coast, where they committed prodigious thefts and robberies, but this person exceeded all that ever dwelt in other Islands, though execrable and profligate villains; for he did not only ravage and depopulate the sear-coast, but buried the largest regions and most ample kingdoms in their own ruins, sending thousands to hell by his butcheries. He made incursions for many miles continuance, that is to say, in those countries that are included in the territories of Darien and the Provinces of Nicaraqua, where are near five hundred miles of most fertile land in the world, and the most opulent for gold of all the regions hitherto discover'd. And although Spain has been sufficiently furnished with the purest gold, yet it was dig'd out of the bowels and mines of the said countries by the Indains, where (as we have said) they perished.

This Ruler, with his accomplices found out new inventions to rack, torment, force and extort gold from the Indians. One of this captains in a certain excursion undertaken by the Command of his Governor make depredations, destroy'd forty thousand persons and better exposing them to the edge oft the sword, fire, dogs and variety of torments; of all which a religious man of the Order of St. Francis, Francisus de S. Romano, who was then present was an eye-witness. Great and injurious was the blindness of those presided over the Indians; as to the conversion and salvation of this people; for they denied in effect what they in their flourishing discourse pretended to, and declar'd with their tongue what they contradicted in their heart; for it came to this pass, that the Indians should be commanded on the penalty of a bloody war, death, and perpetual bondage, to embrace the Christian Faith, and submit to the obedience of the Spanish King; as in the Son of God, who suffered death for the redemption of all mankind, had enacted a law, when he pronounced these words, "Go and teach all Nations" that Infidels, living peaceably and quietly in their hereditary native country, should be impos'd upon plain of confiscation of all their chattels, lands, liberty, wives, children, and death itself, without any precedent instruction to confess and acknowledge the true God, and subject themselves to a King, whom they never saw, or heard mention'd before; and whose messengers behav'd themselves toward them with such inhumanity and cruelty as they had done hitherto. Which is certainly a most foppish and absurd way of proceeding, and merits nothing but scandal, derision, nay Hell itself. How suppose this notorious and profligate Governor had been impower'd to see the execution of these edicts perform'd, for of themselves they were repugnant both to law and equity; yet he commanded (or they who were to see the execution thereof, did it of their own heads without authority) that when they phansied or proposed to themselves any place, that was well stor'd with gold, to rob and feloniously steal it away from the Indians living in their cities and houses, without the least suspicion of any ill act. These wicked Spaniards, like thieves came to any place by stealth, half a mile off of any city. town or village, and there in the night published and proclaim'd the edict among themselves after this manner:

You Cacics and Indians of this continent, the inhabitants of such a place, which they named; we declare or be it known to you all, that there is but one God, one hope, and one King of Castile, who is Lord of these countries; appear forth without delay, and take the oath of allegiance to the Spanish King, as his vassals.

So about the fourth watch of the night, or three in the morning these poor innocents overwhelm'd with heavy sleep, ran violently on that place they named, set fire to their hovels, which were all thatcht, and so, without notice, burnt men, women and children; kill'd whom they pleas'd upon the spot; but those they preserv'd as captives, were compell'd through torments to confess where they had hid the gold, when they found little or none at their houses; but they who liv'd being first stigmatized, were made slaves; yet after the fire was extinguished, they came hastily in quest of the gold. Thus did this wicked man, devoted to all the infernal furies, behave himself with the assistance of profligate Christians, who he had lifted in his service from the 14th to the 21, or 22, year, together with his domestick servants and followers, from whom he received as many portions, besides what he had from his slaves in gold, pearls, and jewels, as the Chief Governor would have taken, and all that were constituted to execute any kind of Kingly office followed in the same footsteps; every one sending as many of his servants as he could spare, to share in the spoil. Nay, he that came hither as Bishop first of all did the same also, and at the very time (as I conjecture) the Spaniards did depredate or rob this Kingdom of about ten hundred thousand Crowns of gold; yet all these their thefts and felonies, we scarce find upon record that three hundred thousand Castilian Crowns ever came into the Spanish King's coffers; yet there were about eight hundred thousand men slain; the other tyrants who governed this kingdom afterward to the three and thirtieth year, depriv'd all of them of life that remain'd among the inhabitants.

Among all those flagitious acts committed by this Governor while he rel'd this Kingdom, or by his consent and permission this must by no means be omitted; A certain Casic, bestowing on his a gift, voluntarily, or (which is more probably) induced thereunto by fear, about the weight of nine thousands Crowns, but the Spaniards not satisfied with so fast a sum of money, sieze him, fix his to a pole, extended his feet, which being mov'd near the fire, they demanded a larger sum; the Casic overcome with torments, sending home, procur'd three thousands more to be brought and presented to them, but the Spaniards, adding new torments to new rage and fury, when they found he would confer no more upon them, which was because he could not, or otherwise because he would not, they expos'd him for so long to that torture, till by degrees of hear the marrow gusht out of the soles of his feet, and so he dyed thus they often murder'd the Lords and Nobles with such torments to extort the gold from them.

OF THE PROVINCE OF NICARAQUA

Editor Note: While many of the nations the Spanish came to dominate were productive and beautiful, their greed quickly turned them into wastelands. Nicaragua is one such example.

The said tyrant an. Dom. 1522 proceeded farther very unfortunately to the subjugation of conquest of this province. In truth no person can satisfactorily or sufficiently express the fertility, temperateness of the climate, or the multitude of the inhabitants of Nicaraqua, which was almost infinite and admirable, for this region contain'd some cities that were four miles long, and the abundance of fruits of the earth (which was the cause of such a concourse of people) was highly commendable. The people of this place, because the country was level and plain, destitute of mountains, so very delightful and pleasant, that they could not leave it without great grief, and much dissatisfaction, they were therefore tormented with the greater vexations' and persecutions, and forced to bear the Spanish tyranny and servitude, with as much as they were masters of; Add farther that they were peaceable and meek spirited. This tyrant with these accomplices of his cruelty did afflict this nation (whose advice he made use of in destroying the other Kingdoms) with such and so many great damages, slaughters, injustice, slaver, and barbarism, that tongue, though of iron, could not express them all fully. He sent into the province (which is larger than the country of Ruscinia) fifty horsemen, who put all the people to the edge of the sword, sparing neither age nor sex upon the most trivial and inconsiderable occasion. As for example, if they did not come to them with all possible speed when called, and bring the imposed burthen of Mahid (which signifies corn in their dialect)or if they did not bring the number of Indians required to his own, and the service or rather servitude of his associates. And, the country being all campaign or level, no person was able to withstand the hellish fury of their horses.

He commanded the Spaniards to make excursions, that is, to rob other provinces, permitting and granting these thieving rogues leave to take away by force as many of these peaceable people as they could, who being iron'd (that they might not sink under the burthen of sixty or eighty pound weight) it frequently happened, that of four thousand Indians, six only returned home, and so they dyed by the way; but if any of them chanced to faint, being tired with over-weighty burthens, or through great hunger and thirst should be seized with a distemper; or too much debility and weakness, that they might not spend time in taking off their fetters, they beheaded them, so the head fell one way, and the body another. The Indians when they spied the Spaniards making preparations for such journeys, knowing very well that few, or none returned home alive, just upon their setting out with sighs and tears, burst out into these or the like expressions.

Those were journeys, which we traveled frequently in the service of Christians, and in some tract of time we return'd to our habitations, wives and children, but now there being no hope of return, we are forever depriv'd of their sight and conversation. It happened also, that the same President would dissipate or disperse the Indians de vovo at his own pleasure, to the end (as it was reported) he might violently force the Indians away from such as did infest or molest him; and dispose of them to others, upon which it fell out, that for the space of a year complete, there was no sowing or planting, and when they wanted bread, the Spaniards did by force plunder the Indians of the whole stock of corn that they had laid up for the support of their families, and by these indirect courses above thirty woman oppressed with insufferable hunger, depriv'd her own son of his life to preserve her own.

In this province also they brought many to an untimely end; loading their shoulders with heavy planks and pieces of timer, which they were complell'd to carry to a haven forty miles distant in order to their building of ships, sending them likewise unto the mountains to find out honey and wax, where they were devour'd by tygers, nay they loaded women impregnated with carriage and burthens fit for beasts. But no greater pest was there that could unpeople this province, than the license granted the Spaniards by this Governor, to demand captives from the Casics and Potentates of this region for at the expiration of four or five months or as often as they obtain'd leave of the Governor to demand them, they deliver'd them up fifty servants, and the Spaniards terrified them with menaces, that if they did not obey them in answering their unreasonable demands, they should be burnt alive, or baited to death by dogs. Now the Indians are but slenderly stor'd with Servants, for it is much if a Casic hath three of four in his retinue, therefore they have recourse to the subjects and when they had in the first place seized the orphans, they required earnestly and instantly one son of the parent, who had but two, and two of him that had but three, and for the Lord of the place satisfied the desires of the tyrant, not without the effusion of tears and groans of the people, who (as it seems) were very careful of their children. And, this being frequently repeated in the space between the year 1523 and 1533, the kingdom lost all their inhabitants, for in six or seven years time there were constantly five or six ships made ready to be freighted with Indians that were sold in the regions of Panama and Perusium where they all dyed, for it is by daily experience prov'd and known, that the Indians when transported out of their native country into any other, soon dyed because they are shortened in their allowance of food, and the task impos'd on them no ways dimished, they being only brought for labour. And, by this means, there have been taken out of this province five hundred thousand inhabitants and upward, who before were Freemen, and made slaves, and in the wars made on them, and the horrid bondage they were reduc'd unto fifty or sixty thousand more have perished, and to this day very many still are destroy'd. Now, all these slaughters have been committed within the space of fourteen years inclusively, possibly in this province of Nicaraqua there remains four or five thousand men who are put to death by ordinary personal oppressions, whereas (according to what is said already) it did exceed other countries of the world in multitude of people.

Fig. 3 Feeding human body parts to the dogs

Fig. 4 The Spaniards wiping out an entire village

OF THE KINGDOM AND PROVINCE OF GUATEMALA

This tyrant at his first entrance here acted and commanded prodigious slaughters to be perpetrated; notwithstanding which, the Chief Lord in his Chair or Sedan attended by many Nobles of the City of Ultlatana, the Emporium of the whole Kingdom, together with trumpets, drums and great exultation, went out to meet him, and brought with them all sorts of food in great abundance, with such things as he stood in most need of. That night the Spaniards spent without the City, for they did not judge themselves secure in such a well fortified place. The next day he commanded the said Lord with many of his peers to come before him, from whom they imperiously challenged a certain quantity of gold; to whom the Indians return'd this modest answer, that they could not satisfie his demands, and indeed this region yeilded no golden mines; but they all, by his command, without any other crime laid to their charge, or any legal form of proceeding were burnt alive. The rest of the Nobles belonging to other Provinces, when they found their Chief Lords who had the supreme power were expos'd to the merciless element of fire kindled by a more merciless enemy; for this reason only, because they bestow'd not what they could not upon them, viz. gold, they fled to the mountains (their usual refuge) for shelter commanding their subjects to obey the Spaniards, as lords, but withal strictly and expressly prohibiting and forbidding them to inform the Spaniards of their flight or the places of their concealment. And, behold a great many of the Indians addrest themselves to them earnestly requesting they would admit them as subjects, being very willing and ready to serve them. The Captain replyed that he would not entertain them in such a capacity, but instead of so doing would put every individual person to death, if they would not discover the receptacles of the fugitive Governours. The Indians made answer that they were wholly ignorant of the matter, yet that they themselves, their wives and children should serve them; that they were at home, they might come to them and put them to death, or deal with them as they pleas'd. But the Spaniards, O wonderful! went to the towns and villages, and destroy'd with their lances these poor men, their wives and children, intent upon their labour, and as they thought themselves secure and free from danger. Another large village they made desolate in the space of two hours, sparing neither age, nor sex, putting all to the sword without mercy.

The Indians perceiving that this barbarous and hard-hearted people would not be pacified with humility, large gifts or unexampled patience, but that they were butcher'd without cause, upon serious consultation took up a resolution of getting together in a body, and fighting for their lives and liberty; for they conceiv'd it was far better, (since death to them was a necessary evil) with sword in hand to be kill'd by taking revenge of the enemy, then be destroy'd by them without satisfaction. But when they grew sensible to their wants of arms nakedness and debility, and that they were altogether incapable of the management of horses, so as to prevail against such a furious adversary, recollecting themselves, they contriv'd this strategm to dig ditches and holes in the high-way into which the horses might fall in their passage, and fixing therein purposely sharp and burnt posts, and covering them with loose earth, so that they could not be discern'd by their riders, they might be transfixed or gored by them. The horses fell twice or thrice into those holes, but afterward the Spaniards took this course to prevent them for the future, and made this a law, that as many of the Indians of what age or sex soever as were taken, should be cast into these ditches that they had made. Nay they threw into them women with child, and as many aged men as they laid hold of, till they were all fill'd up with carkasses. It was a sight deserving commiseration, to behold women and children gauncht or run through with these posts, some were taken off by spears and swards, and the remained expos'd to hungry dogs, kept short of food for that purpose, to be devour'd by them and torn in pieces.

Fig. 5. Vicious dogs tearing the Indians to pieces

They burnt a potent Nobleman in a very great fire, saying, that he was the more Honour'd by this kind of death. All which butcheries continued seven years, from 1524 to 1531. I leave the reader to judge how many might be massacred during that time.

Among the innumerable flagitious acts done by this tyrant and his co-partners (for they were as barbarous as their principal) in this kingdom, this also occurs worthy of an afterism in the margin. In the Province of Cuztatan in which S. Saviour's City is seated, which country with the neighboring sea coasts extends in length forty or fifty miles, as also in the very City of Cuzcatan, the metropolis of the whole province, he was entertain'd with great applause; for about twenty or thirty thousand Indians brought with them hens and other necessary provisions, expecting this coming. He, accepting their gifts, commended every single Spaniard to make choice of as many of these people, as he had a mind to, that during their stay there, they might use them as servants, and forced to undergo the most servile offices they should impose on them. Every one cull'd out a hundred, or fifty, according as he thought convenient for his peculiar service, and these wretched Indians did serve the Spaniards with their utmost strength and endeavour; so that there could be nothing wanting in them but adoration. In the mean time this Captain requir'd a great sum of gold from their Lords (for that was the load-stone attracted them thither) who answered, they were content to deliver him up all the gold they had in possession, and in order thereunto the Indians gathered together a great number of spears gilded with Orichalcum, (which had the appearance of gold, and in truth some gold in them intermixt) and they presented to him. The Captain ordered them to be toucht, and when he found them to be Orichalcum or mixt metal, he spake to the Spaniards as followth: 'Let that nation that is without gold be accursed to the pit of Hell. Let every man detain these servants he elected, let them be clapt in irons, and stigmatiz'd with the brand of slavery! which was accordingly done, for they were all burnt, who did not escape with the Kings Mark. I myself saw the impression made on the son of the chiefest person in the city. Those that escap'd with other Indians, engaged the Spaniards by force of arms, but with such ill success, that abundance of them lost their lives in the attempt. After this they return'd to Guatemala, where they built a city, which God in his judgement with three deluges, the first of water the second of earth, the third of stones, as big as half a score oxen, all concurring at one and the same time, laid level with its own ashes. Now all being slain who were capable of bearing arms against them, the rest were enslav'd paying so much per head for men and women as a ransom; for they used no other servitude here, and then they were sent into pecusium to be sold, by which means together with their slaughters committed upon the inhabitants, they destroy'd and made a desert of this kingdom, which in breadth as well as length contains one hundred miles, and with his associates and brethren in iniquity, four millions at least in fifteen or sixteen years, that is, from 1524 to 1540 were murdered and daily continues destroying the small residue of that people with his cruelties and brutishness.

It was the usual custom of this tyrant, when he made war with any city or province, to take along with him as many of those Indians he had subjugated as he could, that they might fight with their country-men; and when he had in his army twenty, or sometimes thirty thousand of them, and could not afford them sustenance, he permitted them to feed on the flesh of other Indians taken prisoners in war; and so kept a shambles of man's flesh in his army, suffered children to be kill'd and roasted before his face. They butcher'd the men for their feet and hands only; for these members were accounted by them dainties, most delicious food.

He as the death of many by the intolerable labour of carrying ships

Fig. 6. The Spaniards feeding the Indians the flesh

by land, causing them to transport those vessels with anchors of vast weight from the Septentrional to the Mediterranean Sea, which are one hundred and thirty miles distant; as also abundance of great guns of the largest fort, which they carried on their bare, naked shoulders, so that opprest with many great and ponderous burthens, (I say no more than what I saw) they dyed by the way. He separated and divided families, forcing married men from their wives, and maids from their parents, which he bestow'd upon his Marriners and Soldiers, to gratifie their burning lust. All his ships he freighted with Indians, where hunger and thirst discharg'd them of their servitude and his cruelty by a welcome death. He had two companies of soldiers how hackt and tore them in pieces, like thunder from heaven speedily. O how many parents has he robb'd of their children, how many wives of their husbands, and children of their parents? How many adulteries, rapes, and what libidinous acts hath he been guilty of? How many hath he enslav'd and opprest with insufferable anguish and unspeakable calamities? How many tears, sighs and groans hath he occasion'd? To how many has he bin the author of desolation, during their peregrination in this, and of damnation in the World to come, not only to Indians, whose number is numberless, but even to Spaniards themselves, by whose help and assistance he committed such detestable butcheries and flagitious crimes? I supplicate Almighty God, that he would please to have Mercy on his soul, and require no other satisfaction than the violent death, which turn'd him out of this world!

OF THE KINGDOM OF JUCATAN

Editor Note: The savagery of the conquering Spaniards is almost unimaginable in its horrifying acts of inhumanity to man, including but not limited to rape, murder, butchery, and evil so despicable it is difficult to ascribe to human beings.

An impious wretch by his fabulous stories and relations to the King of Spain was made prefect of the Kingdom of Jucatan, in the year of our Lord 1526; and the other tyrants to this very day have taken the same indirect measures to obtain offices, and screw or wheedle themselves into publick charges or employments for this pretext, and authority, they had the greater opportunity to commit theft and rapine. This Kingdom was very well peopled, and both for temperature of air, and plenty of food and fruits, in which respect it is more fertile than Mexico, but chiefly for honey and wax, it exceeds all the Indian countries that hath hitherto bin discover'd. It is three hundred miles in compass. The inhabitants of this place do much excel all other Indians, either in polities or prudence, or in leading a regular life and morality, truly deserving to be instructed in the knowledge of the true God. Here the Spaniards might have erected many fair cities, and liv'd as it were in a Garden of Delights, if they had not, through covetousness, stupidity, and the weight of enormous crimes rendered themselves unworthy of so great a benefit. This tyrant, with three hundred men began to make war with these innocent people, living peaceable at home, and doing injury to none, which was the ruin of a great number of them. Now because this region affords no gold, and if it did the inhabitants would soon have wrought away their lives by hard working in the mines, that so he might accumulate gold by their bodies and souls, for which Christ was Crucified; for the generality he made slaves of those whose lives he spared. and sent away such ships as were driven thither by the wind of report, loaden with them, exchanging them for wine, oyl, vinegar, salt pork, garments, pack horses and other commodities, which he thought most necessary and fit for his use. He proposed to them the choice of fifty virgins, and she that was the fairest or best complexioned he bartered for a small cask of wine, oyl, vinegar or some inconsiderable quantity of salt pork, the same exchange he proferred of two or three hundred well-disposed young boys, and one of them who had the mind or presence of a princes son, was given up to them for a cheese, and one hundred more for a horse. Thus he continued his flagitious course from 1526 to 1533, inclusively, till there was news brought of the wealth and opulence of the region of Perusia, whither the Spaniards marcht, and so for some time there was a cessation of this tyranny, but in a few days after they returned and acted enormous crimes, robbed, and imprisoned them and committed higher offences against the God of Heaven; nor have they ye done, so that now these three hundred miles of land so populous (as I said before) lies now uncultivated and almost deserted.

No solifidian can believe the particular narrations of their barbarism, and cruelty in those countreys. I will only relate two or three stories which are fresh in my memory. The Spaniards used to trace the steps of the Indians, both men and women with curst currs, furious dogs; an Indian woman that was sick happened to be in the way in sight, who perceiving that she was not able to avoid being torn in pieces by the dogs, takes a cord that she had and hangs her self upon a beam, tying her child (which she unfortunately had with her) to her foot and no sooner had she done, yet the dogs were at her, tearing the child, but a priest coming that way baptiz'd it before quite dead.

When the Spaniards left this kingdom, one of them invited the son of some Indian Governour of a city or province, to go along with him, who told him he would not leave or desert his native countrey, where upon he threatened to cut off his ears if he refus'd to follow him. But the youth persisting resolutely, that he would continue in the place of his nativity; he drawing his sword cut off each ear, notwithstanding which he persever'd in his first opinion, and then as if he had only pincht him, smilingly cut off his nose and lips. This rogue did lasciviously boast before the Priest, and as if he had merited the greatest applause, commended himself to the very Heavens, saying he had made it his chief trade or business to impregnate Indian women, that when they were sold afterward, he might gain the more money by them.

In this kingdom or (I'm certain) in some province of New Spain, a Spaniard hunting and intent on his game, phancyed that his beagles wanted food, and to supply their hunger snatcht a young little babe from the mother's breast, cutting off his arms and legs, cast a part of them to every dog, which they having devour'd, he threw the remainder of the body to them. Thus it is plainly manifest how they value these poor creatures, created after the image of God, to cast them to their cannibal curs. But that which follows (if possible) a sin of a deeper dye.

Editor's Note: Although some of the priests and religious leaders were able to effectively teach the natives about the God of the Christians, their success was short-lived by the barbarisms of the invading armies.

Thus to the great joy and hope of these Priests reducing them to the knowledge of Christ they were received by the inhabitants of this Kingdom that surviv'd the heat and rage of the Spanish cruelties, but behold eighteen horse and twelve footmen by another way crept in among them, bringing with them many Idols, which were of great weight, and taken out of other regions by force. The Commander in Chief of these Spaniards summoned one of the dynasts or rulers of that province which they entered into, to appear before him, and command him to take these Idols with him, distribute them through his countrey and exchange every single Idol for an Indian man or woman; otherwise he would make war against him. The above said Lord compelled to it by fear did so accordingly with a command, that his subjects should adore worship and honour them, and in compensation send Indians male and female into servitude. The terrified people delivered up their children, and by this means there was an end made of this sacrilegious merchandize, and thus the basic satisfied the greedy desires of the (I dare not say Christian) Spaniards. One of these sacrilegious robbers was John Garcia by name, who being very sick and at the pint of death, had several idols hid under his bed, and calling his Indians that waited on him, as a nurse, commanded her not to party with those Idols at a small rate for they were of the better sort, and that she should not dispose of them without one Indian, for each Idol by way of barter. Thus by this his private and nuncupative Last Will and Testament distracted with these carking cares, he gave up the ghost; and who is it that will not fear his being tormented in the darkest and lowest Hell? Let us now consider what progress in religion the Spaniards made, and what examples of Christianism they gave, at their first arrival in America, how devoutly they honoured God, and what expense of sweat and toil they were at to promote his worship and adoration among the Infidels. Let it be also taken into serious consideration, whose sin is the greater, either Joroboam's, who made all Israel to sin, and caused two Golden Calves to be erected, or the Spaniards who traffick and trade in Idols like Judas, who was the occasion of such great scandals. These are the good deeds of the Spanish Dons who often, nay very often to feed their avarice, and accumulate gold have sold and still do sell, denied and still do deny Jesus Christ our Redeemer.

The Indians now finding the promises of the religious, that the Spaniards should not enter into this countrey, null and void; nay that the Spaniards brought Idols from other places to be put off there; when as they had delivered up their own to the priests to be burnt, that there might be only worship of the true God established among them; they were highly incensed against these Friars, and addressed themselves to them in these words following : 'Why have you deceived us, binding your promises with false protestations, that the Spaniards should not be admitted to come hither? And why have you burnt our Gods, when others are brought from other regions by the Spaniards? Are the God of other provinces more sacred than ours?'

The Friars was well as they could (though they had little to return in answer) endevou'd by soft language to appease them, and went to these thirty Spaniards, declaring the evil actions they were guilty of, humbly supplicating them to withdraw themselves from that place. Which they would by no means condescend to, and what is most flagitious and wicked perswaded the Indians, that they were introduc'd by those Priests, which being made known to them, these Indians resolved to be the death of these Monks, but having notice thereof by some courteous Indians, they stole from thence by night and fled, but after their departure the truth of the matter and the Spanish malice being understood they sent several messengers who followed them fifty miles distant beseeching them in the name of the Indians to return and begging pardon for the ignorant mistake.

The Priests relying on their words, returned, and were caress'd like angles sent from Heaven, and continued with them (from whom they received a thousand kindnesses) four or five months. But when the Spaniards persisted in their resolution not to quit the place, although the Vice-Roy did use all endeavours and fair means to recall them, they were proclaim'd traitors, guilty of High Treason and because they continued still exercising tyranny and perpetrated nefarious crimes, the Priests were sensible they would study revenge, though it might be some considerable time before they put it in execution, fearing that it might fail upon their own heads, and since they could not exercise the function of their ministry securely and undisturbed by reason of the continual incursions and assaults made by the Spaniards, they consulted about their departure, and did leave this kingdom accordingly which remain'd destitute of all Christian Doctrine and these poor souls are at this day involv'd in the obscurity of their former misery and ignorance, they being deprived by these accursed Spaniards, of all hopes of remedy, and the irrigation of divine knowledge, just like young withering plants for want of water; for in that very juncture of time, when these religioso's took leave, they embraced the doctrine of our faith with the greatest fervency and eagerness imaginable.

OF THE PROVINCE OF ST. MARTHA

The Province of St. Martha was rich in the neighboring Golden Mines, and a fruitful soil, nay the people were very expert and industrious in those mine-works. Upon this account, or temptation it was, that from the year 1540 to 1542, abundance of tyrants sailed thither, laying waste the whole country by their depredations, slaughtering the inhabitants at a prodigious and bloody rate; and robbing them of all their gold, who dayly fled to their ships for refuge, moving sometime to one place, and sometime to another. And, thus those provinces were laid waste, the greatest outrages being committed on the sea shore, which lasted till the year 1523, whither the Spaniards then came to seat themselves, and fis[t] their intended habitation. And, because it is a plentiful region and opulent withal; it was subjected to several rulers, who like infernal fiends contended who should obtain the Palm, by out-staining the sword of his predecessor in innocent blood; insomuch, that from the year 1529 to this very day, they have wasted and spoiled as much good ground as extended five hundred miles, and unpeopled the countrey.

If I design'd to enumerate all the impieties, butcheries, desolations, iniquities, violence's, destructions and other piacula and black enormities committed and perpetrated by the Spaniards in this province, against God, the King, and these harmless nations; I might compile a voluminous history, and that shall be completed, if God permit my glass to run longer, in his good time. It may suffice for the present to relate some passages written in a letter to our King and Lord by a Reverend Bishop of these provinces, dated the 20th of May An. Dom. 1541, wherein among other matters he thus words it[:]

'I must acquaint your Sacred Majesty, that the only way to succour and support this tottering region is to free it from the power of a father in law, and marry it to a husband who will treat her as she ought to be, and lovingly entertain her, and that must be done with all possible expedition too, if not, I am certain that she will suddenly decay and come to nothing by the covetous and sordid deportment of the Governours,'

And, a little after he writes thus:

'By this means your Majesty will plainly know and understand how to depose the prefects or Governours of those regions from their office if they deserve it, that so they may be alleviated and eas'd of such burthens; which if not perform'd in my opinion, the body politick will never recover its health. And this I will make appear to your Majesty that they are not Christians, but Devils; not Servants of God and the King, but traitors to the King and Laws, who are conversant in those regions. And, in reality nothing can be more obstructive to those that live peaceably, then inhumane and barbarous usage, which they, who lead a quiet and peaceable life, too frequently undergo, and this is so fastidious and nauseous to them, that there can be nothing in the world so odious and detestable among them as the name of a Christian; for they term the Christians in their language "Yares", that is, "Devils"; and in truth are not without reason; for the actions of those that reside in these regions, are not such as speak them to be Christians or men, gifted with reason, but absolute Devils, hence it is, that the Indians, perceiving these actions committed by the heads as well as members, who are void of all compassion and humanity, do

judge the Christian laws to be of the same strain and temper, and that their God and King are the authors of such enormities. Now to endeavour to work upon them a contrary perswasion is to no purpose; for this would afford them a greater latitude and liberty to deride Jesus Christ and his laws. Now the Indians who protect and defend themselves by force of arms, think it more eligible, and far better to dye once, than suffer several and may deaths under the Spanish power. This I know experimentally, Most Invincible Casar.'
And he adds farther:

'Your Majesty is more Powerful in subjects and servants, who frequent these Kingdoms, then you can imagine. Nor is there one Soldier among them all, who does not publickly and openly profess, if he robs, steals, spoils, kills, burns His Majesties subjects, 'tis to purchase gold. He will not say that he therein does your Majesty great service, for they affirm they do it to obtain their won share and dividend. Wherefore, Most Invincible Casar, it would be a very prudential act for your Majesty to testifie by a rigid correction and severe punishment of some malefactors, that it is disservice to you for your subjects to commit such evil acts, as trend to the disobedience and dishonour of the Almighty.'

What you have read hitherto is the relation of the said Bishop of St. Martha, epitomized and extracted from his letters, whereby it is manifest, how savagely they handle these mild and affable people. They term them warlike Indians, who betake themselves to the mountains to secure themselves from Spanish cruelty; and call them Country Indians, or Inhabitants, who by a dreadful massacre are delivered up to tyrannical and horrible servitude, whereby at length they are become depopulated, made desolate, and utterly destroy'd; as appears by the Epistle of the prementioned Bishop, who only gives us a slight account or essay of their persecution and sufferings. The Indians of this country use to break out into such words as these, when they are driven, loaded like brutes through the uncouth wayes in their journeys over the mountains, if they happen to faint through weakness, and miscarry through extremity of labour, (for then they are kicked and cudge'd, their teeth dashed out with the pummels of their swords to raise them to go on without respiration, or time to take breath, and all this with the following increpation, or upbraiding and taunting words,'O what a wicket Villain art thou?') I say they burst out into these expressions, 'I am absolutely tir'd kill me, I desire to dye, being weary of my life as well as my burthen and journey!' And this not without deep heart-breaking sighs, they being scarce able to draw or breathe out their words, which are the characteristically notes, and infallible of the mind drowned in anguish and sorrow. M[a]y it please our merciful God to order the discovery of these crimes to be manifested to those persons, who are able and oblig'd to redress them.

OF THE PROVINCE OF CARTHAGENA

This province is distant Fifty Miles from the Isle of St. Martha westward, and situated on the confines of the country of Cenusia, from whence it extends one hundred miles to the Bay of Uraba, and contains a very long tract of land southward. These provinces from the year 1498 to this present time were most barbarously us'd, and made desert by murder and slaughter, but that I may the sooner conclude this brief summary. I will not handle the particulars; to the end I may the better give an account of the detestable villanies that ruin'd other regions.

OF THE PEARL COAST, PARIA AND TRINITY-ISLE

The Spaniards made great spoils and havock from the Parian Coast to the Bay of Venecuola, exclusively, which is about two hundred miles. It can hardly be exprest by tongue or pen how many, and how great injuries and injustices, the inhabitants of this sea-shore have endur'd from the year 1510, to this day. I will only relate two or three peculiar criminal acts of the first magnitude, capable of comprehending all other enormities that deserve the sharpest torments, wit and malice can invent, and so make way for a deserved judgment upon them.

A nameless Pirate of the year 1510, accompanied with a parcel of sixty or seventy, arriv'd at Trinity-Island, which exceeds Sicile, both in amplitude and fertility, and is contiguous to the Continent on that side where it toucheth upon Paria, whose inhabitants, according to their quality, are more addicted to probity and v[i]rtue, than the rest of the Indians; who immediately published an Edict, that all the inhabitants should come and cohabit with them. The Indian Lords and subjects gave them a debonair and Brotherly reception, serving them with wonderful alacrity, furnishing them with dayly provisions in so plentiful a manner, that they might have sufficed a more numerous company; for it is the mode among Indians of this New World, to supply the Spaniards very bountifully with all manner of necessaries. A short time after the Spaniards built a stately house, which was an appartment for the Indians, that they might accomplish their premeditated designs, which was thus effected. When they were to thatch it, and had rais'd it two mens height, they inclos'd several of them there, to expedite the work, as they pretended, but in truth that they who were within, might not see those without; thus part of them surrounded the house with sword in hand that no one should stir out, and part of them entered it, and bound the Indians, menacing them with death if they offered to move a foot; and if any one endeavoured to escape, he was presently hackt in pieces; but some of them partly wounded, and partly unwounded getting away, with others who went not into the house, about one hundred and two hundred betook themselves to another house with bows and arrows; and when they were all there, the Spaniards secur'd the doors, throwing in fire at another place, and so they all perished. From hence they set sail to the Island of St. John with near upon one hundred and eighty slaves, whom they had bound, where they sold one half of them, and thence to Hispaniola, where they dispos'd of the rest. Now when I taxed this Captain with wickedness and treachery in the very Isle of St. John, he dismist me with this answer 'Forbear good Sir, I had this in commission from those who sent me hither, that I should surprize them by them by the spetious pretense of peace, whom I could not sieze by open force' And in truth this same Captain told me with his own mouth, that in Trinity-Isle alone, he had met with a father and mother in civil usage, which he uttered to his greater confusion and the aggravation of his sins. The monks of our Order of St. Dominic on a certain time held a Consult about sending one of their Fraternity into this Island, that by their preaching they might instruct them in the Christian Faith, and teach them the way to be sav'd, of which they were wholly ignorant. And to this end they sent thither a religious and licentiate in Theologie, (or Doctor in Divinity, as we term it among us) a man famous for his vertue and holiness with a Laic his Associate, to visit the country, converse with the inhabitants, and find out the most convenient places for the erection of Monasteries. As soon as they were arriv'd according to custom, they were entertain'd like Coelestial Messengers, with great affection, joy and respect, as well as they could, for they were ignorant of their tongue, and so made use of signs, for the present.

It hap[p]ned that after the departure of that vessel that brought these religious men, another came into the Port, whose crew according to their hellish custom, fraudulently, and unknown to the religious brought away a Prince of that Province as captive, who was call'd Alphonsus, (for they are ambitious of Christian name) and forthwith desire without farther information, that he would baptize him; but the said Lord Alphonsus was deceitfully overperswaded to go on board of them with his wife and about seventeen more, pretending that they would give him a collation; which the Prince and they did, for he was confident, that the religious would by no means suffer him [to] be abus'd, for he had no so much confidence in the Spaniards; but as soon as they were upon deck, the perfidious rogues, set sail for Hispaniola, where they were sold as slaves. The whole country being extremely discompos'd, and understanding that their Prince and Princess were violently carried away, addressed themselves to these Religioso's who were in great danger of losing their lives; but they being made to understand this unjust action, were extraordinarily afflicted, and 'tis probable would have suffered death, rather than permit the Indians to be so injuriously dealt with, which might prove an obstruction to their receiving of, and believing in God's Word. Yet the Indians were sedated by the promises of the Religious; for they told them, they would send letters by the first ship that was bound of Hispaniola, whereby they would procure the restitution and return of their Lord and his retinue. It pleased God to send a ship thither forthwith, to the greater confirming of the Governours damnation, where in the letters they sent to the Religious of Hispaniola, letters containing repeated exclamations and protestations, and protest against such actions, but those that received them denied them justice, for that they were partakers of that prey, made of those Indians so [u]njustly and impiously captivated. But when the Religious, who had engag'd to the inhabitants, that their Lord Alphonsus should be restor'd within four months, and found that neither in four, nor eight months he was return'd, they prepar'd themselves for death, and to deliver up their life to Christ, to whom they had offer'd it before their departure from Spain: Thus the innocent Indians were revenged on the innocent Priests; for they were of opinion, that the Religious had a hand in the plot, partly, because they found their promises that their Lord should return within four months, ineffectual, and partly because the inhabitants made no difference between a Religious Frier and a Spanish rogue. At another time it fell out likewise, through the rampant tyranny and cruel deeds of evil-minded Christians, that the Indians put to death two Dominican Friers, of which I am a faithful witness, escaping my self, not without a very great miracle, which transaction I resolve silently to pass over, least I should terrifie the reader with the horror of the fact.

In these provinces, there was a city seated on the Bay of Codera, whose Lord was call'd Higueroto, a name, either proper to persons or common to the rulers of the place. A Cacic of such signal clemency, and his subjects of such noted vertue, that the Spaniards who came thither, were extraordinarily welcome, furnished with provisions, enjoying peace and comfort, and no refreshment wanting; but a perfidious wretch got many of them on board, and sold them to the Islanders of St. John. At the same time I landed upon that Island, where I obtained a sight of this tyrant, and heard the relation of his actions. He utterly destroy'd that land, which the rest of the Spaniards took very unkindly at his hands, who frequently play'd the Pirate, and rob'd on that shore, detesting it as a wicked thing, because they had lost that place, where they use to be treated with as great hospitality and freedom, as if they had been under their own roof. Nay, they transported from this place, among them, to the Isles of Hispaniola and St. John two millions of men and upward, and made the coast a desert.

It is most certainly true, that they never ship off a vessel freighted with Indians, but they pay a third part as tribute to the sea, besides those who are slaughter'd when found in their own houses. Now the source and original of all this is the ends they have propos'd to themselves. For there is a necessity of taking with them a great number of Indians, that they may gain a great sum of mon[e]y by their sale. Now the ships are very slenderly furnished with provisions and water in small quantity, to satisfie few, left the tyrants, who are term'd owners or proprietors of ships should be at too great expence in victualling their vessels, nay they scarce carry food enough with them to maintain the Spaniards that manage the vessel, which is the reason so many Indians dye with hunger and thirst, and of necessity they must be thrown over-board; Nay one of them told me this for a truth, that there being such a multitude of men thus destroy'd a ship may sail from the Isle of Lucaya to Hispaniola, which is a voyage of twenty leagues and upward, without chart or compass, by the sole direction or observation of dead fluctuating carkasses.

But afterward, when arriv'd and driven up into the Isle whither they are brought to be sold, there is no person that is in some small measure compassionate, but would be extremely mov'd and discompos'd at the sight; viz. to spie old men and women, together with naked children half starv'd. Then they separate parents from children, wives from their husbands, about ten or twenty in a company, and cast lots for them, that the detestable owners of the ships may have their share; who prepare two or three ships, and equip them as a fleet of Pirates, going ashore ravaging and forcing men out of their houses, and then robbing them, but when the lot of any one of them falls upon a parcel, that hath an aged or diseased man, the tyrant, whose allotment he is, usually bursts out, as followth 'Let this old fellow be damn'd, why do you bestow him upon me; must I think you, be at the charge of his burial? And this sickly wretch, how comes he to be one of my allo[t]ted portion must I take care for his cure? Not I.'   Hence you may guess what estimate and value the Spaniards put upon the Indians, and whether they practise and fulfil[l] that Divine Heavenly precept injoying mutual love and society.

There can be nothing more cruel and detestable then the tyrannical usage of the Spaniards towards the Indians in their pearl-fishing; for torments undergone in the unnatural exenteration and tearing out with paracidal hands the richer bowels of our common Mother, or the inward cruciating racks of the most profligate, heaven daring desperado can admit of no comparison with these, although the extracting or digging for gold is one of the sharpest subterranean drudgeries, they plunge them down four or five ells deep under water, where swimming about without breathing, they eradicate and pull up Oisters, wherein the pearls are engendred. Sometimes they rise up to the superfities of the water with nets full of Oisters for respiration and air, but if these miserable creatures stay but a little more then is ordinary to rest themselves the hangman is immediately upon them in a Canow or small boat, who bearing them with many stripes drag them by the hair of the head under water, that they may drudge again at their expilcation or pearl fishing. Their food is fish, and the same which contains the pearls and Cassabus made of roots with a few Mahids, the bread of that countrey; in the former there is little or no nutriment or substance, and the other is not made without great trouble, nor for all this have they a sufficient allowance thereof to support nature. Their lodging or bed is the earth confined to a pair of stocks, for fear that they should run away. And it frequently happens that they are drown'd with to toil of this kind of fishing and never more seen, for the Tuberoms and Maroxi (certain Marine Monsters that devour a complete proportioned man wholly at once) prey upon them under water. You must consider with all, that it is impossible for the strongest constitution to continue long under water without breathing, and they ordinarily dye though the extreme rigro of the cold, spitting blood which is occasioned by the too great compression of the breast, procreated by a continued holding breath under water, for by too much cold a profluvium of blood follows. Their hair naturally black is changed into a combust, burnt or sun-colour like that of the Sea Wolves, their shoulders and backs covered, or overspread with a saltish humor that they appear rather like monsters in human shape then men.

They have destroy'd all the Lucayans by this intolerable or rather diabolical exercise, for the accustomary emolument or gain of lucre, and by this means gain'd the value of fifty, sometimes one hundred Crowns of every individual Indian. They sell them (though it is prohibited) publickly; for the Lucayans were excellent swimmers, and several perished in this Isle that came from other Provinces.

OF THE KINGDOM OF VENECUELA

Our Sovereign Lord the King in the year 1526, over-perswaded by fallacious appearances (for the Spaniards use to conceal from His Majesties knowledge the damages and detriments, which God himself, the Souls and state of the Indians did suffer) intrusted the Kingdom of Venecuela longer and larger then the Spanish dominions, with its Government and absolute jurisdiction to some German merchants, with power to make certain capitulations and conventions, who came into this Kingdom with three hundred men, and there found a benign mild and peaceable people, as they were throughout the Indies till injured by the Spaniards. These more cruel then the rest beyond comparison, behav'd themselves more inhumanely then rapacious tygres wolves and lyons, for they had the jurisdiction of this Kingdom, and therefore possessing it with the greater freedom from control; lay in wait and were the more vigilant with greater care and avarice to understand the practical part of heaping up wealth, and robbing the inhabitants of their gold and silver, surpassing all their predecessors in those indirect ways, rejecting wholly both the fear of their God and King, nay forgetting that they were born men with reasonable faculties.

These incarnate devils laid waste and desolate four hundred miles of most fertile land, containing vast and wonderful provinces, most spatious and large valleys surrounded with hills, forty miles in length, and many towns richly abounding in gold and silver. They destroy'd so many and such considerable regions, that there is not one supernumerary witness left to relate the story, unless perchance some that lurkt in the caverns and womb of the earth to evade death by their inhumane swords embrew'd in innocent Indian blood, escaped. I judge that they by new invented and unusual torments ruinated four or five millions of souls and sent them all to hell. I will give a taste of two or three of their transactions that hereby you may guess at the rest.

They made the supreme Lord of the Province a Slave, to squeeze his gold from him, racking him to extort his confession who escaping fled into the mountains, their common sanctuary, and his subjects lying absconded in the thickets of the woods, were stir'd up to sedition and tumult or mutiny. The Spaniards follow and destroy many of them, but those that were taken alive and in their power were all publickly sold for slaves by the common Crier. They were in all Provinces they came into entertained and welcomed by the Indians with songs, dances and rich presents but rewarded very ungratefully with bloodshed and slaughter. The German Captain and tyrant caused several of them to be clapt into a thatcht house, and there cut in pieces; but some of them to avoid falling by their bloody and merciless swords, climb'd up to the beams and rafters of the house, and the Governour, hearing it (O cruel Brute?) commanded fire to be put to it and burnt them all alive, leaving the region desert and desolate.

They also came to another stately province, bordering on St. Martha; whose inhabitants did them may egregious and notable services, bestowing on them innumerable quantities of gold besides many other gifts, but when they were upon departure, in retribution of their civil treating and deportment the German tyrant, commanded that all the Indians, with their wives and children if possible, should be taken into custody; inclosed in some large capacious place, and that there it should be signified unto them, whosoever desired to be set at liberty should redeem himself at the will and pleasure (as to price) of the unjust Governour, or at a certain rate imposed upon himself, his wife and every child's head; and to expedite the business prohibited the administration or allowance of any food to them, till the gold required for redemption was paid down to the utmost grain. Several of them sent home to discharge the demanded price of their redemption, and procur'd their freedom, as well as they could by one means of other, that so they might return to their livelihood and profession, but not long after he sent other rogues and robbers among them to enslave those that were redeemed.

To the same goal they are brought a second time, being instigated or rather constrained to a speedy redemption by hunger and thirst; thus many of them were twice or thrice taken, captiv'd and redeemed; but some who were not capable of depositing such a sum, perished there. Farthermore this tyrant was big with an itching desire after the discovery of the Perusian Mines, which he did accomplish. Nay, should I enumerate the particular cruelties, slaughters, &c. committed by him though my discourse would not in the least be contrariant to the truth, yet it would not be believed and only stupifie and amaze the reader.

This course the other tyrants took who set sail from Venecuela and St. Martha (with the same resolution of detecting the Perusian Golden, consecrated houses as them they esteemed) who found the fruitful region so desolate, deserted, and wasted by fire and sword, that those cruel tyrants themselves were smitten with wonder and astonishment at the traces and ruins of such prodigious devastations.

All these things and many more were prov'd by witness in the Indian Exchequer, and the Records of their Testimony were ent[e]red in that Court, though these execrable tyrants burnt many of them that there might be little or nothing prov'd as a cause of those great devastations and evils perpetrated by them. For the Minister of Justice who have hitherto lived in India, through their obscure and damnable blindness, were not much solicitous about the punishment of the crimes and butcheries which have been and are still committed by these tyrants, only they may say possibly because such a one, and such a one hath wickedly and barbarously dealt with the Indians, that is the reason so great a summ of Crowns in money is diminished already or retrenched from His Majesties Annual Revenue, and this general and confused proof is sufficient (as they worthily conceive) to purge or repress such great and heinous crimes. And though they are but few, are not verified as they ought to be, nor do they attribute and lay upon them that stress and weight as they ought to do, for if they did perform their duty to God and the King; it could not be made apparent as it may be, that these German tyrants have cheated and rob'd the King of three millions of gold and upward;

and thus these enemies to God and the King began to depopulate these regions and destroy them, cheating his Majesty of two millions of gold per annum, nor can it be expected, that the detriment done to his Majesty can possibly be retriev'd as long as the Sun and Moon endures, unless God by a miracle should raise as may thousands from death to life, as have bin destroy'd. And these are the temporal dammages the King suffers. It would be also a work worthy the inquiry into, to consider how many cursed sacrileges and indignities God himself have been affronted with to the dishonour of this name. And what recompense can be made for the loss of so many souls as are now tormented in hell by the cruelty and covetousness of these brutish German tyrants. But I will conclude all their impiety and barbarism with one example, viz. That from the time they ent[e]red upon this country to this very day, that is, seventeen years, they have remitted many ships fraighted with Indians to be sold as slaves to the Isles of St. Martha, Hispaniola, Jamaica, and St. John, selling a million of persons at the least. I speak modestly and still do expose to sale to this very year of our Lord 1542, the King's Council in this Island seeing and knowing it, yet what they find to be manifest and apparent they connive at, permit and countenance, and wink at the horrid impieties and devastations innumerable which are committed on the coasts of this Continent, extending four hundred miles in length, and continues still together with Venecuela and St. Martha under their jurisdiction, which they might easily have remedied and timely prevented.

OF THE PROVINCES OF FLORIDA

Three tyrants at several times made their entrance into these provinces since the year 1510 or 1511, to act those crimes which others, and two of these three made it their sole business to do in out regions to the end, that they might advance themselves to higher dignities and promotions than they could deserve, by the effusion of blood and destruction of these people; but at length they all were cut off by a violent death, and the houses which they formerly built and erected with the cement of human blood, (which I can sufficiently testifie of these three) perished with them, and their memory rot[t]en, and as absolutely washed away from off the face of the earth, as if they had never had a being. These men deserted these regions, leaving them in great distraction and confusion, nor were they branded with less notes of infamy, by the certain slaughters they perpetrated, thought they were but few in number than the rest. For the just God cut them off before they did much mischief, and reserv'd the castigation and revenge of those evil which I know, and was an eye-witness of, to this very time and place. As to the fourth tyrant, who lately, that is, in the year 1538, came hither well-furnished with men and ammunition, we have received no account these three years last past; but we are very confident, that he, at this first arrival, acted like a bloody tyrant, even to extasie and madness, if he be still alive with his follower, and did injure, destroy, and consume a vast number of men (for he was branded with infamous cruelty above all those who with their assistants committed crimes and enormities of the first magnitude in these Kingdoms and Provinces) I conceive, God hath punished him with the same violent death, as he did other tyrants. But because my pen is wearied with relating such execrable and sanguinary deeds (not of men but beasts) I will trouble my self no longer with the dismal and fatal consequences thereof.

These people were found by them to be wise, grave, and well disposed, though their usual butcheries and cruelties in oppressing them like brutes, with heavy burthens, did rack their minds with great terror and anguish. At their entry into a certain village, they were welcomed with great joy and exultation, replenished them with victuals, till they were all satisfied, yielding up to them above six hundred men to carry their bag and baggage, and like grooms to look

after their horses. The Spaniards departing thence, a Captain related to the Superiour tyrant returned thither to rob this (no diffident or mistrustful) people, and pierced their King through with a lance, of which wound he dyed upon the spot, and committed several other cruelties into the bargain. In another neighboring town, whose inhabitants they thought, were more vigilant and watchful, having had the news of their horrid acts and deeds, they barbarously murdered them all with their lances and swords, destroying all, young and old, great and small, Lords and subject without exception.

Of the New Kingdom of GRANADA

Many tyrants there were, who set sail from Venecuela, St. Martha, and Carthagena, hastening to the Conquest of Perusia, Anno Dom. 1539, and they accompanied with many more going farther from this region, endeavored to penetrate into the heart of this countrey, where they found about three hundred miles from Carthagena and St. Martha, many admirable Provinces and most fruitful land, furnished with an even-tempered or meek-spirited people, as they are in other parts of India; very rich in gold and those sorts of precious stones known by the name of emeralds; to which Province they gave the name of Granada, upon this account, because the tyrant who first arrived in these regions, was born in the Kingdom of Granada belonging to these parts; now they that spoiled these provinces with their rapine being wicked, cruel, infamous butchers, and delighting in the effusion of humane blood, having practically experimented the peculiar and grand enormities perpetrated among the Indians; and upon this account their diabolical actions are so great, so many in number, and represented so grievously horrid by circumstantial aggravations, that they exceed all the villanies committed by others, nay by themselves in other regions. I will only select and cull out a few out of so great a number which have been transacted by them within these three years, for my present purpose.

A certain Governour, because he that went to commit depredations and spoils in the Kingdom of Granada, would not admit him, as a companion in his robberies and cruelties, set up an Inquisition, and produced proofs confirmed by great evidence, whereby he palpably lays open, and proves the slaughters and homicides he committed, and persists in to this very day, which were read in the Indian Courts of Judicature, and are there now recorded.

In this Inquisition the witnesses depose, that when all these Kingdoms enjoy'd peace and tranquility, the Indians serv'd the Spaniards, and got their living by constant day-labour in tilling and manuring the ground, bringing them much gold, and many gems, particularly Emeralds, and what other commodities they could, and possessed, their cities and dominions being divided among the Spaniards, to procure which is the chiefest of their care and pains; and these are the proper measures they take to obtain their proposed ends, to wit, heaping and treasuring up of gold and riches.

Now when all the Indians were under their accustomed tyranny: A certain tyrant, and Chief Commander, took the King and Lord of the whole Countrey, and detain'd him captive for six or seven months, demanding of him, without any reason, store of gold and Emeralds. The said King, whose name was Bogoca, though fear, promised him a house of gold, hoping, in time, to escape out of his clutches, who thus plagu'd him, and sent some Indians for gold, who frequently and at several times brought him a great quantity of gold, and many jewels; but because the King did not, according to his promise, bestow upon him an apartment made of pure gold, he must therefore forfeit his life. The tyrant commanded him to be brought to tryal before himself, and so they cite and summon to a tryal the greatest King in the whole region; and the tyrant pronounced his sentence, that unless he did perform his Golden Promise he should be exposed to severe torments. They rackt him, poured boiling soap into his bowels, chain'd his legs to one post, and fastened his neck to another; two men holding his hands, and so applyed the scorching heat of the fire to his feet; the tyrant himself often casting his eye upon him, and threatening him with death, if he did not give him the promised gold; and thus with these kind of horrid torments, the said Lord was destroy'd; which while they were doing, God being willing to manifest how displeasing these cruelties are to his Divine Majesty, the whole city, that was the stage on which they were acted, was consumed by fire; and the rest of the Captains following his example, destroy'd all the Lords of that region by fire and faggot.

Once it fell out, that many Indians addressed themselves to the Spaniards with all humility and simplicity, as they use to do, who thinking themselves safe and secure, behold the Captain comes into the city, where they were to do their work, and commands all these Indians slipping and taking their rest, after supper, being wearied with the heavy drudgery of the day, to be slain by the sword: And this stratagem he put in practice, to make a greater impression of fear on all the minds of the inhabitants; and another time a certain Captain commanded the Spaniards to declare upon oath, how many Casics and Indians every individual person had in his family at home, who were presently lead to a publick place, and lost their heads; so there perisht, that bout, four or five hundred men. The witnesses depose this of a particular tyrant, that by beating, cutting off the hands and noses of many women as well as men, and destroying several persons in great numbers, he exercised horrid cruelties.

Then one of the Captains sent this bloody tyrant into the Province of Bogata, to inquire who succeeded that Prince there, whom he so barbarously and inhumanely murder'd, who traveling many miles in this countrey, took as many Indians as he could get, some of which because they did not tell him who was successor of this deceased Prince, had their hands cut off, and others were expose to hunger-starv'd currs, to be devour'd by them, and as many of them perished miserable.

Another time about the fourth Watch, early in the morning he fell upon several Casics, Noblemen and other Indians, who lookt upon themselves to be safe enough, (for they had their faith and security given, that none of them should receive any damage or injury) relying upon this, they left the mountains their lurking places, without any suspicion or fear. and returned to their cities, but he seized on them all, and commanding them to extend their hands on the ground, cut them off with his own sword, saying, that he punished them after this manner, because they would not inform him what Lord it was, that succeeded in that Kingdom.

The inhabitants of one of these Provinces, perceiving that four or five of their Governours were sent to the other world in a fiery vehicle or chariot, being terrified therewith, took to the mountains for sanctuary, there being four or five thousand in number, as appears by good evidence; and theforesaid Captain sends a tyrant, more cruel than any of the rest after them. The Spaniards ascend the mountains by force (for the Indians were naked an unarm'd) proclaiming peace, if they would desist and lay down their arms, which the Indians no sooner heard, but quitted their childish weapons; and this was no sooner done but this sanguinary Spaniard sent some to possess themselves of the fortifications, and they being secur'd, to attaque the Indains. Thus they, like wolves and lyons, did rush upon this flock of sheep, and were so tired with slaughter, that they were forced to desist for a while and take breath, which done, the Captain commands them to fall to it gain at the same bloody rate, and precipitate all that survived the butchery, from the top of the mountains, which was of a prodigious height; and that was perfrom'd accordingly. And the witnesses farther declare upon oath, that they saw the bodies of about seven hundred Indians falling from the mount at one time, like cloud abscuring the air, who were all broken to pieces.

This very tyrant came once to the city Cota, where he surprized abundance of men, together with fifteen or twenty Casics of the highest rank and quality, whom he cast to the dogs to be torn limb-meal in pieces, and cut the hands of several men and women, which being run through with a pole, were exposed to be viewed and gaz'd upon by the Indians, where you might see at once seventy pair of hands, transfixed with poles; nor is it to be forgotten, that he cut off the noses of many women and children.

"The witnesses farther depose, that the cruelties and great slaughters committed in the aforsaid new Kingdom of Granada, by this Captain, and other tyrants, the destroyers of mankind, who accompany him, and have power still given them by him to exercise the same, are such and have power still given them by him to exercise the same, are such and so hainous, that if his Majesty does not opportunely apply some remedy, for the redress and prevention of such mischiefs for the future, (since the Indians are daily slaughtered to accumulate and enrich themselves with gold, which the inhabitants have been so rob'd of, that they are now grown bare, for what they had, they have disposed to the Spaniards already) this Kingdom will soon decay and be made desolate, and consequently the Land being destitute of Indians, who should manure it, will lye fallow and incultivated.

And, here is to be noted, how pestilential and inhumane the cruelty of these tyrants hath been, and how violently exercised, when as in two or three years space, they were all slain, and the countrey wholly desolate and deserted, as those that have been eye-witnesses can testifie; they having acted like merciless men, not having the fear of God and the King before their eyes, but by the instigation of the Devil; so that it may well be said and affirmed, not one person will be left alive, unless his Majesty does retard, and put a stop to the full career of their cruelties, which I am very apt to believe, for I have seen with these very eyes of mine, many Kingdoms laid waste and depopulated in a small time. There are other stately Provinces on the confines of the New Kingdom of Granada, as Popayan and Cali, together with three or four more above five hundred miles in length, which they destroyed, in the same manner, as they have done other places, and laid them absolutely waste by the prementioned slaughters, who were very populous, and the soil very fruitful. They who came among us from those regions, that nothing can be more deplorable or worthy of pity and commiseration, then to behold such large and great cities totally ruinated, and intombed in their own ashes, and that in a city adorn'd with 1000 or 2000 fabricks, there are hardly now to be seen 50 standing, the rest being utterly demolished, or consum'd and leveled to the ground by fire and in some parts regions of 100 miles in length, (containing spacious cities) are found absolutely destroyed and consumed by fire.

Finally, many great tyrants who came out of the Perusian Kingdoms by the Quitonians travelled to the said new Kingdom of Granada and

Popayan, and by Carthagena and the Urabae, they directed their course to Calisium, and several other tyrants of Carthagena assault Quito, who joyn'd themselves in an intire body and wholly depopulated and laid waste that region for the space of 600 miles and upward, with the loss of a prodigious number of poor souls; nor as yet do they treat the small remnant of so great and innocent a people with more humanity then formerly.

I desire therefore that the readers who have or shall peruse these passages, would please seriously to consider whether or no, such barbarous, cruel and inhumane acts as these do not transcend and exceed all the impiety and tyranny, which can enter into the thoughts or imagination of Man, and whether these Spaniards deserve not the name of Devils. For which of these two tings is more eligible or desirable whether the Indians should be delivered up to the Devils themselves to be tormented or the Spaniards? That is still a question. Nor can I here omit one piece of villany, (whether it ough to be postpon'd or come behind the cruelty of brute animals, that I leave to decision). The Spaniards who are conversant among the Indians bred up curst curs, who are so well instructed and taught they at first sight, fly upon the Inhabitants tearing them limb by limb, and so presently devour them.

Editor's note: The chronicler of these outrages then implores the reader to consider what consequence ought to befall the perpetrators of such infamy.

Now, let all persons whether Christians or not consider, if ever such a thing as this reacht the ears of any man, they carry these dogs with them as companions where ever they go, and kill the fettered Indians in multitudes like hogs for their food; thus sharing with them in the butchery. Nay they frequently call one to the other, saying, 'Lend me the fourth part of one of your slaves to feed my dogs, and when I kill one, Iwill repay you!' As if they had only borrowed a quarter of a hog or sheep. Others, when they go a hunting early in the morning, upon their return, if you ask them what sport had you to day at the game? They will answer, enough, enough, for my dogs have killed and worried 15 or 20 Indian vassals. Now all these things are plainly prov'd upon those inquisitions and examinations made by one tyrant against another. What I beseech you, can be more horrid or barbarous?

But, I will desist from writing any longer at this time, till some messenger brings an account of greater and blacker impieties (if greater can be committed) or else till we come to behold them again, as we have done for the space of forty two years with our own eyes. I will only make this small addition to what I have said that the Spaniards, from the beginning of their first entrance upon America to this present day, were no more solicitous of promoting the preaching of the Gospel of Christ to these Nations, then if they had been dogs or beasts, but which is worst of all, they expressly prohibited their addresses to the Religious, laying many heavy impositions upon them dayly afflicting and persecuting them, that they might not have so much time and leisure at their own disposal, as to attend their preaching and divine service; for they lookt upon that to be an impediment to their getting gold, and raking up riches which their avarice stimulated them so boundlessly to prosecute. Nor do they understand any more of a God, whether he be made of wood, brass or clay, then they did above an hundred years ago, New Spain only exempted, which is a small part of America, and was visited and instructed by the Religious. Thus they did formerly and still do perish without true faith, or the knowledge and benefit of our Religious Sacraments.

I Frier Bartholomeas de las Casas or Casaus of the Order of St. Dominick who through the mercy of God am arriv'd at the Spanish Court, cordially wishing the expulsion of Hell or these Hellish acts out of the Indies; fearing least those souls redeemed by the pretious blood of Christ, should perish eternally, but heartily desiring that they may acknowledge their Creator and be saved; as also for the care and compassion that I ever had for my Native Countrey Castile, dreading least God should destroy it for the many sins committed by the Natives her children, against faith, honour and their neighbours: I have a length upon the request of some persons of great quality in this Court, who are fervently zealous of the Honour of God, and moved with pity at the calamities and afflictions of their neighbours (though I long since proposed it within my self, and resolved to accomplish it, but could not, being distracted with the avocatons of multiplicity of constant business and employment, have leisure to effect it) I say I have at length finished this Treaties and Summary at Valencia, Decemb. 8. An. Dom. 1542, when they were arrived at the height, and utmost degree of executing violences, oppressions, tyrray, desolations, torments, and calamities in all the aforesaid regions, inhabited by the Spaniards (though they are more cruel in some places than others) yet Mexico with its confines were more favourably treated than the rest of the Provinces. And indeed no man durst openly and publickly do any injury to the inhabitants; for there some Justice, (which is no where else in India) though very little is done and practiced; yet they are grievously opprest with intolerable taxes. But I do really believe, and am fully perswaded that our Sovereign Lord Charles the Fifth, Emperour and King of Spain, our Lord and Prince, who begins to be sensible of the wickedness and treacheries, which have been, and still are committed against this miserable nation, and distressed countries contrary to the will and pleasure of God, as well as His Majesties that he will in time, (for hitherto the truth hath been concealed and kept from his knowledge, with as great craft, as fraud and malice) totally extirpate and root up all these evils and mischiefs, and apply such proper medicines as may purge the Morbifick and peccant humours in the body politick of this New World, committed to his care and Governement as a lover and promoter of peace and tranquility. God preserve and bless him in all his attempts, that he may remedy the distempers of the Christian Church, and crown him as last with Eternal Felicity, Amen.

After I had published this Treatise, certain laws and constitutions, enacted by his Majesty then at Baraclona in the Month of December, An. Dom. 1542, promulgated and published the year ensuing in the City of Madera, whereby it is provided, (as present necessities requir'd) that a period be put to such great enormities and sins, as were committed against God and our neighbours, and tended to the utter ruine and perdition of this New World. These Laws were published by his Majesties order, several persons of highest authority, Councellors, learned, and conscientious men, being assembled together for that purpose, and many debates made at Valedolid about this weighty affair, at length by the unanimous consent and advice off all those who had committed their opinions to writing, they were made publick who traced more closely therein the Laws of Christ and Christianity, and were judged persons pure, free from and innocent of that stain and blemish of depriving the Indians of their treasures by theft and rapine, which riches had contaminated and sullied the hands, but much more the souls of those who were enslav'd by those heaps of wealth and covetousness, now this obstinate and hot pursuit after wealth was the original of all those evils committed without the least remorse of check of conscience.

These laws being thus promulgated, the Courtiers who promoted these tyrants, took care that several copies should be transcribed, (though they were extremely afflicted to see, that there was no farther hopes or means to promote the former depredations and extortions by the tyranny aforesaid) and sent them to several Indian Provinces. They, who took upon them the trouble and care of extirpating, and oppressing by different ways of cruelty, as they never observed any method or order, but behav'd themselves most inordinately and irregularly, having perused these Diplomata or Constitutions, before the new made Judges, appointed to put them in execution, could arrive or be landed, they by the assistance of those (as 'tis credibly rumou'd, nor is it repugnant to truth) who hitherto favour'd their criminal and violent actions, knowing well that these Laws and Proclamations must necessarily take effect, began to grow mutinous, and rebel, and when the Judges were landed, who were to execute these mandates, laying aside all manner of love and fear of God, were so audacious as to contemn and set at nought all reverence and obedience due to their King, and so became traytors, demeaning themselves like blood-thirsty tyrants, destitute and void of all humanity.

More particulary this appear'd in the Perusian Kingdoms where An. Dom. 1542, they acted such horrid and stupendous enormities, that the like were never known or heard in America, or throughout the whole world before that time: Nor were they only practised upon the Indians, who were mostly destroy'd, but upon themselves also, God permitting them by his just judgement to be their own executioners, and sheath their swords in one anothers bowels. In like manner the other parts of this New World being moved by the example of these rebels, refused to yield obedience to those laws. The rest pretending to petition his Majesty turn rebellious themselves; for they would not voluntarily resign those estates, goods and chattels they have already usurped, nor willingly manumit those Indians, who were doomed to be their slaves, during life; and where they restrain'd the murdering sword from doing execution, they opprest them gradually with personal vassalage, in just and intolerable burthens; which his Majesty could not possible hitherto avert or hinder, because they are all universally, some publickly and openly, others clancularly and secretly, so naturally addicted to rob, thieve and steal; and thus under pretext of serving the King, they dishonour God, and defraud his Imperial Majesty.

Here the author having finished the matter of fact in this compendious history, for confirmation of what he has here written, quotes a tedious and imperfect epistle (as he styles it) beginning and ending anonymous withal, containing the cruelties committed by the Spaniards, the same in effect as our author has prementioned, now in regard that I judge such reiterated cruelties and repeated barabarisms are offensive to the reader, he having sailed already too long, and too far in an Ocean of innocent Indian blood: I have omitted all but two or three stories not taken notice of by the author. One of the tyrants (who followed the steps of John Ampudia, a notorious villain) gave way to a great slaughter of sheep the chief food and support of the Spaniards as well as Indians, permitting them to kill two or three hundred at a time, only for their brains, fat, or suet, whose flesh was then altogether useless, and not fit to be eaten; but many Indians, the Spaniards friends and confederates followed them, desiring they might have the hearts to feed upon, whereupon they butchered a great many of them, for this only reason, because they would not eat the other parts of the body. Two of their gang in the Province of Peru killed twenty five sheep, who were sold among the Spaniards for twenty five Crowns, merely to get the fat and brains out of them: Thus the frequent and extraordinary slaughter of their sheep above a hundred thousand head of cattle were destroy'd. And upon this account the region was reduced to great penury and want, and at length perished with hunger. Nay the Province of Quito, which abounded with corn beyond expression, by such proceedings as these, was brought to that extremity that a Sextarie or small measure or wheat was sold for ten Crowns, and a sheep at as dear a rate.

This Captain taking leave of Quito was followed by a poor Indianess with loud cries and clamours, begging and beseeching him to not to carry away her husband; for she had the charge of three children, and could not possibly supply them with victuals, but they must inevitably dye with hunger, and though the Captain repulsed her with an angry brow at the first; yet she approacht him a second time with repeated cries, saying, that her children must perish for want of food; but finding the Captain inexorable and altogether unmov'd with her complaints, and her husband not restor'd, through a piguant necessity wedded to despair; she cut off the heads of her children with sharp stones, and so dispatcht them into the other world. Then he proceeded farther to another city, and sent some Spaniards that very night to take the Indians of the city of Tulilicui, who next day brought with them above a hundred persons; some of which (whom he lookt to be able to carry burthens) he reserved for his own and his soldiers service, and other were chain'd and perished in their fetters; but the little infants he gave to the Casic of Tulilicui, above said to be eaten up and devoured, whose skins are stuft with ashes and hung up in his house to be seen at this very day. And in the close of this letter he shuts up all with these words, 'tis here very remarkable and never to be forgotten, that this tyrant (being not ignorant of the mischiefs and enormities executed by him) boastingly said of himself. 'They who shall travel in these Countreys fifty years hence, and hear the things related of me, will have cause to say or declare that never such a tyrant as I am marched through these regions, and committed the like enormities.'

Now not to quit the stage without one comical scene or action whereon such cruelties have been lively personated, give me leave to acquaint you with a comical piece of grammatical learning in a Reverend Reigioso of these parts, went thither to convert the West-Indies, Pagans, which the author mentions among his reasons and replications, and all these I pass by as immaterial to our purpose, many of them being repeated in the narrative before.

The weight and burthen of initiating the Indians into Christian Faith lay solely on the Spaniards at first; a ignorant, and foppish fellow, was under examination before us (and he had one of the most spatious cities committed to his charge as well as the care and cure of the souls of the inhabitants) whether he understood how to fortifie himself with the sign of the Cross against the wicked and impious, and being interrogated what he taught, and how he instructed the Indians, whose souls were intrusted to his care and conduct; he return'd this answer, that if he damn'd them to the devil and furies of hell, it was sufficient to retrieve them, if he pronounced these words: Per Signin Sanctin Cruces! A fellow fitter to be a Hogherd than a Shepherd of souls.

This deep and bloody American tragedy is now concluded, and my pen choakt up with Indian blood and gore. I have no more to say, but pronounce the Epilogue made by the author, and leave the reader to judge whether it deserves a Plaudite.

The Spaniards first set sail to America, not for the honour of God, or as persons moved and merited thereunto by servant zeal to the true faith, nor to promote the salvation of their neighbours, nor to serve the King, as they falsely boast and pretend to do, but in truth, only stimulated and goaded on by insatiable Avarice and Ambition, that they might for ever domineer, command, and tyrannize over the West Indians, whose Kingdoms they hoped to divide and distribute among themselves. Which to deal candidly in no more or less intentionally, than by all these indirect wayes to disappoint and expel the Kings of Castile out of those Dominions and Territories, that they themselves having usurped the Supreme and Regal Empire, might first challenge it as their right, and then possess and enjoy it.

The Full Translation of the Padilla Plates by Jose Davila

To all those who have ears, listen! The anointed God, METCH, speaks. His words are as fire, with power to mold and perfect those who heed. He is the anointed one, the God of the celestial boat, who speaks Holy Scriptures. He teaches the correct way of life that will bring brilliance and enlightenment to those who heed. Such ones will be beatified in Heaven. His words are such power, that they reach to the depth of the underground sanctuary of the other world.

Mankind are sons of God, but have become corrupt and filthy. To these the Holy One speaks, that they might learn the correct way of life. He does not destroy them, but goes among them as a Shepherd preparing to rise from the waters and from the earth. The holy ones, who are righteous, [H]e will bring forth with a body of flame and fire.

The wicked who reject his word will remain in their graves, in the underground chambers of the other world, cared for by the ancient earth god SEKER.

This Sky God, who loves mankind, descended from the sun to be born on earth and live among men. He is the [L]ord of creation, [L]ord of truth and light, lord of justice and mercy. He descended to put in order the paths and roadways for man. From the celestial regions he descended to die, to give the living and the dead, truth and exaltation in the heavens.

You rise from your grave in the mountains, oh [G]od of the spirit, you who never knew corruption; you have defeated death, to be exalter as lord of justice and righteousness. You sit in glory on your throne. You are the judge who weighs on the scales and measures man actions. You select and settle accounts. Some you reject and cast out.

To the worthy you allot estates and bestow crowns of glory. Oh [G]od of justice, your sacrifice is for all mankind. You have opened up the graves of the dead. These shall be lifted up to be judged of you in holiness. You have broken the earth and kept open the doorway, that all may rise, because of your free offering.

We sing praises and give honor bowed down with gratitude for this great gift. Mankind could not regenerate themselves, they had no power to do so, but the [L]ord of creation opened the door for regeneration and all will be raised at one time or another. They will be as numerous as the stars in the heavens.

This [G]od whose celestial boat was wrecked upon the cross, bestows a gift for righteousness. This gift is a divine body, like that of the first born. There will be a time when the bodies of the dead will rest in their graves, but not all will have a peaceful wait. There are two places wherein the spirits dwell awaiting regeneration. Some souls are in anguish, others enjoy a state of rest. Since there is opposition in all things the force of evil has been present in man from the beginning. There must needs be a place for these two opposing conditions, good and evil, one is called heaven, the other METNAL or hell. Nevertheless those prisoners in hell are being taught the correct way of life and truth. They are being prepared for regeneration. A plan is being presented for their acceptance or rejection.

The three [G]ods in heaven, earth and the spirit world, descended through the underworld, to teach, mold and prepare the dead for a return to life. These [G]ods have power to open the mouths of the dead and give them life again. Those who remain impure will be judged, by the [G]od who descended from the sun. He will pass righteous judgment upon the wicked. These souls will remain in METNAL. Those who have listened to the councils of the [G]ods, will be given light and guidance. These are the harvest of the labors of [G]od. Through their obedience they are reclaimed and led to the doorway.

The [G]od of generation[s] will receive as his seed this nation of foreign people, who were lost and found, through obedience. They have been formed and molded in the image and likeness of [G[od. They will serve [H]im and in time break out of the earth hastily, in a moment, as youthful gods. Breaking the earth they hover light as air. Their figures are radiant. In a moment they are taken by the hand, by a group of gods, that help the dead and floating in the air they approach the throne of [G]od.

Those who have prayed and supplicated the gods of heaven will be received as their seed even as their children. They will be given a kind of garment pertaining to a divine body that will be eternal. These just ones are formed with the qualities of virtue, even the qualities of [G]od. They will be crowned with power and authority for they have proved worthy to wield such power.

Those who are filthy and evil will be held back, in their graves, rejected by the just [G]od, to remain for a time prisoners of the devil. They are as sleepers in their impurity and dishonor. They suffer humiliation and shame, in a state of helpless inactivity. One day they shall be brought before the tribunal to be judged. They judgment will be given according to the acts that have been recorded in the books, as has been commanded.

These wicked ones were and are slaves of the devil, chained to him by their own choice. They were free to cho[o]se. No one forced wickedness upon them. They are the thieves, liars, murderers, luscious ones and those who say one thing and mean another. These lost souls will await their judgment through a thousand years of peace, then they will stand their trial in court. The books will be opened, their acts will be weighed and measured, and justice will be done, by the [G]od of truth and light. This [G]od loved all men and would have had them as his seed, through obedience, but these rebellious ones were free to choose and they sought to serve the devil. Their misfortune will be to suffer a second death. They will be condemned to pass the time with the personified darkness, wailing their lot in pain and suffering, cast out forever into darkness beyond the sight of the divine group who were found worthy.

There will be great sadness over the loss of these wayward ones. No joy will be felt because of their fall. Where God dwells, they can never come but great gladness will fill the courts because of those who were found worthy. These will have their healthy bodies renewed as shining temples. They will be crowned with glory. These are the virtuous ones formed in the image and likeness of God, persons of light and knowledge. These are glorious beings full of joy and happiness praising their God. These holy ones enter into the protecting gates of heaven, where all is peace and love. They are safe from all evil amid beauty and adornments beyond mortal description. Their mansions are allotted, according to their virtue.

The sacrifice of the only begotten is fully realized in this highest glory. Those who inhabit it are counted as [H]is children. They will multiply within their family. On the other hand the wicked will be confined without, guarded by a lake of fire. They will have no increase. Their splendor will be destroyed as an unopened bud is killed by the worm.

When the time has passed for mankind to work out his place in eternity, the one who controls, directs and supervises this earth's movements, will place a barrier of force to give peace to the world that it may rest from war and destruction for a thousand years. Some righteous ones will wait and remain to the last laboring. They will be lifted up high in greatness before the eyes as a group of gods.

After the peaceful period, of a thousand years the earth as it is now known, will come to an end. This orb will be transformed into an abode of beings of light. It will be changed by the visit of the great [G]od who will grace it by His presence. This planet will glow and burn like the Sun. It will have light in itself, to take its place in the celestial ocean. This was decreed and ordained by God from the beginning.

At this time when the Father visits this planet His posterity will be transformed into [G]ods, beings of light, wise and instructed folk, crowned in light as splendid youthful, Gods, men of righteousness, that adore truth and justice, clothed with virtue and character, in the likeness of [G]od. These have the privilege of eternal increase, multiplying in the life to come. Theirs is the right to associate with the God of heaven. They can praise Him for the things that exist. They will shout with joy and sing hymns of praise to the great God who changed the world into a lake of truth and flaming fire, for the benefit of his children. This glorified earth will circle in its orbit as a shining sun. It will be a place of celestial flame and fire and the cr[y]stal scepter, a glorious temple of light, where the [G]od of the soul and the first born will come to this earth. Baba will remain exalted as the God and ruler of this planet.

Happy and fortunate will be those who overcome evil and choose the correct way of life, as was taught by the [F]irst [B]orn. These will be resplendent and beautiful souls—even as Gods. They will dwell in this glorified earth forever—co-creators of other planets, peopled by their spiritual offspring, continuing eternally creations in the universe.

Analysis of the Manti Tablets

by Ray Matheny, Ph.D. and William James Adams, Jr., M.A.

O N JANUARY 20, 1970, CLYDE Pritchet of the [BYU]Zoology depart-ment brought to me four tablets made of light colored limestone, each containing Semitic-like inscriptions. In order that we might not overlook any important discoveries that could provide us with more information on the scriptures of the New World, an investigation was made of these tablets.

FIELD EXAMINATION

The owner of the tablets [John Brewer] claimed to have found them sealed in the earth in an archaeological context. He said that he had hunted for arrowheads in the Manti area for many years, searching the same places repeatedly, always finding new things. One technique that he used was to turn over flat rocks and look under them for concealed arrowheads which others had not thought to do. He claimed to have been using the above technique two years previous to our investigation along the west bank of the Sevier River, a few miles northwest of Manti, Utah. [Note: The Sevier River does not run northwest of Manti Utah but the Sanpitch River does.] Under a stone which the owner of the tablets lifted up he saw two flat stones sticking upright out of a small depression of the ground. He further stated that he had dug these stones up and discovered that they had peculiar markings on them. This dis-covery further stimulated him to dig at the spot to about "waist deep" where he found the remainder of the tablets.

On January 21, 1970, Clyde Pritchet, Dale Berge of the [BYU] Anthropology and Archaeology department, James Walker of Photographic Services, and myself went to the spot where the owner of the tablets claimed that he had found them. We thoroughly examined the earth and found a shallow depression. Excavation at that spot showed clearly that the earth there had not been disturbed and consisted of shallow topsoil overlying what appeared to be Pleistocene gravel. We encountered a large stone about one foot below the surface, which was well rounded from stream course action and which had not been moved since it was naturally deposited there.

We dispute the claim that a recent excavation had been made at the spot where the owner of the tablets says he found them. Also, we dispute the claim that any archaeological context existed for the two upright standing stones. There simply was not any evidence for any excavation having taken place by man at the place claimed. [Note: They did not go to the place Brewer told them to go].

LABORATORY EXAMINATION OF THE TABLETS

The tablets are light brown in color and are slightly lighter in hue than the stones found in the Manti Temple. The temple stones have been exposed to the atmosphere for about 80 years and have turned darker with time, although some stones have remained a light hue, or where lighter when qua[r]ried. Some fresh scuff marks appear on the surface of the Manti Tablets exposing a whitish lime-stone. The inscription on the thickest stone (BYU 71-40.1, Chart I) is not as fresh as the scuff marks on the surface, but contains fine sand.

The stones were cleaned only in part in order to maintain control over observation. Cleaned parts of the inscription reveal that they are lighter in color and fresh looking. The surface color is darker and suggest that it was prepared some time before the inscriptions were made.

Inscription marks are so distinctive that they must have been made with a hard metal tool. A low power binocular microscopic examination shows that a sharp tool was used gouging out the stone in successive strokes. A deep center gouge is visible along with two to three gouge marks on the slope. A radius in each end of the gouge of the marks shows tool entry and exit. A dash on the top line of one tablet was made by pressing the cutting implement into the stone on the right side, and then moving it to the left. Other marks examined are not as clear as this one to indicate the mode of tool movement.

Metal is found on the surface of the thick tablet that appears to be solder or lead. No metal particles are found in the gouges of the inscriptions, indicating that an extremely hard metal tool was used in cutting the stone. [Note: Remember, they cleaned parts of the inscriptions]. Experiments show that mild carbon steel leaves traces of metal on limestone when it is pressed hard on the surface, but that stainless steel, such as that used for dental picks, leaves no trace.

Workmanship of making the inscriptions is not of the high quality, but has produced irregular marks. These marks suggest the difficulty in making them and show that the engraver lost patience [!] on occasion.

Two of the four tablets were partially coated with pine pitch obscuring some of the inscriptions. The pitch was thick and did not seep into any of the inscription marks. White bleached cotton fibers are found impressed into the pine pitch. The cotton appears fresh and not old. One tablet shows the weave of cotton cloth impressed into the pitch. Pitch on both tablets is hard and brittle. Pitch must have been soft when first wrapped in cotton cloth. Pine pitch is a honey color and is not darkened and cracked from age, nor does it show evidence of exposure to moisture and soil for a long period of time.

The pitch was easily dissolved by soaking in zylol for a few hours in order to expose all of the inscriptions. The fast action of zylol further suggests recent treatment of the tablets rather than a long term interment in the soil as claimed.

From the technological point of view I conclude that the tablets are of recent manufacture, using modern tools.

OTHER TABLETS FROM THE MANTI AREA

In 1964, several limestone tablets bearing Semitic-like inscriptions were shown to me, which were [purportedly] found in a cave near Manti. These tablets are in the museum at the department of Anthropology, University of Utah (Salt Lake City). They contain inscriptions similar to those described above.

Examination of these University of Utah tablets suggests recent and clumsy manufacture with crude drawings in addition to inscriptions. Recently inscribed lead tablets were brought to my attention that were supposedly found in the mountains near Manti. These lead tablets contain a small script similar to that of the stone tablets, reputedly to have come from the same area. Interestingly, the same person who found the four inscribed tablets discussed herein also found the lead plates.

I think that it is clear that someone is in the business of manufacturing inscriptions in the Manti area for his own entertainment in hopes of exciting the Latter-day Saints into some foolish action. The inscriptions found on the tablets have their own story to tell.

LINGUISTIC ANALYSIS
by William James Adams, Jr.

I wish to thank the symposium committee for this invitation to discuss the Manti Tablets in conjunction with Dr. Ray Matheny. I also wish to thank two graduate students, Paul Jesclard for preparing the autographs and LeGrand Davies for preparing frequency sign lists. Finally, I wish to thank the College of Religious Instruction for the financial aid they gave.

After Dr. Matheny's archaeological analysis, the burden of language falls on me. Following the archaeological suggestion of a fraud, the first approach was to search for authentic inscriptions which the forger could have copied. Because of the Semitic-like appearance of the inscriptions, a search of Palestinian inscriptions was made. This proving fruitless, Demotic and Hieratic Egyptian were considered. This again proved fruitless. I then sampled the writing systems of the world often finding a sign or two like the signs in the Manti Tablets but never an exact comparison and no authentic inscriptions which could have been copied. In America, the Manti Tablets were compared to such inscriptions as the Davenport Stone, the Kinderhook Plates, etc., but again no direct comparison. Thus, from this exhaustive search, I must conclude that the Manti Tablets contain an inscription which is unique in and of itself.

With this development, the second approach was that of decipherment. Here I followed the techniques used for decipherments in the past—such as that used by Champollion in deciphering Egyptian, by Brotefend and Rawlinson in deciphering Addadian, and by Ventris in the decipherment of Cretan Linear B. The first problem in decipherment is the direction of writing. It might be good to envision a type-written page of English. The margin where we begin to read from is straight whereas the other margin is ragged. This is well seen in CHARTS I and VI where the left margin is straight and the right margin is jagged. Thus we can conclude that the inscriber wrote from left to right. Also you will notice that the bottom line of CHARTS I and VI fall short of the left margins. This tells us that these two lines are the end of the text and thus the bottom line. This again is what we see in English where we never expect the last line of a paragraph to reach the left margin.

With the direction of writing determined the next step indicated by past decipherments was to prepare frequency sign lists. For this purpose I found Tablets 1 and 2 most alike and Tablets 3 and 4 most alike. Tablets 1 and 2 contain some one hundred signs and Tablets 3 and 4 contain some two hundred signs. From this I concluded that the script was representing syllables (syllabic) and was not an alphabetic script.

The next step is to note the groupings in which the individual signs cluster. This has been one of the major keys to past decipherments. Champollion noted clusters which he assumed were Egyptian names. Rawlinson noted clusters which he assumed meant "NAME, king of kings, lord of lords, king of the whole earth," and Ventris noted clusters of signs at the ends of words in lists which he assumed were Greek case endings. This key of clustering is well illustrated in CHART VII. This is a part of the Code of Hammurabi and contains about as many signs as one of our Manti Tablets. The whole code is written with about 250 different signs. In the upper corner are two signs read as a-na. The cluster is repeated twice more as indicated. Part way down the right column is two signs which begin the line and are read i-na. This cluster of signs is repeated again near the bottom of the right column as indicated. As I looked for repeated clusterings of signs in the Manti Tablets I found only the dash and triangle seen near the end of line 3, Tablet 1 and near the middle of line 4, Tablet 1 (See CHART I.)

Now, as I have noted, authentic scripts have frequently recurring clusters of signs. This is even true of authentic scripts so far undeciphered such as Cretan Linear A. Years before Rawlinson deciphered Akkadian; Grotefend had noted the clusterings I have noted on CHART VII. But with these Manti Tablets, I have been able to find only one cluster of two signs repeated twice. What then can we conclude from this situation? From a language point of view I believe that we must conclude that the Manti Tablets are not authentic and thus a fake. Instead of a meaningful script, we have here the hap hazardous and meaningless scratchings of a forger and frauder. Thus, as a scholar of languages, my conclusion is in full harmony with the archaeological conclusions of Dr. Ray Matheny.

Brewer Tablets Alphabet by Lyman Platt

Lyman Platt, PhD, author of *World Book of Generations* was shown transcripts of the characters found on the various tablets discovered in a cave near Manti, Utah. Following is his analysis and background of how this alphabet could have found its way to Utah in a cave with large mummies and other artifacts discovered by Johnny Brewer in the 1950s in Sanpete County.

BREWER TABLETS ALPHABET CHARACTERS

It is my best estimate that there are thirty-two characters in the language on the Brewer tablets, showing that it is indeed an alphabet. Given the type of migration the Jaredites did after leaving Babylon, going north, crossing an interior sea and then coming to the Pacific Ocean, most likely in northern China, it is possible that the thirty-two characters represent a forgotten alphabet that the Chinese used prior to creating glyphs. As I have studied the glyphs on the Chinese, I can see how certain strokes represent words and ideas formed by the glyphs; these glyphs didn't come about all at once as the beginning of a language; they had to develop over time. It is my conclusion that at the time the Jaredites were among the Chinese, they were using an alphabet similar or equal to what we see on the Brewer plates, and the Jaredites copied it because it was easy to use.

TOWER OF BABEL AND THE UNIVERSAL FLOOD

The confusion of tongues at the Tower of Babel actually occurred about 1996 B.C., not the date given by most Mormon historians (See

World Book of Generations, page 64). That puts some interesting prophets within the Tower of Babel. Noah and Japheth were both contemporaries of that date, Noah dying in 1996; and Japheth living until 1896. He could easily be the founder of the Chinese race; certainly they are his descendants. If so, we must ask what was the language he and Noah brought with them through the Flood; and during the approximately 300 year interim from the Flood to the Tower of Babel, did that language change.

At the end of the first 100 years after the Flood, mankind had spread from its beginnings at Ararat throughout the Fertile Crescent, into adjoining parts of Africa, the Mediterranean, Anatolia, the steppes of Asia, and throughout the southern climes as far as China. Shortly after that they spread to the Americas, into Europe, and then into the islands of the sea and the far reaches of the continents. Within another 100 years, the world was explored in most of its regions and settlements begun in all major areas of the world. The descendants of Noah quickly diversified even before the Tower of Babel. Their intermarriage, new religious ideas, and technological developments were important to this diversification. Very few remained true to the doctrines as taught by Noah, Japheth, Shem, and Ham. Many of their children, and most of their grandchildren strayed from these doctrines to worship their own gods (*World Book of Generations*, page 116).

Given the time period in question, it was most likely the famine set prior to the confusion of tongues at the Tower of Babel in 1996 that caused Abraham, along with other righteous men, to be inspired as to the locations to which they were to travel.

Hugh Nibley in *The World of the Jaredites*, page 175 states: "The weather of Asia is the great central driving mechanism of world history. It is only in recent years that men have begun to correlate the great migrations of history, with their attendant wars and revolutions [and death], with those major weather crises such as the great wind and drought of 2300 - 2200 B.C. and the world floods world floods of 1300 B.C., which we know to have taken place in the course of recorded history. The 349-year period immediately after the flood (2345 B.C.) was a period of mutual understanding and of a common spoken language initially. All the people of the earth as they expanded had full use of the technologies and knowledge of the ark family. As nearly as can be determined, this language has been identified by modern philologists as the

Keltemin language. This was the language of the patriarchs. "For death hath come upon our fathers; nevertheless we know them, and cannot deny, and even the first of all we know, even Adam. For a book of remembrance we have written among us, according to the pattern given by the finger of God; and it is given in our own language" (*Pearl of Great Price*, The Book of Moses 6:45-46).

In another place it states: "And a book of remembrance was kept, in the which was recorded, in the language of Adam, for it was given unto as many as called upon God to write by the spirit of inspiration; and by them their children were taught to read and write, having a language that was pure and undefiled (The Book of Moses 6:5-6).

Pre-Flood archeological digs show a great diversity of language among the pre-deluvians. Noah may have brought more than one writing system with him through the Flood. These spread early after the Flood.

Again, Nibley shows in his work quoted about (page 275), that at Uruk, presumably a post-Flood settlement, a discovery has been made where "parent forms" of writing appear, not by any gradual process of evolution, but "suddenly and without warning there appear fifteen hundred signs and pictographs scratched on clay. They seem to have been written and used without hesitancy," showing that writing was already well-established *somewhere* in the world, and that somewhere would seem to be in the region of the north of "Mesopotamia."

There are a number of secular and scriptural scholars who maintain a position of a common language. Hutton Webster says, for example: "More than a century ago Occidental philologists discovered that Sanskrit, the ancient speech of the Aryans in India, was distantly connected with the classic Greek and Latin. All the Indo-European languages, both living and 'dead' have now been shown to be related. They must have sprung from some parent language no longer adequately represented by any one of them" (*History of Civilization, Ancient & Medieval* [Boston: D.C. Heath and Company, 1947], page 20).

So, in conclusion, the Brewer writing could easily have been an alphabet taken by the Chinese to China prior to the Tower of Babel, during the drought period. Was it original Adamic? The Hebrews claim Hebrew is based on original Adamic and there is some proof of this in studies made of this ancient language. However, most agree that Hebrew derived from Phoenician, which in turn is very ancient and shows possibilities of having derived from Adamic. We must conclude that the Brewer writing is part of an ancient writing system brought by the Jaredites to the Americas, probably from China, and that it was one of the writing systems used in Mesopotamia prior to the Chinese migration.

That it is an alphabet is certain. That it has the potential of being the original Adamic is uncertain. There are no records to compare it with that have yet been discovered anywhere in the world. We are not so lucky with this script as we were with the Rossetta Stone and Egyptian.

http://www.friendsofsabbath.org/Further_Research/British-Israel2/2.Mormon%20Lost%20Tribes%20books/1.List%20of%20 books_by_LDS.htm

Petroglyphs are images created by removing part of a rock surface by incising, picking, carving, or abrading, as a form of rock art. Outside North America, scholars often use terms such as "carving", "engraving", or other descriptions of the technique to refer to such images. Petroglyphs are found worldwide, and are often associated with prehistoric peoples. The word comes from the Greek word petro-, basis of the word "petra" meaning "stone", and glyphein meaning "to carve", and was originally coined in French as pétroglyphe.

The term petroglyph should not be confused with petrograph, which is an image drawn or painted on a rock face.

Endnotes

1. Excerpts from the papers and Journals of Zula Brikerhoff, author of many unpublished manuscripts and "God's Chosen People of America" 1971.

2. Courtesy of Ancient American Magazine; Wayne May Publisher.

3. Lost Treasures on the Old Spanish Trail, George A. Thompson, 1985.

4. Ibid

5. Information supplied by Daniel Lowe, author, explorer.

6. References on Giants from multiple sources.

7. Uncovering The Mysteries Of Your Hidden Inheritance, Robert A. Balaicius, 2001.

8. Dr. Paul Cheesman Papers. Brigham Young University Harold B. Lee Library, Special Collections.

9. Ibid

10. Wayne May, Publisher/Editor.

11. Ibid

12. The Mound Builders. Henry Clyde Shetrone, 1930, pg, 115

13. Ibid. pages 199 - 201.

14. The Cave of Many Faces. Russell Burrows and Fred Rhydholm, 1991.

15. Milton R. Hunter Photographs. In possession of Author.

16. Michigan Artifacts. In possession of Author.

17, Lyman Platt Papers:

"It is my best estimate that there are thirty-two characters in the language on the Brewer tablets, showing that it is indeed an alphabet. Given the type of migration the Jaredites did after leaving Babylon, going north, crossing an interior sea and then coming to the Pacific Ocean, most likely in northern China, it is possible that the thirty-two characters represent a forgotten alphabet that the Chinese used prior to creating glyphs. As I have studied the glyphs on the Chinese, I can see how certain strokes represent words and ideas formed by the glyphs; these glyphs didn't come about all at once as the beginning of a language; they had to develop over time. It is my conclusion that at the time the Jaredites were among the Chinese, they were using an alphabet similar or equal to what we see on the Brewer plates, and the Jaredites copied it because it was easy to use.

The confusion of tongues at the Tower of Babel actually occurred about 1996 B.C., not the date given by most Mormon historians (See *World Book of Generations*, page 64). That puts some interesting prophets within the Tower of Babel. Noah and Japheth were both contemporaries of that date, Noah dying in 1996; and Japheth living until 1896. He could easily be the founder of the Chinese race; certainly they are his descendants. If so, we must ask what was the language he and Noah brought with them through the Flood; and during the approximately 300 year interim from the Flood to the Tower of Babel, did that language change.

At the end of the first 100 years after the Flood, mankind had spread from its beginnings at Ararat throughout the Fertile Crescent, into adjoining parts of Africa, the Mediterranean, Anatolia, the steppes of Asia, and throughout the southern climes as far as China. Shortly after that they spread to the Americas, into Europe, and then into the islands of the sea and the far reaches of the continents. Within another 100 years, the world was explored in most of its regions and settlements begun in all major areas of the world. The descendants of Noah quickly diversified even before the Tower of Babel. Their intermarriage, new religious ideas, and technological developments were important to this diversification. Very few remained true to the doctrines as taught by Noah, Japheth, Shem, and Ham. Many of their children, and most of their grandchildren strayed from these doctrines to worship their own gods (*World Book of Generations*, page 116).

Given the time period in question, it was most likely the famine set prior to the confusion of tongues at the Tower of Babel in 1996 that caused Abraham, along with other righteous men, to be inspired as to the locations to which they were to travel.

Hugh Nibley in *The World of the Jaredites*, page 175 states: "The weather of Asia is the great central driving mechanism of world history. It is only in recent years that men have begun to correlate the great migrations of history, with their attendant wars and revolutions [and death], with those major weather crises such as the great wind and drought of 2300 - 2200 B.C. and the world floods of 1300 B.C., which we know to have taken place in the course of recorded history.

The 349 - year period immediately after the flood (2345 B.C.) was a period of mutual understanding and of a common spoken language initially. All the people of the earth as they expanded had full use of the technologies and knowledge of the ark family. As nearly as can be determined, this language has been identified by modern philologists as the Keltemin language. This was the language of the patriarchs. "For death hath come upon our fathers; nevertheless we know them, and cannot deny, and even the first of all we know, even Adam. For a book of remembrance we have written among us, according to the pattern given by the finger of God; and it is given in our own language" (*Pearl of Great Price*, The Book of Moses 6:45-46). In another place it states: "And a book of remembrance was kept, in the which was recorded, in the language of Adam, for it was given unto as many as called upon God to write by the spirit of inspiration; and by them their children were taught to read and write, having a language that was pure and undefiled (The Book of Moses 6:5-6).

Pre-Flood archeological digs show a great diversity of language among the pre-deluvians. Noah may have brought more than one writing system with him through the Flood. These spread early after the Flood.

Again, Nibley shows in his work quoted about (page 275), that at Uruk, presumably a post-Flood settlement, a discovery has been made where "parent forms" of writing appear, not by any gradual process of evolution, but "suddenly and without warning there appear fifteen hundred signs and pictographs scratched on clay. They seem to have been written and sued without hesitancy," showing that writing was already well-established *somewhere* in the world, and that somewhere would seem to be in the region of the north of "Mesopotamia."

There are a number of secular and scriptural scholars who maintain a postion of a common language. Hutton Webster says, for example: "More than a century ago Occidental philologists discovered that Sanskrit, the ancient speech of the Aryans in India, was distantly connected with the classic Greek and Latin. All the Indo-European languages, both living and 'dead' have now been shown to be related. They must have sprung from some parent language no longer adequately represented by any one of them" (History of Civilization, Ancient & Medieval [Boston: D.C. Heath and Company, 1947], page 20).

So, in conclusion, the Brewer writing could easily have been an alphabet taken by the Chinese to China prior to the Tower of Babel, during the drought period. Was it original Adamic. The Hebrews claim Hebrew is based on original Adamic and there is some proof of this in studies made of this ancient language. However, most agree that Hebrew derived from Phoenician, which in turn is very ancient and shows possibilities of having derived from Adamic. We must conclude that the Brewer writing is part of an ancient writing system brought by the Jaredites to the Americas, probably from China, and that it was one of the writing systems used in Mesopotamia prior to the Chinese migration. That it is an alphabet is certain. That it has the potential of being the original Adamic is uncertain. There are no records to compare it with that have yet been discovered anywhere in the world. We are not so lucky with this script as we were with the Rossetta Stone and Egyptian."

18. Jerry Mower (Sanpete County) and Gary Taylor (Weber County, since passed) both who decided that they were the protectors of all the ancient sites in Sanpete County, Utah are credited with the destruction.
19. A spirit met us at the recovery site and it stayed with the tablets until they were taken from us.
20. Elder Futhark & Futhorc runes. Thought to be the oldest version of the Runic alphabet.
21. *America B.C.*. Dr. Barry Fell, 1989, Chapter 3.
22. Courtesy of *Ancient American Magazine* and Publisher Wayne May.
23. *Tayos Gold: The Archives of Atlantis*, Stan Hall, 2006.
24. Photos by author.
25. Drawings in possession of author.
26. NEXUS www.nexusmagazine.com

Cited Works

Brinkerfoff, Zula. *God's Chosen People of America,* 1971.

Burrows, Russell 1991. *The Mystery Cave of Many Faces,* 1991.

Budge, E.A. Wallis "Dover edition 1993" *An Egyptian Hieroglyphic Reading Book for Beginners.*

Churchward, Albert. *Signs & Symbols of Primordial Man.* 1913.

Deloria, Vine. *Red Earth, White Lies: Native Americans and the Myth of Scientific Fact.* 1997.

Ellis, Peter Berresford. *The Druids.* 1994.

Farley, Gloria 1995. *In Plain Sight.* 1995.

Fell, Barry, *America B.C.: Ancient Settlers in the New World.* 1989.

Fell, Barry. *Saga America*, 1980.

Hall, Stan. *Tayos Gold: The Archives of Atlantis.* 2006.

Harris, James Roy. *Southwestern American Indian Rock Art and the Book of Mormon.* 1991.

Hopkins, Sarah Winnemucca. 1883. *Life Among the Piutes: Their Wrongs and Claims.* 1883.

Jenkins, Timothy R. *The Ten Tribes of Israel.* 1883.

Jewell, Roger. *Riding The Wild Orb.* 2001.

Jewell, Roger. *Ancient Mines of Kitchi-Gummi: Cypriot/Minoan Traders in North America.* 2011.

May, Wayne 2002. *THIS LAND: Zarahemla and the Nephite Nation.* 219 pages.

May, Wayne 2004. *THIS LAND:Only One Cumorah.* 225 pages.

May, Wayne 2005. *THIS LAND: They Came from the EAST.* 225 pages

May, Wayne 2009. *THIS LAND: AMERICA 2,000 B.C. TO 500 A.D.* 263 pages.

Mann, Charles C. *1491: New Revelations of the Americas before Columbus.* 2006.

Martineau, LaVan. *The Rocks Begin to Speak.* 1973.

May, Wayne N. *Ancient American Magazine* Vol. 11, Number 68.

Menzies, Gavin. *1434: The Year A Magnificent Chinese Fleet Sailed To Italy And Ignited The Renaissance.* 2008.

Nielson, Richard, Wolter, Scott. *The Kensington Rune Stone: Compelling New Evidence.* 2008.

Osmon, Rick. *The Graves of the Golden Bear: Ancient Fortresses and Monuments of the Ohio Valley.* 2011.

Platt, Lyman D. *The World Book of Generations: A Genealogical History,* Volume 1. 1996.

Porter, Bruce, Meldrum, Rod. *Prophecies & Promises: The Book of Mormon & The United States of America.* 2009.

Ruskamp, John A. Jr. *Asiatic Echoes: The Identification of Chinese Pictograms in North American Rock Writing.* 2011.

Ruskamp, John A. *Asiatic Echoes: Addendum* 2012.

Rydholm, Fred. Michigan *Copper: The Untold Story.* 2006.

Slifer, Dennis. *Guide to Rock Art of the Utah Region.* 2000.

Shetrone, Henry Clyde. *The Mound-Builders.* 1930.

Smith, Eathan. *View of the HEBREWS 1825.* 1825.

Smith, Michael E. 1996. *The Aztecs.* 1996.

Squier, E.G. *Antiquities of New York.* 1851.

Thompson, Gunnar 1996. *The Friar's Map of Ancient America 1360 AD.* 1996.

Waddell, L.A. *The Phoenician Origin of Britons Scots & Anglo-Saxons.* 1924.

Waddell, L.A. 1925. *The Indo-Sumerian Seals Deciphered.* 1925.

Wakefield, Jay S., Reinoud M. De Jonge. *Rocks & Rows: Sailing Routes across the Atlantic and the Copper Trade.* 2005.

Wolter, Scott. *The Hooked X: Key to the Secret History of North America.* 2008.

List of Figures

26. Photo by Dr. Julian Fell describing the of Three Kings Panel and Phoenicians.

27. Three Kings Panel break down.

28. Large close-up of Chief or King at the Three Kings Panel site.

29. Manti King, as drawn by the son of John Brewer at Sanpete County, Utah.

30. Manti Queen, as drawn by the son of John Brewer at Sanpete County, Utah.

31. Copper head with strange inscriptions on it found in the Brewer Cave at Sanpete County, Utah.

32. KAWEAH Alphabet used by early cultures in California.

33. KAWEAH Alphabet continued.

34. Obverse of Slate tablet Chart 1 with characters from Sanpete County, Utah.

35. Chart II.

36. Chart III.

37. Reverse of Slate tablet Chart IV with characters from Sanpete County, Utah.

38. Obverse of Slate tablet Chart V with characters from Sanpete County, Utah.

39. Gray slab thought to be from either the Lenape or Alligewi.

40. Lady Elche of the West, discovered at Richfield, Utah by men digging a water well.

41. The actual Lady Elche that was discovered at Elx, Spain.

42. Gold Lady of Elche reproduction.

43. Hopi Maiden with similar hair style of the Lady Elche.

44. The Tecaxi -Calixtahuaca Head.

45. Copper Head Piece used by the Hopewell and Adena warriors.

46. Hopewell grave with skeleton with copper head plate.

47. Another skeleton showing the head plate.

48. Copper Breast Plate worn by the Hopewell and Adena warriors.

49. Copper ingot from mounds.

50 & 51. Bronze axes discovered in area mounds in Ohio.

52. Copper Tablets.

81. Bronze Axe.

82. Black Slate Gorgets.

83. Black Slate depicting the "Tower of Babel".

84. Black Slate depicting "Death and Destruction".

85. Black Slate depicting "War & Peace".

86. Black Slate depicting "Noah's Flood".

87. Is this Jesus?

88. The Crucifixion.

89. Ogam Script.

90. Similar to Phoenician script.

91. Type of Charm.

92. Ancient Algonquin.

93. Negro man. (Unknown if this individual came from Africa).

94. Old world style portrait stone. Part of the Burrows Cave artifacts.

95. Obverse side of the "Davenport Stone".

96. Davenport Stone #2.

97. Manti or Brewer's Cave Copper Tablets noted as the "Scorpion Plates".

98. Manti or Brewer's Cave Copper Tablets with strange design.

99. Brewer's Cave artifact.

100. Strange Medallion.

101. An elaborate design.

102. Possible pieces of ancient currency.

103. Lead amulet.

104. Other lead artifacts from Brewer's collection.

105. Dr. Jesus Padilla Orozco Claimed these tablets found by him came from the State of Oaxaca, Mexico.

106. Padilla artifact - obverse side.

107. Padilla artifact - reverse side.

108. Padilla artifact - obverse side.

109. Padilla artifact - reverse side.

110. Padilla artifact, Character Guide.

111. Dodge Canyon Lead Tablets, discovered in an ancient stone foundation in Sanpete County, Utah.

202. Crespi with large gold sheet with many inscriptions and figures on it.

203. Crespi artifacts.

204. Crespi artifacts that some think are fakes.

205. Tablet. Very impressive!

206. The "Kincaid Egg" thought to have originated in the Grand Canyon.

207. More of the Kincaid Egg.

208. Knife Sketch as described.

209. Goblet Sketch as described.

210. John W. Powell, who put American Antiquities in the basement of the Smithsonian Institution.

Annotated Bibliography
A Synopsis of other Publications by the Author

Rumors, Facts and Fictions of Ancient America: Written Records, Hieroglyphs, Pictographs, Artifacts and Other Remarkable Discoveries of North, Central and South America, 2018

Utah's Hidden Treasure: Outlaw Loot in Every County, 2017

Treasures of the Ancients: Recent Discoveries of Ancient Writings in North America, 1996, 2013

Voices of the Ancients, 2012

Out of the Dust: Utah's Lost Mines and Treasures, 2006

Nachi: Man of Justice, Son of Warrior, 2001

Of Men and Gold: The History and Evidence of Spanish Gold Mines in the West, 1994

La Mina Del Yutas: The Lost Josephine Mine (out of print)

OF MEN AND GOLD: THE HISTORY AND EVIDENCE OF SPANISH GOLD MINES IN THE WEST, 1994

This account deals mainly with the Lost Josephine Mine; its history from its beginning to its untimely demise. A revised edition with 69 additional pages adds to the historical overview of the meanings and functions of signs and symbols and rock cairns and monuments used primarily by Spanish miners and explorers. Many scholars and historians refuse to believe that early Spanish explorers looking for mineral came as far north as Northern Utah. This research proves that they did in fact come north into Utah's High Uinta Mountains west near present day Kamas to eastern Utah at or near the town of Vernal.

Work books and journals have been found proving that these Spaniards had been coming to Northern Utah since 1718 when A Don Diego Garcia son of Don Pedro and brother to Jose Garcia exploring (Yutas) minerals; Jose Garcia being the founder of the Josephine Mine on Hoyt Peak near present day Kamas, Utah.[1]

At the time of the rediscovery of the mine by John W. Young in 1943, a mining engineer employed by Young made the statement that the mining methods used in one of the tunnels was pre-Columbian, meaning the technique was of an ancient form. Artifacts discovered in the old mine by Young made him think the mine was once mined by people of an ancient origin.

According to a Spanish document[2] discovered by Professor Russell R. Rich, its contents proved that this mine was none other than the Josephine of Martinique, the Empress. The document was found in the Archive of the Indies with the work book and a map. The map brought Professor Rich to Hoyt Peak. The document describes the mine in detail and how rich it was at that time and even told of a large cache buried deep in its hidden caverns. One of the early prospectors with John Young discovered an ancient Roman Coin in the pit of the mine.[3] This find suggests that miners before the Spaniards worked the old mine's ore veins.

The author is considered an expert when it comes to deciphering Spanish signs and symbols that were used during the 18th and 19th centuries pertaining to prospecting, gold, silver and mining techniques. In this book he gives an overall view of signs and symbols as well as old alphabet letters used by the Spaniards as well.

[1]Research for Garcia family-and related documents from Sp. arc-Royal Library arc-de Indies Mex. Mine & Mint rec's. Viceroy letters. New Mexico's Governors letters.

[2]Professor Russell Rich had left a document and a map at BYU (Brigham Young University) at Provo, Utah. This document proved without a shadow of doubt that the mine east of Kamas, Utah was indeed the "Lost Josephine Mine." Once in our hands we took the document up to the University of Utah at Salt Lake City, Utah. The document was presented to Professor Jonathan Stowers whose office was in Room 104 of the Department of Languages at Spencer Hall on campus. We made an appointment to have the document examined. Stowers and a Professor Handcock, the latter being born and raised in Mexico and understood the language. After careful study and research we were contacted by Stowers to come get the document. There with the document was a declaration of authenticity waiting for us. It read: "The document appeared to be genuine and authentic. It could only have been written by a Spanish speaking person of that time period

who was acquainted with the phraseology and use of the language. It's author was of normal education and not a scholar, as were most clergymen or priests of that time, but he was well schooled in the language, typical of men of his position with the military who most probably worked his way up through the ranks to become that of an officer. The use of singulars in conduction with plurals, as in this document, was very typical of many documents obtained from that time period, at the turn of the nineteenth century, it was commonplace. Several words in the document are also no longer used but were commonly used at that time."

[3]The Roman coin discovered in the old mine was an Antoninianus Copper Piece coated with silver, minted under the rule of Gallienus, Augustus of Rome, A.D. 259 - 268.

TREASURES OF THE ANCIENTS: RECENT DISCOVERIES OF ANCIENT WRITINGS IN NORTH AMERICA, 1996, 2013

This book has seven chapters dealing with the likes of the Sanpete Mummy Cave[1], the Kinderhook Plates[2], a Middle Bronze Age Tablet of the Wasatch[3], the Unknown Nation[4], The Padilla Plates[5], Mystical Writings and Lost Treasures[6] and Other Writings, Artifacts and Conclusions[7].

[1]Sanpete Mummy Cave is the story of Earl John Brewer of Moroni, Utah who discovered a cave near the town of Manti that housed not only stone boxes filled with ancient records on lead and copper tablets and plates, but two large mummies of a man and a woman. The story gives a close look at Brewers journey into this complex and exciting adventure through his personal journal.

[2]The Kinderhook Plates story has raised eyebrows throughout the country for years. It was Robert Wiley, of Kinderhook, Pike County, Illinois who had three dreams in succession that there was a buried treasure near his home. The dreams were so implanted in his mind that he had a hard time thinking of anything else! Eventually he, along with two members of The Church of Jesus Christ of Latter-day Saints, began excavating the site where Wiley said the treasure cache lay hidden. They eventually uncovered six brass bell like plates with strange inscriptions on them.

[3]The Middle Bronze Age Tablet was discovered east of Salt Lake City, Utah by a young man hunting mule deer early in 1980, who when descending off a ledge dislodged a rock that sent him tumbling down the hill some 20 feet. Being a young man he suffered no harm but his inquisitive mind told him to check out the hole left by the dislodged rock. As he and members of his hunting party got up to the hole they noticed it was squared out; manmade looking. He looked into the hole and could see that it went back in farther than he anticipated. He noticed at this point, a shiny object back in a ways, so he carefully extended his arm into the hole and grabbed the object. Bringing it out of the hole the party was stunned to see that it was an oblong metal object with strange writing on it. The writing proved to be an ancient cuneiform script but undecipherable.

[4]The Unknown Nation reveals a marvelous period in early American history where hundreds and thousands of metal and stone artifacts were discovered from earthen mounds in Michigan. These artifacts had several different styles of script and illustrations that were beautiful, depicting scenes from Biblical times down to about 400 years after Christ was born. These ancient records are referred to as the Michigan Tablets.

Not only tablets and plates but giant skeletons with metal head and leg armor were discovered. Some of these giants measured over eight feet.

[5]In 1961, two missionaries from The Church of Jesus Christ of Latter-day Saints by the names of Richard L. Averett and Gerald Kammerman, happened to knock on the door of Dr. Jesus Padilla, a well known and respected physician. This family was wealthy and well known in town. The two missionaries had been assigned to the village of Cuautla, Mexico, where the Padilla family had made their home. They were greeted by Mrs. Padilla who invited the two young men into her home so they could deliver their message. As customary, after the formalities were over, the missionaries handed the Padilla's a copy of the pamphlet entitled: *El Libro de Mormon: La Historia de las Americas Antes de Colon.* Dr. Padilla thumbed through the pamphlet until he came upon page five where he stopped and stared at the picture at the bottom of the page that had an artist's rendition of

the gold plates uncovered by the Prophet Joseph Smith. The drawing was of the plates stacked and bound with three gold rings. Also on that page was a copy of the Anthon transcript. Elder Averett later stated that, "While thumbing through the tract Dr. Padilla saw the characters of the Anthon transcript and exclaimed that he believed what the missionaries were telling him because he had discovered in a pre-Columbian tomb a set of gold plates with similar writing. He then showed us the three small gold phylacteries with the small hinges that Mrs. Padilla wore on her wrist. Each was inscribed with twenty five characters not unlike the characters on the tract. A small hinge was on the plates at the time and the remains of red fingernail polish were also visible."

[6]East of Fillmore, Utah there is a small canyon known as Chalk Creek. On a hill above the creek is a large rock outcropping that has strange hieroglyphic characters cut deep in the rock face. Researcher Jose Davila made this site his personal project to prove it was the site of hidden tablets and treasure left by the Book of Mormon Moroni. His translation of the inscribed rock has since been proven wrong but the story of how he came to such a conclusion is no less interesting and captivating.

[7]A discovery of ancient lead tablets in eastern Utah leads to a remarkable adventure as to who, what and why these cuneiform inscriptions were left in an earthen mound. To date nobody has been able to come up with a viable transliteration of the writing. Fakes are the norm when academia is left wondering. Yet these tablets carbon dated to the 12th century! What are they doing in Utah?

Voices of the Ancients, 2012

This volume begins with a critique of three theories concerning the origins of the first inhabitants of ancient America, those being 1) the trans-oceanic migration viewpoints, 2) the Bering Sea Land bridge migrations from Siberia, and 3) the aliens from outer-space contact and settlement hypothesis. The author quickly demolishes the outdated Bering Sea Land bridge notions with common sense and logic. Although extra-terrestrial contact may be unpalatable to some, it is the paradigm of many American Indian cultures, particularly the Ute people. Eleven beautiful color photographs for Chapter 1 show rock carvings of what appear to be space craft, alien beings, and enigmatic script. These pictographs and many other were discovered on Ute property on a large stone mound that will probably never be excavated. But the pictographs are still under investigation.

This country was indeed inhabited and explored by many different cultures and races for thousands of years before Columbus. The people of what would become the Eastern U.S., starting with the maritime "Red Paint People" of New England (ca 5,000 BCE), the inhabitants who erected large dolmens as the same time as in Britain and the "Old Copper Culture" of northern Michigan and Lake Superior (ca 3,000 BCE). The late Fred Rydholm[1] is quoted as stating that Scandinavians came and traded for copper ingots from the Algonquians in the area around 1700 BCE.

The main focus of *Voices of the Ancients* and the subject matter of the author's research is the cultures who explored the western part of the country. Many Egyptian-type hieroglyphs[2] panels have been discovered, six in Utah alone. Conversations with members of the Ute Tribe in Eastern Utah tell of an ancient race of giants that once visited the land who came from the west and spoke a strange language. Others tell of settlers from Jerusalem[3] who arrived, ca 600 BCE who were ancestors of the modern Indians of North America.

Chapters on the dolmens of Utah,[4] Burrows Cave,[5] the Michigan tablets,[6] and the Father Crespi treasures of Ecuador,[7] are all equally intriguing. Most ancient America investigators are familiar with the stone ruins and dolmens of New England, but not many are aware of the dolmens found in Utah. Accusations of fakery of the Michigan tablets fail to explain the sheer volume of the thousands of tablets that were discovered from hundreds of earthen mounds that make them unlikely to be frauds; equally so with the Crespi collection and plates of gold and silver.

[1] *Michigan Copper; the Untold Story; A History of Discovery*, 2006, Winter Cabin Books & Services Publisher, Fred Rydholm, author.

[2] At least 29 sites have been identified throughout the western part of America. Interestingly, some are at or near the high water mark of ancient Lake Bonneville, therefore ships or large boats could have made landfall nearby.

[3] The Book of Mormon (The Church of Jesus Christ of Latter-day Saints) tells of a people who left Jerusalem by revelation to go to a new

land especially set aside for people who were descendants of Jacob (Israel), particularly the tribe of Joseph.

[4]"Dolmen" a Neolithic tomb or monument consisting of a large flat or rounded stone laid across upright stones; a cromlech.

[5]In 1982, Russell Burrows of Olney, Illinois, stumbled onto the opening of a vertical shaft in southern Illinois. What he allegedly discovered was a tomb full of artifacts that predated European colonization by thousands of years. The tomb represented Egyptians and other cultures that apparently came to North America circa 2500 BCE.

The Mystery Cave of Many Faces: A History of Burrow's Cave, Russell Burrows and Fred Rydholm, 1992

[6]Commonly known as the "Michigan Tablets" these began to be unearthed in the mid-19th century in the state of Michigan and later in adjoining states such as Ohio and Illinois. Early in the 1960s, Elder Milton R. Hunter of The Church of Jesus Christ of Latter-day Saints acquired a large collection of these unusual artifacts gathered by Father Savage, a Catholic Priest from Detroit, Michigan. First discovered in 1858, these "plates" continued to be found until the early 20th century in over 27 counties throughout the state of Michigan and neighboring states.

This Land: They Came from the East, Wayne N. May, 2005. Published by Ancient American Archaeology Foundation; Trashing America's 'Politically Incorrect' Prehistory; F. Rydholm, Issue No. 32 *Ancient American Magazine.*

[7]Carlo Crespi Croci was born in Legnana, near Milan, Italy, on May 29, 1891, but not from a rich family of dukes and royalty. He became a novice in Foglizzo (Turin), and was ordained in Verona at age twenty-six. After receiving a Masters Degree at the University of Padua with a thesis in anthropology, he eventually made his way to Cuenca, Ecuador.

During his time there he was instrumental in constructing the Instituto "Cornelio Merchan", an imposing, four-storied boys' elementary and trade school, becoming its first director. Crespi once told a journalist that his impulse to create a museum came from having encountered an ancient potsherd during excavations for the foundation of "Cornelio Merchan." The same interviewer then asked him, "Is it certain that Padre Crespi has been sold things that have no scientific value; that they swindle you?" To this he answered: "En somma, permitame. Esto no lo ponga. Todavia hay en Cuenca mucha gente que pasa hambre. Y el P. Crespi lo sabe…" ("In summary, permit me, don't put that down. In Cuenca there are still many people who experience hunger. And Padre Crespi knows." Crespi went on buying or receiving incredible artifacts from natives of the region. Eventually he had the greatest collection of Old World Artifacts of anyone in South America.

ANCIENT AMERICA